Bed/Time/Story

Bed/Time/Story

JILL ROBINSON

RANDOM HOUSE NEW YORK

Author's Note: It was neither my need nor my intention here to reveal the private stories of others, so names have been changed.

All rights reserved under International and Pan-American Copyright Conventions. Published in the United States by Random House, Inc., New York, and simultaneously in Canada by Random House of Canada Limited, Toronto.

Library of Congress Cataloging in Publication Data
Robinson, Jill, 1936-
  Bed/time/story.
  I. Title.
PZ4.R66248Be [PS3568.02898] 813'.5'4 74-8578
ISBN 0-394-48803-2

Manufactured in the United States of America
9 8 7 6 5 4 3 2
First Edition

For my husband

My gratitude to the following for their support and encouragement:

My daughter
My son

Robert Loomis
Gloria Friedman
Lynn Nesbit

PART ONE

California

I saw him walking.

He had the lean-to walk of a tall person who doesn't want to knock over the world with his tallness, who's leaning over a bit to see you.

Far, far below the window that juts out like the prow of a ship over the Santa Monica Canyon with the sea gleaming through the fog, I saw him walking and I thought, "This cannot be for me."

My friend Karen had called, earlier this evening. "I've got an insane mathematician here," she said. "A friend of ours from New York. He's pacing the floor upstairs. But remember, this is just for fun, not for real and I'll send him over . . . wait, I'll put him on."

If Karen said "insane," it did not just mean what you might call "off-beat." It could well be taken to mean the other side of certifiable. I was going to ask, "What does he look like?" remembering Karen's last referral.

I didn't ask because she had given me some long lectures about my Hollywood standards. I had explained to her about my father's private projection room, where the images of his beautiful employees glittered at me from the silver screen.

"What matters," she had said, dismissing my best stories, "is who the person is to you. The feelings . . . can this person love?"

"Too much talk of love and feelings going on," I said. "I'm

basing it all on appearances. At least you can see right away . . ." My father, a considerate movie-studio executive, had said that "Beauty is as beauty does." And in the secrecy of his tower library, reached only by a spiral staircase, he had told me the classic Hollywood fables. They somehow had the same moral: the best thing you can get out of being a star is some real estate in the San Fernando Valley. But my father had failed to convince me.

And, as for love, my mother had told me it was beautiful:

I see her standing so straight with her gorgeous little body in one of the pure-silk gowns my father gives her. Standing looking in the mirror, hating her face. A pencil is poised in her hand, she returns to what she was telling me. Because I do not seem to understand, she draws a picture. "This," she says, "is a penis." It looks like a dear, fat mushroom.

Most real ones sneaked up to you like snakes, insinuating, then bounding at you suddenly for the kill. One was like a thunderbolt, striking my thigh in the night. Thud. To announce it wanted in. And then there was the aristocratic one, slender and swift as a jeweled dagger. Coldly in and out before it warmed, spitting at me with a sneer upon its face.

Somewhere there was a gentle man with a cock that wore a jaunty grin and stayed long enough for you to get to know him.

And so I had talked very hopefully to Karen's insane mathematician on the phone. His name, he said, was Larry Robinson.

"I'll probably call you Lawrence. Do you like it with a 'u' or 'w'?" This was exactly my most annoying thing to do. Digging in, immediately. Especially since he did not sound as if he was pacing. He also sounded thin.

"It really is Lawrence. Spelled with a 'w.' Why don't I come over in a while, okay?"

"About a half-hour," I said, "would be fantastic. I'm a writer,

I guess Karen has told you, and I'm just finishing up this chapter of my new book. It's an historical novel set in 2005— I've done a lot of research on triage, futurists' scenarios and . . ."

As a mathematician he would be interested in futurists.

I had to make it clear: I am involved in my work. I will not make demands on you. I probably would have slipped in something about my magazine column, my radio show and having the second most hate mail in Los Angeles if his breathing hadn't indicated he hated phones and didn't want to talk any more.

I put on several different outfits. The advantage of not knowing who you are is you can attempt to be all things to all men . . . or women. My mother saw me always glancing in every mirror, every window; in the gleaming blades of knives. She said, "Jill is vain." She did not know I was looking to see who would be there this time.

Since Karen and Mike lived only a block away, my suspicions about this Larry's enthusiasm were gorgeously reinforced when two hours later he had not arrived.

I went from my son's room to my daughter's and back. Wright and Emily. Looking at them, shadowing their curved bodies with my hand, putting my face close enough to feel their warmth. Each child had a cat in its bed. A warm uncritical shape to be next to. That, I thought, is almost enough to have.

"You're so ambitious," my mother once said, not really paying attention. This was only an idle criticism.

"I have to be."

"I remember energy. Being tormented by painting; so much junk." We don't talk to each other any more. We complain at each other—at a distant spot somewhere over the left ear.

"But you used to be ambitious. You worked hard." I remembered the studio. The rolls of Belgian linen canvas. The smell of linseed oil. Turpentine. I would not tell her how fondly I remembered all of that at this point.

"I love you, baby dear" was all she said.

"I know."

And she does. But she loves him best by far and with a fierce loyalty that was probably the most helpful thing she ever taught me.

I took off the beige pants with the sea-green sweater. They were perhaps too reminiscent of army colors or hospital colors, in case he had been either of those places recently.

Perhaps I should have said I would come over to where he was. By now I would have met him at least.

I changed clothes once more. Blue and cream was better; Shetland-blue seemed right for an East Coast math person.

Still he was not coming.

By then I had clipped a couple more chunks off my speed gum, for which I drove two hours every week. The amphetamine puts everything in sharper focus. Every detail is important. Move this Mexican painted box just here, into the glow of the red glass light. Shove the astrology booklets I've written into a drawer. Put that copy of my first book under the couch. Hide all evidence of *Cosmopolitan* articles—slip the tear sheets, the notes on the latest rewrite in between the pages of art books. Then I place my tapes on the corner of the desk. I can mention they are interviews from my radio show. I will select the political ones. Turn the labels out so he will see the names of Eastern antiwar leaders he will have heard of.

Fresh flowers. With speed, I am able to leap the landlord's fence and clip an armload of fat white roses off his hedges. I put them in soup bowls and set them, then, in wicker baskets so he would not see the porcelain bowls from the old wedding and think I was too expensive.

I put one basket on my desk and then sat on the couch to see how the roses looked. If that one looked weary, perhaps, or this one too indifferent with its back to him. To a Hollywood person even roses have their good sides.

The speed gum was developed by a pediatrician in Banning; it was a blessing for someone who couldn't get a straight prescription; another way of playing Keep Away with what was really happening. I was getting back on again.

Of course, I was still only taking, say, ten to fifteen milligrams a day and that's cool. For writing, it was a different matter entirely; then you put on your formal amphetamines. It had been little more than a year since I got myself locked up.

"When did you start taking amphetamines?" the doctor had asked at the hospital.

"When I was six."

He writes down "Age six."

He looks at me. "Did you say six?"

"Ephedrine is synthetic amphetamine, or vice versa. I was on it for asthma." Six months after I left the hospital I had gotten my radio show, which seemed an acceptable substitute for speed. All the listeners calling in—a vast argumentatve audience. Moderate stardom.

At the hospital the doctor had continued, "Who brought you here?"

"Jordan. Because I smashed all the mirrors in the house. Because of the stripes on my arms and legs." Jordan of Zenda was my other self, a cavalier; a fearless androgyne. I considered him/her part of an interior cinema repertory company that played roles in books, in dreams—in fantasies I sometimes acted out. Mercury, swift critic, once resembled Gore Vidal and I wanted only to be a terrific boy so I could hang around with him, and so forth. Fame was the goddess-mother—a cool, dark woman with a long, slow smile. I could never separate the longing to be from the longing to have—and longing meant the lust to bed.

I talk about finding me. I don't think I wanted that to happen at their expense. The trick was to find someone who would appreciate Jordan, Fame and Mercury as much as I did and would let me deal with their needs and interests, some of which moved like shadows below consciousness, leaping out of sight when touched.

By the time I was eighteen, I had given up. There are some

parts, you figure, you just won't be able to share. Some people really demand that there are these private corners. Yes. But I wanted one person to understand. (To permit?) An alter ego is not the answer either. Jordan, for instance, despised Jill and had nothing but contempt when she married. "I am running away." I said to my mother after six weeks of marriage, "to Greenwich Village, where I can be a dyke." My mother, outraged, slapped me. I thought I meant to say, "Where I can be a writer."

I had tried, at the hospital that time, to explain all this to the doctor. He was more interested in the symptom. "Do you still see the stripes?" he asked again.

"Are you asking whether we still feel we are becoming a zebra?"

We noticed that, at last, we had attracted his attention.

The alarming thing about what was classified as borderline schizophrenia was that in a small dark corner, a terrified but rational animal was obliged to observe what was happening and unable to exercise any restraints. It wasn't a great animal, mind you, a woodchuck, perhaps.

My father flew in from New York, where he and my mother had moved when Hollywood ended. I had arranged to be out of the hospital before he came. I did not want to see him cry, holding his folded immaculate handkerchief over his eyes with his stylish performer's hands. (It is not from out of nowhere that Lawrence's hands would have a special appeal.)

But I was glad I looked gaunt and haggard. "For God's sake," I used to scream at his photograph, "with all this craziness—at least why aren't we rich like everyone else!"

Listen, a lot of the others didn't have it either—the money that lasts. The fame fraud is so complete that all the Hollywood kids think everyone else has money. It is the suburban delusion. But then, suburbia was invented by Hollywood. The lush small-town sets designed by hungry young men who fled West from the Depression to create the prototype for the middle-

American dream. And generations of kids growing up guilt-ridden by their rage at not having enough and angered at adults who, having provided it all, reminded them that they not only did not appreciate it but did not deserve it. "You have so much," the generic Hollywood child was told, "that you don't know what Real Life is like." But then, when we would try to find out: "You have broken our hearts . . . rejected everything we have tried to tell you, to give you, to show you. And we worked so hard too . . ." Hollywood even designed the Generation Gap to go with the dream.

But I was not particularly surprised any more by Real Life. It did not seem unusual to wait two and a half hours for an insane mathematician.

And so, on this fog-softened night in Santa Monica, I watched this man walking slowly down the street and thought, "He belongs to my life."

I looked at myself reflected in the window against the night sky, superimposed like a giantess over this princely man in the tweed jacket walking up the road to my house, and I thought again, "No, this cannot be for me."

He said, as he stepped in the door, smiling, "It took me a little longer to get here."

"Oh," I said, "I was so involved with my work I didn't notice."

What I really wanted to say was, "Listen, when do I get to touch you?"

He looked like: the young socialist poet from the Village in the thirties; the troubled young Scottish nobleman crossing windswept moors; a troubadour passing a locked-up castle, singing quietly of the plague; an introspective, unusually pensive Kennedy. His soft-focus lighting, his ambience, indicated the use of black-and-white film.

He was going to be more than a midweek fill-in for Current-and-Choice, who had a kind of sexual calendar similar to his Catholic fertility ideas, but with permits limited solely to Friday or Saturday nights. Choose one. This was a way to guarantee there would be No Involvement.

I used to have a collection of cocktail napkins which all had "No Involvement" written on them. The letters had been heavily graven into the paper by three different men at three different times in the dim light of three different clubs.

But I would rather tell you about Lawrence.

Now I am sitting on the couch with him. We are holding drinks and cigarettes—a hand unoccupied might reach out. As long as you hold a drink, light a cigarette, the other one can't go away. That's Single People Magic.

I remember the sigh of relief when a man would light another cigarette. I'd have one, too, and take longer. No one goes mid-cigarette.

Lawrence had his own set of magic games. His silence is of interest here; silence in his graceful gestures. Silence in his walk.

When the time came to refill our drinks, he emptied ice trays and did it quietly. He did not have to pound them against the counter.

So he made no sounds. I wondered if, in sunlight, he would leave a shadow.

He looked at the baskets of the white roses and touched the leaves of the ones on the coffee table. I watched his long fingers curl lightly about the silky green leaves and then move to brush the roses with more of an enclosing gesture, the shape of a hand cupping a breast. We caught each other's eyes. He smiled at me directly, did not pretend it was an accident or throw me any stupid line. He nodded his head abruptly, just once up and quickly down: an interior decision, and then he changed the subject back to the roses.

"They remind me," he said, "of the Chrysanthemum Problem, which is that the leaves will turn brown if you spray them or if you don't, and I've never been able to remember which it is. But it's a good thing to discuss. I suppose, when you don't want to get into war stories . . ."

"War stories?"

"Two old colonials—officers—meeting at a club exchanging adventures. Each one has to tell a more ferocious story indicating a more heroic past. We do that, too."

So I decided not to terrify him with my tales of rapine and horror. "Actually," I said, "the Chrysanthemum Problem applies to many things. It also becomes the problem of the hard-boiled eggs—I mean hard-cooked, which the cookbook people are very testy about. It's different but I think it relates to the Chrysanthemum Problem and is even more complex in that if you do start the eggs in cold water—or if you don't—the shells will or will not come off more easily and the yolks will or will not have green rims."

"Then you do understand the Chrysanthemum Problem," he said.

We did not exchange war stories, although the Scotch and

speed made me an unreliable witness. There was this time lapse, something I often experienced when I was anxious to please. Like all anxiety, this, too, was accompanied by a drink to come down. Or is, perhaps, the other anxiety I have in mind—interchangeable—to me? The anxiety concerning Fame.

I next found myself next to Lawrence in a restaurant on the Pacific Coast Highway. A restaurant I always was taken to on the First Date. A sort of screen test—the place to case me, without the commitment of taking me into town.

Lawrence was not casing me. He was just hungry. He may have asked me to fix him something, but I don't think so—it is too revealing. I cook too well and it is often interpreted as loving.

"How did we get here?" I asked.

He looked puzzled. "You asked your neighbors next door to listen for your children, and then we walked over to Karen and Mike's and picked up the VW. You missed that part?"

"Not really—I wasn't concentrating. You know how to drive?"

"Well, sure . . ."

So he knew about realities such as ordering, paying for things, driving and, presumably, tipping. On whatever star he had fallen from, I assumed such things weren't necessary. I liked that way of putting it, so I asked him, "What star did you fall from?"

Without a beat, he answered, "Santa Barbara. Actually I was born in Oxnard. A doctor there was a specialist in natural childbirth, which was unusual then." He wasn't going to say any more about that.

"Well," I said, "that's fortunate, because Oxnard scans better than Santa Barbara. And 'Oxnard,' he says, 'is the name of his star . . .' "

"The interior Munchkin." He had a grin that jumped off to the side and with a quick skip landed in a dimple. When could I touch him was not enough; where to begin.

Then everything faded out again and I was aware only of

the closeness of a tweed sleeve. He poured the rest of my Scotch into his empty glass. "Hey, don't try to keep up with me." Such a very gentle voice, with a thin border of amusement hand-painted swiftly around the edge, like the kind of stationery one refers to as letter paper.

"Oh, I'm not. I'm not."

"Do you always put out your cigarette in your salad?"

Mortification. And that terrible inward head shaking and blinking you go through when there's simply been too much. I went to the john and quickly chewed off another corner of speed. Cold water on the wrists. And to complete the five-minute Quick Beauty Pickup: a little fast floor nap. Very effective. Just wedge the forehead into the coldest corner. Tightly. Take deep breaths. Everything will turn black, then silver, then sort of blue . . . and you can get up and start right off refreshed.

But I did make up my mind to cool it. Somehow the most important thing in my life—for the rest of the night—was not to frighten this Lawrence Robinson away. I must remember not to overwhelm his Anglo-Saxon sensibility with Hollywood stories; not for an instant to let him suspect about the Shopping (the amount of shoes). It must be obvious somehow that money was certainly of no interest to me, and that I am so sensibly on to the total fraud of celebrity and the futility of fame. God knows.

Primarily, I should be quiet; should let him do the talking. I tried that, when I returned, eyes gleaming—competence zipping through my veins, and there was too much silence. "I'm talking too fast?"

"Well, we're not going anywhere right now. So don't rush so . . ." He ordered two more stingers, which I realized were both for him; he was a heavy drinker, I supposed, one of those men with a hollow leg. You could never tell if they were drunk. Or was it that they never got drunk. He smiled and stretched his long arms and legs, then stared out at the rocks below. At the waves.

"It's dangerous down there." I had to say something. "Rip tide, probably. A little peril to go with your vacation. Gives a touch of suspense to a day on the beach. Rip tide. You would look lovely in the water. Like a merman. Am I talking slower?"

"What are your three favorite plays?"

"I don't know if I can actually think of three, which is terrible, I mean I can think of three titles of plays, but not three I've actually seen or read—you changed the subject. You didn't like being a merman?" Such evident anxiety; always leaking out before I can catch it.

"I can't swim. Enough to get out, I guess, if I found myself in the water, but it's something I try to get around." I did not feel, with him, that he was just being patient with me, that one wrong step or word would be the end.

"Just write down three plays," he said.

But as he took a pen from his pocket, handed me a cocktail napkin and took one for himself, I wondered if there would be a play called *No Involvement*. I did not want him to be just added to the collection. I should have kept talking fast no matter what. When you let silence come by too early on, men assume you want to go to bed and then that means you're easily had; it also means they're likely to get involved.

We exchanged plays. *Hamlet* was on both lists.

"That," he said, "is the point. It almost always is."

"But I'm not sure if it is one of mine, actually. It's just one I have actually seen; the movie, of course."

"Everyone identifies with Hamlet—it's always safe to give a character a sad childhood. Most adults like to think their own childhoods were secretly sadder than everyone else's."

"I suppose so. I always felt guilty about that. I didn't have any of the problems: dead parents, poverty—the facts that would make sadness valid. To look at it, the childhood was happy. It was just the child that was sad. You had some acceptable excuses to go with your sadness, I think."

Was that what I had seen when I saw him walking, coming down my street?

"It was not a great childhood. I guess not. I was more angry than sad. But even allegedly happy children are angry a lot of the time. There is so much they aren't allowed to do."

Lawrence Robinson and children. I had a feeling they moved too fast and might frighten him. I could see him, in the back of the top shelf of the bookcase, peering out with very wide eyes, like one of the cats we kept getting.

We drove back, after a while, down the Pacific Coast Highway.

It runs parallel with the California person's aorta. Should be listed on anatomy charts. I seemed to begin and end everything on the Highway. To make all decisions at sixty miles an hour.

It is especially fine on nights such as this, when there is no one else out; no distant headlights. Even though Lawrence was driving, being with him had all the positive qualities of being alone.

He turned up the Channel Road, past the shanty bars, the stucco cabin restaurants, dwarfed by their neon lights, the Tumble-Inn motel, the lead-ins to the street where I lived, in the house with the window cantilevered out far enough so a woman sitting at her desk there could see someone walking.

This Lawrence, I thought, he needs protecting. A lot of calm and quiet. And having me only leads to chaos.

He stopped the car and turned the key to switch it off. The car was still.

"Take a deep breath this time," I said to Jordan, who wears the horns in that interior repertory company I mentioned.

"I want you," he said. And he put his arms around me in the big, happy hug of a child.

"Let's," I said, leaping out of the car, unbuttoning my cardigan as I dashed up the stairs to my house, three at a time, "go where there's more room."

This was exactly against my rule. To sleep with someone at home—it was to worry about later.

We had our clothes off very fast. He assumed I was capable of taking off my own clothes, which I liked. I cooperate with almost any idea, of course, but I liked this feeling of being friends getting undressed, of not being his doll.

I would not fake tonight. He would know instantly and recognize it as part of a how-to-get-your-man kit. The kind of thing I wanted him to believe I didn't do. The light came up from the street lamp and came in through that flying window like moonlight, and as he leaned so gracefully to place his clothes on the back of a chair, I saw how perfectly formed he was—the curve of his back as he bent slightly sideways. His motions seemed automatically to assume the classic form. If we had been playing statues, I could have said "Freeze" at any point, and sculpted him just in that instant of marble and you would see what I mean.

It is not just this Hollywood sensibility. I think we love men's bodies when they're beautiful more than we say. It is, perhaps, that men are too shy to be looked at and adored, too afraid we might turn into their mothers and hiss at them, in a moment of spite, "You're vain!" And tell their fathers, who will bellow, "What's this I hear (have feared) about you not being a real man!" Or that we will turn into middle-aged wives and shriek (because they do not fuck us every night), "You must be a goddamn latent homosexual!" A latent person, after all.

Oh, Lawrence. As I reached out for him I did believe I would find I was holding only empty air and long-gone wishes.

There was none of the gaunt look of a tall man; not a bone out of proportion, from his squared, slender shoulders to his fine, slim ankles. His thighs and legs had the well-modeled shapeliness of a son—a boy.

Even with the help of the speed and the drink he made me shy a little because, although he had had even more to drink, he too seemed shy. Or that's how I interpreted it when he spent a lot of time kissing my face and stroking my hair. And brushed his lips across my collarbone, discovering, I wanted to tell him, a new erogenous zone in the process. (I made a note that he should repeat that often.)

He touched me everywhere at first as if he were making a preliminary sketch to be filled in later in bolder strokes. So sweet he was that when his hand went strolling lightly down my stomach and through the underbrush it was like a friend going to meet a dear, old roommate. It was not like a tiger pouncing to score and furrow the meat for more efficient consumption. And so legs trained to do what they were told, opened wide like arms.

"This hand knows what is what and where is where," she said to her commander, her superego, the Wac Sergeant, sitting at her broad wooden desk in my brain.

But as Lawrence drew his lips over my thighs to add such subtle detail to his handcrafted finery, the Wac Sergeant snapped her ruler on the desk. "Attention! What have we here: a splayed frog, laid out for dissection?" And the Wac Sergeant with modern audio-visual techniques at her command, superimposed a slide of rape—from her up-to-date files—on my consciousness.

So I pulled gently on his arms and shoulders, sliding under him, lifting his hands away from what might be a lengthy pursuit—and boring. I wanted to be comfortable to Lawrence because he felt so comfortable to me. He fitted into and around me and the shape of him became the shape of me and his smiling kisses returned my own scent back to me. His arms swept around my back and somehow I felt lifted up to him, suspended under him, carried under his belly like a possum, protected as he loped through to home. He made me feel we might just get there, for he didn't gallop in desperation; his pace was slow and wide and deep and rolling and I didn't have to hang on for the fear of being thrown off, or breathe hard for the fear of suffocating. There was an umbilical fondness and nourishment to be derived from this attachment.

And he looked down at me with a narrowing smoky look in his blue cat eyes. He let me have his mouth again to feel his sighs right down through my throat and to taste me while feeling him and that fantastic mixing of identities and the excitement of feeling his transfusion, of feeling as you do when you give someone exactly the right present—the tightening of his arms, cockscends gently going deeper . . . He did want me, really me, in some urgent search.

I sent a message down to hold him, and she listened, startled, for once, from her vow of ambivalence, she welcomed him. And she kept him securely wrapped and held through his free-fall pain. A fast spin—orgasm—a dangerous feeling that had long ago convinced me I would only trust myself to drive.

And then side by side, we lay and watched each other's faces. He kept his arms around me and punctuated his rest by brushing his lips occasionally across my head or shoulders. Slowly he fell asleep and I rested in his arms, feeling rocked and filled and wanted, for when I turned even slightly on the narrow couch, he shaped himself to the way I needed to move and held me even closer.

Most men get hot and stretch and snore, and two at least had given me the house rule which was they "do not sleep with broads," so "you can sleep on the couch if you like . . . or go home. But I just don't sleep well with other people."

With this Lawrence it was like making love with one's twin brother. It was as though we had shared the womb and the childhood traumas. There were all the conceivable joys—and none of the usual taboos. He did not feel like different skin or cells or external matter to me.

So why did I have this other feeling, sort of subterranean, like a warning light in another room, that something was not quite right; that he was not all he seemed to be. I supposed it was simply because Karen had told me he was insane. Like telling your friend the hypochondriac as you serve the cassoulet that has perfumed the house, "I hope it's all right, the Belgian sausage looked a bit green to me, but I'm sure since it's been cooked for hours . . ."

Be cool, I thought, as I outlined his square jaw down to its delicately tapered chin, the trim flesh molding his ribs, the curve of his loin.

Now, wait now, before you decide this is finally the person you will kill yourself over. Perhaps it was a different signal; I was reading this message wrong. Perhaps it was saying, "Listen, you watch out now. Don't you hurt him."

But that was craziness. The only way I could hurt a man was by marrying him and exposing him to the tall, full horror of what supporting me meant.

Just before dawn I woke up and Lawrence was looking at me. He held my head in both exquisite hands and kissed my face as if I were a friend to be careful about and gentle with, and he said, "You look like a small replica of some Nordic goddess—all golden . . ."

See, he didn't have to say anything like that. He could have nodded kind of knowingly and said, "Listen, you've still got a great body, kid." I really don't know why it seems necessary for men—and it's sad to think about why they do it—to suddenly talk like Bronx truckdrivers when they're making love. Or after, when the educated man remembers he's supposed to stay awake for a few minutes and say something to "the woman."

We clung to each other again. Just holding on as tight as

we could. As I think back to holding him that first time in the shadows of that shiplike room, the typewriter, as always, a sullen witness, I feel the freshness of his weight and his hair and what I am trying to describe is that what I felt was interest, not invasion.

When you go over the past, you find new feelings, as well as events you didn't know were there. It is, I told someone, like looking under my daughter Emily's bed. There's a half a pair of socks, the wrapper from a Milky Way bar, pizza paper, a seriously used turtle, some overexposed Magic Markers . . . and back there, the elusive feeling—the one I almost recognized, but couldn't quite place. The feeling that even though it had nothing to do with terror, it was nevertheless quite appealing.

Sorting out what-happened-when is something like untangling the branches of the sweet basil when they flourished in the peaked winter sun, each eager to tell its own flower. So you go in delicately. Fingertips, not sense of order, gently freeing each green strand from the tangled skein and each yarn seems to know when its turn comes up. Without having to stand in line.

I told Lawrence my position on marriage: "An archaic institution—a piece of paper that locks a man into a lifetime of financial obligation . . . don't you think?"

Then, having made certain he would not feel threatened, I said, "Listen, you wouldn't want to go to this wedding with me tomorrow, would you?" I had, as I said, surely clarified my own opinion. (An opinion, I should admit, that would have been especially interesting to one former husband, Berenger, still plowing his way through a decade of financial chaos created by me. I'll just quickly add here that people who are not yelled at don't shop much.)

To Lawrence, however, such inconsistency was one of the better things you could expect from life. "Fine, fine," he said.

"Marriage," he explained, when he showed up the next day

wearing a rusty black suit, "is a kind of contract that insures you'll get a chance to talk it over at least once more. It's not really unreasonable. Marriage."

We had taken Emily with us to the wedding and were walking through the parking lot in the sunshine, each holding one of her arms so she could leap through the air as we walked, her hair like a cape of golden ruffles flying behind her.

I mentioned somewhere along the gleaming thread of that day that the next weekend I would have to go riding, implying a cowboy actor.

"You might as well because," said Lawrence, picking up the implication, "I don't think there'll be much riding from now on."

The very fact that he made further contact with a woman while his liquids were still coursing through all her infinite verities impressed a psychiatrist whom I dropped in on when I had news.

"This one," he said, "sounds like a real heavyweight."

Which is why it sort of confused me when he stole my car.

We slept at Karen and Mike's the next time. Nannie was staying over with Wright and Emily. Nannie had come from Scotland many years before to take care of my children when they were small. Now she would come when she could to visit, to sit, to see if we were all right—and if not, what she could do about it—which was usually everything, including editing. I think I was as attached to her as the children were. I have never felt complete without her, and I believe that Emily's competence and what used to be called "good disposition" come from Nannie.

This time Lawrence and I had had what Nannie referred to as a "real date. He's actually bought you a proper meal?" He had bought me food before, but to Nannie that did not count because it was after midnight. Nannie did not trust Lawrence, even though he did have "a nice way about him."

I told him that night about this Mustang car. Having spent much time in New York, he did not see precisely how a car could be one's trustiest friend.

I bought the car, I told Lawrence, to show I had been paid something for my book. To show my godfather, who had loaned me money to buy a black dress so that I could apply for a position at Saks. In black and pearls. "It isn't easy," my godfather had said, "to make a living from writing." He was sitting in his authentically furnished nineteenth-century house, looking out over the pool with the topiary-tree guardian. A living made from writing.

And my father, too, was now earning a living from writing. In the East, where hardly anyone did that any more. So I'd heard.

Well, I'd also bought Mustang (or made the down payment, which was the same thing), I explained to Lawrence, to impress George, predecessor to someone else. George had the charm of an elf and the beat of the advertising man or the television man who clocks his time for you with his stopwatch. It was like being with the crocodile in Peter Pan. Tick-tick-tick. The rhythm of success.

"Do you have a sense of humor?" Lawrence asked.

"Why? Don't you think so . . ."

"I'm not sure. I know you have wit, but that's different; I'm always interested in what people say about themselves."

"I used to. And then—well, if you'd like to hear a quick war story—George thought I had a sense of humor. Of sorts. It was," I said to Lawrence, "going to be an important night for him. He was trying to sell a pilot to some agents, and some admen sponsor types. George had given me instructions on the phone earlier, 'Look like a million dollars tonight. Black, pearls . . . This is the big time, baby.' He tried, when he was anxious, to pretend he was living in a script from an old movie about Broadway."

I described for Lawrence how it was at the restaurant that night:

Surrounding the haberdashered men in silk suits and cuff links are the women such men refer to as "dolls":

"What's great," George says, with his faster-than-sound grin, "about Jill is she's a hell of a good sport. You couldn't do this with an actress."

He picks up a handful of fettucini and spills it over my head. And we all just roll with laughter.

"It was like just heavy, heavy rain coming, coming down," I told Lawrence, "and I couldn't stop laughing. I couldn't stop laughing. Now, I didn't think that was funny, though. I mean, it was not humor to me."

"Thoreau," Lawrence said, touching my hair as if to brush away any vestiges of fettucini, "wrote, 'Beware of any enterprise requiring new clothes.' I would say, specifically for you: black and pearls."

We did not get back to the business about a sense of humor.

The daybed in Karen and Mike's vast studio was narrower than a couch, but we slept comfortably, even with the addition of their cats coming through the window and napping in among our curves. I walked home around dawn, leaving Mustang for Lawrence.

A day later, when neither he nor Mustang had returned or called, I decided to mention it to Karen.

"Oh, he'll bring it back," she said. "Larry's amoral, but not immoral. It's an important difference."

"I'm glad to hear that."

"It's not that he doesn't like you—I happen to know he's very fond of you."

"Do you also happen to know where he is?"

"No. He's probably trying to work out some things he should have worked out with himself. Look, I told you this was not for involvement. I'm sure when he comes back, he'll explain everything."

"He's married?"

"No." She changed the subject a little too fast. "Listen, you could always call the police."

"Oh, never. No. I just want him to come back. And the car. Cops? Jesus, Karen. I think I love him. I think he's unhappy. That's all."

"He'll be back, then."

At one o'clock three mornings later I was awakened by the slam of Mustang's door. When you spend some time waiting for people in the night, your skill in distinguishing car sounds improves.

I ran out to the carport, pulling on jeans and a sweat shirt as I ran, screaming, "Lawrence . . . Lawrence . . . Laurie . . ." Yelling. He had dropped off the car and left so fast. Mustang was still warm, still making settling-off noises. I ran barefoot down the steps on the side of the bluff to the street, and down the street, faster and faster, in bare feet, thinking, "That is crazy, you are cutting your feet, which means you'll slow down and you'll never get back." But I ran on, stopping only to brush away the worst and sharpest stones and bits of gravel, and I dashed into each bar, staring into the dimness to find him: stared back at like a crazywoman.

"Lawrence," I shouted in at the dark, at the gloom, over the blue neon sound of the jukes. I had the feeling he'd just left somewhere. You do know when you are not going to find someone. I went back very slowly.

The next night: I was speed-sleeping, through odd dreams, prominent with Guilt People suspended in corners in my room, swaying, gray wraiths with troubled, blind eyes. And I had been crying because it was over with him. How much worse it was to have Mustang back, to have all ties cut.

Suddenly: a Guilt Person is moving in my room.

Nightmare sweats; worst terrors confirmed: it is real. Someone is in the room.

"Shhh," he said.

"Laurie."

He sat upon my bed, bending over me and holding me. "I was so scared." I started to cry, again. "Please don't go. Please don't go."

He just held me, lying beside me. He stroked my hair. He kissed my eyes. We didn't make love. He kissed my hands and held them both inside his.

"We fit," he said.

He was saying without saying it that, nevertheless, he had to leave. I walked him to the door.

"I'll be back. I don't know when—just don't move."

The next day Karen swore and paced around her sunny kitchen and said, "Damn him, I think he should have told you. All right." And Karen told me that Nadia had called from London, and he had gone to see her. And that was what he couldn't figure out how to explain.

Nadia was a photographer. They had been married and had filed for divorce before he had come to California. She had gone to North Vietnam. As a person of resourcefulness, he wins.

"He had decided to come here while she was away to see if it was the traveling or each other that was creating the trouble. He really wasn't sure," Karen tried to reassure me, "if he wanted to go back. Or even if she wanted him to. I think it was something he had to do."

Karen poured some coffee. I looked out at the hills of purple lantana, and the mist, soft as his hair. I have to stop thinking of him. This is not a new procedure. It should be easier each time.

"Nadia is a loner," Karen said. To be even more reassuring. That only made Nadia more attractive. Men love women who can amuse themselves for an hour and a half without filing an abandonment suit. ". . . an intellectual," she added.

"She is beautiful, of course. I will just be running this knife across my wrists as you tell me every detail."

"She has lively dark hair, a look of great activity, that English skin, extraordinary green eyes. As for beauty . . ." Karen said. "Sexual magnetism. You can put down the knife, please."

"I've always wondered what that means—'intellectual.'"

"I think," said Karen, "one definition of 'intellectual' is someone who bases action on reason and information, something like that, not emotion or experience. But a further definition might be that an intellectual is one who has never heard any acceptable definition of an intellectual. Including this one."

"At least," I said, realizing I was not an intellectual, "they're not staying here. She would be too large for the cot. And an intellectual like that would reason she couldn't get much sleep on that cot with a tall man and your cats."

"The interesting thing," Karen said, "is you'd probably find her fascinating."

"As another little exercise in masochism?" I stirred my coffee. I wanted a drink, but I'd wait until I got home. It would be a kind of incentive to go back. Listen, I said to myself, don't you get flippy. The first year after divorce a little insanity is permitted. This was now enough. Three years. You be a woman about this. "So," I said, "what do you think, Karen?"

"Listen, I like Nadia. But it may be he seems more secure with you. And she told him once that he was boring. That doesn't seem auspicious. But I've told you. You can't ever tell what Larry's going to do. There was a time when you could, but you can't any more."

The breeze came up from the sea, through the window, ruffling the nasturtium vines tangling around the patio. I felt like a child as we sat, now, on the patio, and I wrapped my arms around my knees: Tell me a story.

Karen and her husband Mike had met Lawrence over ten years before in Texas. Mike and Larry had both been in the Air Force there; both, at the time, teachers in an Air Force training school. Mike had finished his service time earlier and gone on to New York to work with the flourishing new electronics division of a big company.

"Mike says he's got the most brilliant math mind he's ever known. He recruited Larry for the company as soon as he got out of the Air Force."

Her rich voice went on, then she stopped and looked at me. "I'm not sure it's good to keep talking about him. You're obsessing. You're going to be convinced you're in love, when what you've got is a romantic assemblage that has nothing to do with feelings. You're pretending to be wistful when you should be angry."

"I hate thinking. It takes the good out of the longing. Karen, do you really think I'll see him again?"

Everything has always depended on the opinion of the current Authority, which is the person I am talking to at a given moment. How my work is going, how well I am loved, how well I look, whether I will live out the year; all of these questions must be connected, by the umbilical cord of the phone to the ten or fifteen current favored reactors. Before I can cry or smile, before I know if the work is good or bad, I must know what you think.

"You'll see him," Karen finally said, "because you want it to work out that way. I always believe you because you do always get exactly what you want."

"Never! Exactly what I don't want!"

"Because the minute you do, it's not what you want any more. That's very convenient."

"Don't be constructive with me today. Tell me about him. What else do you know?"

"I've told you everything. His mother died when he was three. That would be 1936, She had red hair. Now, what does that tell you? Christ, Jill, ask him. He'll always answer."

"You can ask. That's how you do things. I'm not really like that. Maybe on the air. Not in real life."

"He'll always answer if you ask him a direct question. Do you need cue cards?"

"Oh, Karen. So you do think it will happen . . ." She had implied I would see him again. My whole life was solved.

So I went home and dyed my hair red.

I drove up the Highway a lot during the months I waited. The Highway became me: a solemn, long woman accompanying her pacific lover up the California coast. Each day I drove a little closer to Santa Barbara, trying to get back to his beginnings.

His mother: There must be no more complete torture than to be a mother and to know the moment you are dying that you are leaving your baby a queasy destiny, as unknown as your own, but even worse because, after all, you do know the ways of the world, and as for ways, there can be no worse ones beyond . . . one assumes.

I thought of a mother at Auschwitz, with more guts than I would have, and more basic faith, wrapping her infant inside her clothes on the hooks outside the showers, hoping a tender-hearted guard would find the baby and save it.

I don't think I could die with that question.

Then one evening Karen called and said that Laurie had returned to L.A. and—was working with a research company in the Valley. But Mike and she believed I should give Lawrence time to sort out his feelings. A month went by and he did not call. He was working hard, it was reported. He had bought a used Renault car. I was told that he would call, for sure.

"You should understand," Mike said, "he has some uncomfortable feelings."

"Guilt?" I snapped. "He shouldn't. Unless he never calls and I do die."

"For once," said the chorus of Well-Consulted friends, "show you have some pride." And: "This time you're really asking for trouble." And: "For God's sake, don't call him. If he doesn't have the guts to call you, forget him."

But someone else had said, "Jill, just do what you think feels right to you."

"Will everyone stop talking about feelings!" I screamed. "I don't know what I feel except I love him and I don't know how to tell you how that feels!"

Feelings were not something our family talked about. We said "I love you" to each other as you would say "Hello" and "Goodbye," and a phone call that did not end with "I love you" was a phone call to be repeated, with the question, "Is something wrong?"

And if you said something was wrong, you were usually feeling sorry for yourself. The way to deal with that or any other sadness except legitimate grief, which was only suffered over death, slurs against minority groups, or Republican victories, was to write out the Lists.

The Lists were the Good Things and the Bad Things. And when you were finished, unless I'm wrong (I was told), you'll see there's more on the Good Side. Actually, it was more, "Things to be Grateful For." Which held the implication of the full-dress God. Here are sample lists:

TO BE GRATEFUL FOR	NOT GRATEFUL FOR
1. A healthy, happy child.	1. Being raped, which makes me nauseated in the night still. Because the violence is there waiting. For my own child.
2. Another healthy, happy child.	2. Not being able to support my children as a writer.
3. A beautiful car.	3. Knowing that it still matters more that it is a beautiful car than that I can't pay for it.
4. Being a Gemini because I can talk myself out of committing suicide long enough so that something will have to come along to change my mind anyway.	4. Not being a Leo because they never have to think of suicide at all.
5. A market checker recognized my voice as "that funny girl on the radio who's so mean to all those callers."	5. The fan who said she would know me anywhere because I have my father's nose.
6. Alive parents . . .	6. Worry that the Parent Problem still does matter even though you're over thirty, and after thirty you can't just call it growing pains. And I don't want to call it I-hate-them.
7. Having seen Lawrence.	7. Having seen Lawrence.

No, I don't know what I felt about Lawrence. Except I felt terrified and abandoned with this decision. I didn't know enough about him even to make the Lists (if there's more "Good," I call?). And then, there was the possibility he would say "No," just "No," to anything I had in mind.

Could I handle that? I asked the question, but the answer was irrelevant.

He answered the phone in a low and serious at-work voice I hadn't heard before. "Robinson," he said.

"Robinson," I said, "why don't you just come home?"

He said he would be right over. "Right over" translated here to four hours. He brought everything he owned from a man's entire life: two suitcases. A weekender and what you call a two-suiter. They were new and cheap; to take to places with signs saying "Transients Welcome." I could hear the shirts on cardboard sleds bounding from one side to the other as he walked down the hall to our room.

Our room.

There were four striped shirts, with cuffs and collars so frayed one could consider them fringed; three pairs of black socks gone gray with washing; the tweed sports coat, a pair of slacks that shimmered about the seat with age and use; two shorts, torn and blue; a box of Go pebbles; two packs of playing cards; another tie; dark-blue foulard (he was wearing its partner in dark red with this rusty black suit of his); a copy of *One Flew Over the Cuckoo's Nest* and some stories by a writer called Heinrich Böll.

"Böll . . .?" I asked.

"That's interesting," he said. "Nadia didn't know of Böll either. You'll like these stories."

"Nadia didn't? Well." Although it was over, it was comforting to hear she had a fallibility.

There was also, in Laurie's cases, a fairly new, extremely expensive blue velour terry bath kimono, monogrammed elegantly. The color of his eyes had certainly influenced the selection. From what I had heard of Nadia this, clearly a gift, did not seem to be her cool style.

This was the lavish present of the more insecure lover.

I felt like the children in *Mary Poppins* as they watched the magic satchel being unpacked. For all its emptiness, so full of curiosities. There was a packet of very old letters and a manila envelope.

"All my divorce papers," he said.

"Three?" I seemed to remember he had mentioned he had been married twice before Nadia.

"Yes," he said, examining five socks, none of which seemed to have any immediate relative. So they had, in fact, divorced.

"Children?" I thought I'd slide that in. Sort of as though I were a clerk typing out the living-in permit. Information for the files. Just a formality, really.

"One," he said. He hung up the slacks. "I'll tell you about that—" He didn't have to add "another time." I had never asked him before because I thought if he had never had children, it might have been because he could not have them and he might not want to tell me that. And if he had them, the situation was probably not terrific or he would have mentioned them right away.

I see: Information will be provided as needed.

There were also several dun-colored lawyer-envelopes, collection notices. Turn-off orders. But who that is of any interest does not have such a credit record?

From the manila envelope he drew a photograph of a woman in a thirties dress, a printed crepe with short sleeves and a white collar. Her graceful arms are holding this blond baby with dreamy eyes. She has his face, Laurie's face, just a bit softer. Far-off eyes. That Scottish lyric look: side-stepping grin; the wry comma at the side of the mouth.

"My mother," he said.

So. "Sybil," I said quietly. Had he told me her name before? I could not remember.

When I said it then, just like that, he seemed surprised.

My children were pleased that he would be staying with us. For one thing, as Wright immediately pointed out, "Mom was much nicer when you were going out with her."

Emily dashed about being helpful. "Would you like some more ice, Laurie? Some coffee? Mommy, can I bring him some of the chocolates from under your sweaters? She keeps them there," Emily explained coolly, "so we will not know where they are." Or would he, she wondered, bringing it right out of its cage, like to see her white mouse? "It's really more beige and I can show you how my cat drinks from a real baby bottle . . ."

Wright was even cooler, older. "God, Emily, he doesn't want to hold your mouse!" Then, later, "Larry, do you want to play baseball? My dad and I play on some weekends. Maybe we could set up a game." Wright was making it clear that my friend Lawrence was an augmentation. But not a replacement.

"That would be very fine," Lawrence said, fixing himself another drink. I would have to figure out how to ask him if sometimes he could buy the Scotch. It was expensive for just-drinking, when just-drinking involved the amounts he seemed to use. My just-drinking was only cheap red wine. I could drink it like water. But it wasn't really drinking. As I said, I didn't know how to get into the subject of money. I did not want him to think he was here for that.

"Oh, Mommy, he's nice," Emily whispered, dancing about, much twirling through the house. "Maybe next we could get a pony?"

"I think," Wright said to us later, sitting back in his chair, leg crossed over his knee (if he had had a vest on, his thumbs would have been in it), "that it was a good idea to get a step-father to live in. After all, we get sleep-overs. So Mom can have one. Even"—he was giggling— "on school nights. If she's good."

Wright had learned, when he was about four—"many years ago," he would have said—that adults would be more civil and attentive if you arranged your words in a certain fashion. He understood the importance of delivery over material. He listened carefully to those friends of mine who seemed to capture the most attention.

So, Wright too seemed entranced by the fame game, the fast talk of the talented that masked the ongoing sales pitch. In terms of his splendid wit and companionship, I would not have had it any other way. For him, for growing-up content, I would have wanted it to be easier. I did not like to see the eager panic in his eyes before he spoke, as he built his story—and prowled for the right timing. Laurie could show Wright a little about ease. Emily already shared his tranquillity.

Emily and Laurie accepted. Wright and I battered at life.

My house was in balance.

Do not breathe. Keep these hands still.

On Saturday morning I drove away early to do my radio show. When I returned I saw a note: Laurie and the kids were playing volley ball on the beach with Berenger. And Pat, who was Berenger's woman friend. Berenger had been the father of my children.

I was relieved I had not been there to see how they all explained each other.

Now: Time to go through Laurie's papers.

Sybil. Here is what I learned: Sybil died on May 29, 1936. The day before I was born.

That was something strange.

Sybil: Hair fluffed and, yes, dark-red, in a "hand-coloured in life-like tints" photo. Wearing the white-collared dress; a dress with no collar. A suede jacket. Always with her smiling golden child.

Sybil: A letter from Forest Lawn concerning the payments on her gravestone. Addressed to a Mrs. Matthew Robinson II. The stationery was decorated with the picture of a statue, a gathering of weeping pastoral lovers, called "The Mystery of Life," and this recommendation:

Nothing in Los Angeles gives me a finer thrill than Forest Lawn

(signed) *Bruce Barton*

And there were canceled checks, as well as notes of receipt for payments on the memorial tablet. A ground memorial tablet in Vesperland. There was a note to Laurie wrapped around the check stubs. It was signed "Grandmother." Holding the note, I saw, for one instant, the boy he was . . .

It is 1944.

He is in the kind of room one called a parlor, standing on a carpet printed with roses. He has on a sweater and a starched shirt, with a wide, flat collar. A woman's arm comes into the picture, holding an envelope; it is draped in a plum crepe sleeve. "These records should be kept. We had difficulty enough finding her first gravesite. It took money and time to locate. They were kind and did all they could. But records had been misplaced."

The woman is his grandmother. She puts her arm around his

shoulder. "Now come out to the garden," she says, "and see how nicely the chrysanthemums are doing."

Sybil, lately of Vesperland. B. (?)–d. May 29, 1936. To consider . . .

I put on my bathing suit and ran down to the beach to play ball with everyone.

Laurie was thoughtful. He had provided everyone with paper cups and there was a thermos full of screwdrivers.

Berenger's Pat was playing Anxious Mother, taking Kleenexes from her bikini like clowns come from a car; wiping my children's faces. To be sure, Berenger had told her how bad I am. Taking the children to peace marches on school nights. Exploiting them by talking about what a rotten thing marriage is —right on the air. I've said how next time I'll live with someone in my very own house, with my very own children.

"Emily," Pat suggested, "shouldn't you put a shirt on . . . shoulders look a little red." Pat socked the ball over the net to me, adding, "You really do practice what you preach. I got to hand it to you."

"Oh, I'm sure you will." I was being a little flip as I flipped the ball to Lawrence.

Actually, she liked the kids. And people who like kids assume they—the kids—would be much better off in their hands. No matter what your point of view, that other parent is doing it all wrong.

I tried to be a reasonable person.

I still wanted to goad her to say I am a bad mother so I could eat her in sunlight with steel teeth.

Coming down the beach from the other side was Sue, the current head lady of the PTA. Among my creative cottage industries was the writing/illustrating of the PTA newsletter.

She beckoned me off to a quiet place under the cliff. "I hear," she said, "you're living with a man!" (giggle)

"Yes . . . I love the way the news travels. Look over there."
I pointed to Laurie. "Is that something?"

She squinted. "Cute. Very attractive . . . Listen, I hate to say
anything, but Kent says I— Well, we can't come to your party.
Not with the kids."

She was talking about my children's birthday party. Emily
and Wright had been born almost precisely two years apart.
Every year I gave a huge party, adults and children all together.

"Why not?" I could see it in her expression as she regarded
my houseguest.

"Well . . ." Now she was uncomfortable; she shook her pert
hair. No. I would not make her say it. I skipped through the
sand. But I gave a tight squeeze to Emily and to Wright. And I
looked at Laurie, such a slender, pale god in the sunlight, from
a time before all gods were equipped with suntans and shades.

After the game I helped the children pack up for their weekend with Berenger.

If I believed Sue had a real thinking deformity, why did I
feel defensive? Especially when Berenger glanced over at Laurie.

Damn convention. Next week I would do another show about
why marriage is irrelevant and I would have on a minister and
a conservative marriage counselor to attack. And I would also
have on the head of the whole California PTA. And attack her
for not coming out against the war.

Pat helped Emily into the car. Our eyes met.

"Don't mess with me, baby!" was how I read it. She tied a
good silk scarf neatly around her well-done head.

It would have been more my style to joke about the encounter
with Sue to the whole group. But I was frightened of this Pat.
I had not misplaced this fear; it was sitting—Fear One, Fear
Two—beside her in Berenger's car.

PTA mother. I remembered the list I had made of what my
mother didn't do that I would do:

One: Join the PTA.

Two: (I think.) Make lunches herself and put surprises in

with the sandwiches, including valentine paper napkins on Valentine's Day.

Three: Drive the children to school herself.

Four: Trick or treat. Make the costumes. Go with them, walking. In her own neighborhood.

I looked at Laurie. That was enough to distract me from such thoughts. We took hands as the car went around the bend, and we rushed into our bedroom, got out all our drugs and closed the door so the cats would not get contact high.

We rolled about laughing: tangling hair and kissing so wildly. No inch was left untouched; the morning sun moved past our window. We closed curtains and lit candles. Out of a pocket he pulled a small wooden doll, one opened on the order of the egg-within-egg-within-egg folk-art toys.

"Hash . . . serious hash," he said. I refilled our glasses with Scotch and soda, and we sat on the bed, like kids exchanging treasure collections, sharing morsels of drugs. I found seven amyl nitrite pellets—yellow submarines—and the speed gum, which he said he'd try a corner of.

"If hash," I said, "is like grass, then I'll need more speed, or else I fall asleep. And that's a waste. And besides," I added, "I can be less shy with a little help and tell you things."

Enough drugs and the Censor–Wac Sergeant in my head would pass out; I could sneak off on my own, telling him all the top-secret stuff. "Anyway," I said, arranging myself in the lotus position to distract him from what I was saying, or to distract myself so I could say it, "I can't come. I mean I can but I don't. Not easily."

"I know," he said, sitting across from me on the bed, putting a hand on each shoulder and looking at me very seriously, "it always takes a while. Women don't at first with someone. Usually."

"I know that. Can I call you Laurie? It's better for you . . ." I wondered where all this honesty was coming from when I always lied. "Well, Laurie," I said. Stopped. Then started over, "It was never my best thing to do or easy. But it got worse after this particular bad time. But it wasn't just what happened— it was the terror that when I am not on guard, I find violence. I get hurt. Or I hurt someone. It is as though I've had to freeze my body against destruction. And, I guess, against the good things, too."

I took him with me then; back to the mid-sixties; to the Fourth of July and a party at the Malibu Colony: I have come to the party alone, and with the lean and hungry longing of the freshly divorced, I ask a young screenwriter if he would like to be my lover.

"No," he says, speaking loudly over the din of the Malibu Colony Fourth of July party, the new sound of the Byrds, "for I respect your father too much."

So I have some more to drink.

Although I thought Hollywood had ended when my parents moved to New York, here is a second generation bringing it back; the party is being given by Jane Fonda, who is no longer the best horse rider in school or Henry Fonda's daughter. She has transmogrified into a person arrived. A star.

I want to pretend it is a time warp and I am still the child with all this to look forward to.

But the warp is in achievement. I am still so intent in looking forward, I have not noticed it as almost time to begin looking back.

Stop taking these fast breaths, I tell myself. This is a gathering of old family friends. That is how to see it. But inside this anxious-looking person with the soft frilled hair is the mind of a *Modern Screen* movie-magazine groupie.

I walk back and forth through the plastic film walls that separate the party tent from the house. It is like walking in and out of all our favorite movies, through one scene into another.

Standing here, with my hand affectionately clasping the glass, does not fool anyone. This is a glass. This is not a companion lending weight and balance to my presence.

I am dizzy. Maybe if I lie under the table for a moment. There are many odd ways people listen to such music.

No. There will be questions and I am not well enough to have a quick answer. I will think of one perhaps where it is cooler. On the beach.

My forehead is drenched; the bangs I pulled on all afternoon to make chic and straight are curling up. I am going to pass out.

There is an enormous space of time. I am lying face down on the beach. I hear the people of the party strolling up the beach to their own sand castles. I feel I have been noticed; I think I hear George Cukor point me out. Perhaps it is David Niven he is explaining me to . . .

". . . and she's an alcoholic, you know . . . so sad—for the father is such a decent man."

It's called negative competition. Can you overwhelm your parents' achievements with the public magnitude of your humiliations? I have a long way to go. But one cannot say I am not trying.

With illusion's silence, a limousine seems to come along the beach floating past me at a dreamlike speed. (It is, I see by chrome lettering, a Fellini model.) My elegant, crystalline mother peers from the back seat, horrified. She brandishes a fine red sable paint brush at me.

"Jill!" she says. "Remember who you are." Remember the paternal modifier is what she means. As she wishes to be defined by him, so shall I be.

It becomes so quiet I can hear stars being switched off one by one. Then I hear footsteps coming closer. Someone to help me?

Within the range of my eyes I can see bare feet. It is too much to be expected of me that I should move my head to see whom they belong to. Hands have grabbed my ankles and wrists; trying to lift me.

"Do you think she's someone?" The voice is young.

"No, she's not anyone." That's two voices.

"Just some free-floating broad." Three voices.

There are four blond boys in surfing shorts. They drag me into a very small car. My arms and legs are folded into ways they don't usually go.

I drift out again, straining to consciousness only enough to notice neon signs going by. Now I am lying on a bed. I hear a voice suddenly saying something I do understand, as a phrase reaches you through anesthesia:

"What do you want to do to her next?"

Every woman who's ever been a drunk knows about rape. Just as every man drunk knows about brawling.

Remember the line from school: "When rape is inevitable, lie back and enjoy it."

You don't enjoy it, but if you've ever been slugged by a person larger than you are and felt the tissues of your face stretch and tear and your bones smash like a window shield inside your head, you do lie back.

The instinct is to close the legs, to keep them down and straight as much as possible. So it's more convenient to rape with several friends along, in relay rape there's always someone to hold the hands down. I might hit them. Or try to cover my eyes. It is somehow more effort just to keep my eyes shut. I hate being held down. It is like childbirth: when strangers come near you there—near where it is most mysterious, most dangerous—they must hold down your hands.

It does insure you will not touch yourself. That would be bad.

Every muscle in my hands curls in against awareness. As if these hands see more than eyes. I do not forget the phobic eyes of that compulsive jock above me.

"Go, go," he says, trying to pretend he likes to compete in this game.

I close my eyes. I say, "I'm just a writer. I've got two children."

"I tol' ya she was old."

I try to remember the distinction among the words: Mutilate. Disfigure. Dismember.

"Look, please don't kill me."

I see their teachers interviewed when they are arraigned after the mutilated (or dismembered, but definitely disfigured) body of the divorcee-mother-of-two is found in the Whittier Shopping Center construction site. "Just average boys . . ."

"I've got to finish my book." They must understand. "You can't run out on a book contract."

Being young people, they should like my book. It's political satire.

One is hanging back. He is challenged: "Don't you want to do it, you chicken?" (I do not mind this rejection.)

"Listen," I interrupt. I must insure getting back. "I won't say anything if you just get me to my car . . . I've got two babies." That sounds more affecting than "kids." The rapists, after all, are someone's kids. "Please, please."

"Stop whining—we won't hurt you." Everyone has different standards.

In scenes of violence, in crashes, in rape, there's a time when you take what bits of consciousness you find, and you hide.

I think of that and equate it with how, during a rainstorm that shook my parents' mansion, I had gathered up my dolls as I could find them in flashes of lightning that came through the windows of my dark attic room, and I sheltered them in the curve of my stomach under the covers. I remember all their names. Curly Top. Rowena. I remember how appalled I was when a friend showed me how, with an ice pick, she had made three holes in her doll's bottom. "Get it away," I screamed, "I don't want to see that!"

I wish I had no places now. The minute someone says, "Turn her over," you know you're in for it. Why the hell don't they skip the middlewoman and do it to each other if they want to? "Turn over."

Afterwards I pull my clothes together. That seems the most shameful part because I have to bend and look around under the bed for my shoes. I think they are embarrassed because I am crying. I would have liked to go into the bathroom, but I decide to lie down to die.

They put me back into that car and drop me by the side of the road near enough, they assure me, to where they found me. It's a long, long walk back to the party. When I finally see Mustang parked by the side of the road, I throw my arms around him. It reminds me I am still tangibly me. The car's keys, however, are in my purse, and my purse is in the house, where I can see and hear, by the lights and thumping sounds, that the party is still going on.

It would have been too much to hope that Sonnenberg-the-Kind, self-made town crier and friend to ex-husband Berenger is not the first person to notice me as I come in by the side door.

"You look like you've been raped and murdered," he observes.

I start to cry again.

"You're all bloody and dirty," he continues and I mention six or ten times that he should not speak of this to Berenger.

Then, as other guests gather about, awareness of sympathy and a lot of attention make me tell them what had happened. Tears, I can see, are welling up in the beautiful eyes of a lovely English actor (do I love being affecting because it might effectively get me loved?).

Someone suggests calling the police.

"No," I say.

"They never believe women," says Jane, with her arm around me. Do you want to stay here? Do you want a doctor?"

Her arm is very warm and sturdy for such a thin young arm. For a second I resent her command of my situation— of all situations. It is looks; no. Her daring: when she was twelve she was riding horses naked and cool as a myth.

"We must not call the police," someone said. "The publicity would be bad for Jane."

"That's beside the point," she snaps. It is bravery; as if she had said, "This is now my life: watch how I'm living it." Is it possible to be brave, to be a star and to be in love? At the same time? Or do you have to choose just one?

"I just want to get Mustang's keys and go home," I say. "I just want to go home."

"So," I said to Laurie, "I clicked my ruby slippers three times and here I am." How well he had listened. He kissed my hands.

"California sunshine people," he said, "too much Vitamin C."

"You know," I continued, with this unusual honesty "how they saw a woman in half, those boxes with the door? It's like that. A steel curtain doing a cross section just below my stomach, sort of here . . ." And I drew a line across, an inch or two above the fur. "Well, when I, or when we, make love, it is as if the curtain lifts just a bit so light could come through because you feel so good, but then I remember and it clangs shut again."

"We'll have to do something about that . . ."

I felt relieved. It is easier to share a problem.

"Here," I said when he'd lit the cigarette and shared the drag with me, "come down beside me, to where I can show you how it sometimes works." He lay next to me his legs automatically falling into positions that should be sculptured or sketched.

Moments passed as we lay, sucking in the smoke and feeling the early drift—the spaces in time. I tried to fight my reaction to grass, which was to sleep for as long as I could.

I lost.

When I woke up he was sitting beside me, legs crossed,

giggling, with a jar of honey. He dipped his tongue in, and I sucked it off like a lazy cat. "Energy," he said. I had something to say to that, but by the time I remembered I had forgotten again. Such is how it is, you know, with hash and grass and which is why I didn't like it; speech being, all things considered, the thing I did best, I felt at some disadvantage with that facility impeded. (Inhibited.)

And then, he put the honey everywhere. In and on all places, saucing anatomy's delicacies. On himself. On me. On my breasts, and the feeling there was so strong that the power of speech vaulted through the thick hedges of grass: "Don't stop . . . I can come there."

And so we kept nursing honey off each other with the slow and steady beat of healthy, mildly satiated babies. I could hear the lovely, tiny swallowing gulps—you cover all ages in the sex-play cycle, from nursing infant to death in one terrifying swoop of the sexual plot.

Then he took my hand in his and moved it down onto myself so I could show him how else I could make it happen; he made it easy, so easy, to just be as I would alone, a slow motion cool come came as he cracked the first ammy in its yellow knit sac. He held it under my nose lightly as he took over for the next round. He spun me dizzy, circling faster, harder with a perfect sense of the slow build, his hands and mouth spilling the feeling all over me, moving like the honey in a sweet, heavy tide, heating up and moving faster to a let out kind of graphic rock-and-roll percussion, and it fooled me, it kept on spinning the motor, it didn't kick over. Fantastic!

The perfect terror, time suspends mid-come.

And . . .

On it goes, and I had to have him closer more of him. His eyes were lime-green now. "My satyr," I tried to say before I dove between his legs to find the darkest, deepest place. I felt pregnant with his artful hands—his dazzling mouth went on as I ran all along his narrow aisle, pursuing it as far as I could while licking with some eagerness and stroking with another hand along the path leading to his balls, moving tight and close now, with the tension of flamenco dancers, eyeballs following fantastic dreams with the roll and pitch of REM sleep. There were sighs from far above me and the snap of another ammy. He held it down and I sniffed hard, sucking in the sweet, dangerous fumes. A glance up quickly: to see him lying there, the grin becoming a grimace, dying ammies stuck, like tusks, in his nostrils. "Oh, darling, darling . . ." Was it me or did he call me that? My God. I love him, I love him, I love him, I thought as I moved down harder on him, farther in him, up around him. His arms held tighter, his face was buried in me, the pointed and perfect delicacy of his tongue just right, just right now—circling, spinning around, a mystic war dance circling the little fire, dancing round the small oracle who only tells her best secrets to me, who, with a wanton shudder, said to hell with it, and told him all her stories in a fevered shout, throwing panic like thunderbolts through everywhere, fracturing all light and vision into rays and tiny Persian rugs, minuscule stained-glass windows spiraling down to a whorl of bright light in a tunnel of maroon—all my senses plummeted to the sexual center, a small dot of light, catapulting, like a disconnected planet, tearing down my body from my brain, a disoriented sun fixing itself like a blazing rakish crown on an astonished clit.

"Yes, yes," I screamed and leaped over on him, "I want you inside me now!"

Lamps and bottles or glasses or all of these or none seemed to crash about us as he gripped me in his arms and brought my face down close to share the newest ammy, rough and hard against the wet goodness of his mouth. And then a new army of emotions moved in with heavy stuff. I flipped over on my stomach, pulling on him.

"Get me, get me," I cried, for what we claim to hate the most is what we fear we love the best, and the manly weight of him was on and in me with such a gentle kind of tough pressure in a thundering finish as all the muscles there are clenched like frantic fists, wanting always more and more. I felt him running through me like fluid, flashing Christmas-tree lights all the way. If I spoke now, would I sound like him? I laughed. I yelled. My voice was deep, deep. The hair that lashed my face was wet. He's come, let him be. But he was there for more, we were swimming in garnet starlight, whirling down and down. He pinned me down and whispered reassurances in my ear, holding one more yellow submarine near me, to torpedo my senses.

You could not get closer than this.

We were now inside out of each other.

But I yelled because nothing was enough but pain. "Bite me now, hurt me, hurt me, Hard, hard, hard!" And in an instant, he was out and off and sitting on the edge of the bed, his head in his hands, sobbing. Weeping with the hysteria of the waning ammy-high. Crying like a small boy, with his legs dangling, his beautiful tousled head in his hands. I groped toward him in the oily chartreuse fog that clouds the after-ammy vision—to see him there, this grief-stricken sprite. Crushed water baby.

"What? What, Laurie—what, did I hurt you?"

He shook his head, choking, his shoulders hunched. I put my arms around him, from behind, pressing my breasts against his neck, bending my head on top of his. He reached up his arms now and pulled me around, into his lap, tears ran down his face and he held me like a child, as he took deep breaths to stop crying, like a child, trying to talk at the same time.

"Shhh," I whispered, putting my fingers across his lips.

He shook his head. "I just can't hurt you like that. I won't bite you, I won't hurt you."

"Oh, Laurie—I'm sorry; I told you. I get out of control and," I repeated, "I just get out of control."

We pulled together some glasses that had, it turned out, fallen over, and he poured a drink which we shared, and some straight cigarettes and then we reconnoitered the covers, the pillows, and lay very close to each other.

"I thought," I finally said, "that it was something else that you didn't like, you know?"

"No, no," he said softly, "I wanted to be everywhere. It's the pain I don't understand, just don't understand." He shook his head and swallowed another gulp of Scotch and very flat soda. When Lawrence says "I don't understand," what he means is "I hate it."

Late in the afternoon we woke up and had the mellow post-hash, post-sex giggles and the hard-core food hunger. "One of the reasons I like chicks who have children," he said, "is there is always something to eat."

"Chicks?" I muttered as we padded along the dark hall, our bodies glowing pale in the light of the candle he carried.

"Women," he said.

Then: "You," he added, immediately understanding I had objected not so much to the word, but to the plurality.

"I had the impression," I said, "of a sort of Johnny Appleseed, planting really good comes all across America. I believe it."

"No, no." He smiled, kissing my head as he dealt with the first priority: the ice cubes. "That's not my style."

What, I wondered, is your style? The cats, who had been sniffing under the door, came in now a little contact high, and expressed as much, if not more, interest as I did in the home-made mayonnaise Lawrence decided we needed to have. A very slow and delicate procedure, involving many eggs and most precise addition of olive oil, as I remember. We poured it on romaine lettuce which was there, and Lawrence said, "Only to give it a semblance of decency. We're really just sitting down to a serious plate of mayonnaise."

"If it wasn't homemade," I pointed out, "and therefore kind of French, it would be WASP. Laurie, you really do like women's bodies. I mean, do you know that it's kind of unusual, how did you learn? Did you just know?"

"My stepmother once said something to me that what women want is gentleness. That I must make them feel good. Never any pain."

I sat closer to him, and taking his hands in mine, placed his hands on my breasts. "You have made me feel so good, like I've been lying in the sun everywhere. But that can't be all there is. It can't be all that simple, Laurie." Where, I wondered, had all his sexual perceptions really started from?

He stood in the doorway opening a bottle of white wine as I dashed to the flower bed outside to pick a branch of tarragon for cheese omelettes.

"We had fig trees on our land," he said, remembering.

He would begin, now, to let me see his life:

It is 1946, and for every stretch of orange trees, extending perhaps the length of a city block, there is a block of open land, spindled by a frame house. The Robinsons live in one of these houses, just the boy and his stepmother, now that his father has died.

Lawrence—he is thirteen—is sitting at a wooden table in the shade. His eyes are wide and blue, his neck and jaw line more fragile than they will be when he reaches maturity, but the wide, square cut of the jaw, the catlike breadth is there. It is the chin that is more pointed.

He has a fig in his hand. He blows on it gently to wipe off the beige dust from the edge-of-desert land. His hair is the color of this land also, but gleams as if sand fibers had been polished like gemstones. Lawrence wonders if a fig always contains precisely the same number of tiny fronds. Like the artichoke, which always has the same number of leaves. (He has counted many to be certain the rule is correct.)

Everett sits on the other side of the table. He is a bookkeeper in his late twenties. He had been a friend to Alma's kid brother who was killed before the war ended. Now he handles family accounts for Alma. From the house comes the sound of classical music, heavily overlaid with static. Alma, stepmother to Lawrence, comes out from the house carrying a tray. Everett points out that "fig" is a dirty word in Italian. Alma polishes her fig with a damp cloth and then draws and quarters it. She glares at Everett and Lawrence and says nothing. Part of Alma's resentment of him, Lawrence suspects, is that he is alive, and that her brother is dead, and the other part is that he looks just like his mother. When he is reading, sometimes he looks up and catches his reflection in a mirror, a windowpane or picture frame, he thinks for an instant he sees Sybil.

Lawrence opens a fig gently with his hands, parting the dark, frail skin and drawing the halves slowly away, exposing the sweet pink-and-white fruit. Everett is staring at him with his light eyes. Lawrence sucks off the juices until the skin lies limp in his hand. He does not look up. Alma explains the new financial arrangement she has worked out for Lawrence's keep, based upon an inheritance he had received from his father's side of the family.

"He's smart enough," she says. "That's why he has to learn responsibility. Eighteen thousand dollars!"

The boy just exchanges bored stares with his cat who is now stretching out under the trees.

"Everyone has to pay his own keep, don't they, Larry?"

"Yes, ma'am."

"For room and board. After all, he's got me to look after him."

"Alma, leave this to me, will you? It's tiresome, don't you find, Lawrence?"

Lawrence shrugs, gets up and goes inside. Everett will be staying over again, he figures. The afternoon sun comes through the window, threading carefully through the branches of the fig tree, beyond and through the collection of miniature kerosene lamps Alma keeps on glass shelves in the window. The figs hang like hundreds of full, purple breasts.

He can see also through the living-room window that Everett is following him into the house. There is a kind of positive tension in the air when Everett is in town. A feeling of news, even when there isn't any. His clothes, although they aren't ever new, seem to fall just right. Everett never wears patterns or bright colors. This seems to be something to keep in mind.

Lawrence goes into his room. Everett follows him, saying, "I showed a friend of mine who teaches mathematics up to the college in Claremont and he said those quizzes you made up were excellent. So that's why I mentioned to Alma about you having too many chores. I'm sure she didn't think you'd been complaining to me, you know."

"Thank you," Lawrence says and adds, "I know."

Everett sits on the side of the boy's bed. Lawrence stares at him steadily.

Everett says, "I need to do it, okay? I want to, Larry." His shoulders sag over. "Do you want me just to shut up?"

Lawrence just shrugs and nods. The man does not see the shrug. He has been caressing the boy gently. Now he slips down his trousers and leans over him. Lawrence closes his eyes. Being held is not uncomfortable, and there isn't that much to the rest of it. It would just be better not to . . .

The first time he thought he—his cock—could have been frightened. It was as if he'd broken a kind of pact with it, betrayed him; let someone invade a secret province: he had been Lawrence's own pet, this small bird, growing, flying, coming back. Now someone else is drawing it off, it's spinning now, faster and faster, humming as it disappears, and going off, off— a kite drawn into a tornado, down into a whirlpool, with a whimper. The first time he had moved away quickly and held himself, tears falling. This time he does not cry. He has meant just to please Everett, to be helpful. This is too private a thing . . . for an instant only he looks down. He still half expects to see it is worn off to a tiny point. He covers himself with his hands and shivers.

Everett strokes his back and holds him. The man's trim body now feels vast and hard.

Lawrence feels hairless—small and ineffective. He is afraid of this largeness. Why does he feel this is something he has to do? You should always keep a promise if you can, but he can't remember if this was a promise.

"Come on, now, Larry—just take it. That's right. That's a

good boy. You're doing fine . . . don't you stop, don't you stop."
He pulls the boy's head tighter in, hanging on with fists to the
the boy's silky hair. "Yes, that's so good"—he is speaking faster.
Sounds that are not words . . . his hips pound forward. Lawrence
claws into Everett's thighs to keep him back. His jaws hurt; he's
afraid to let go—he might bite, might hurt. His mouth feels sore;
he can't breathe, but it will not be much longer. It will not last
forever.

And now the boy is lying still, his damp hair combed back.
He looks out his window at his cat silhouetted on the sill against
the color of the sunset sky. Every once in a while he reaches
back with his tongue to dislodge what feels like another hair
caught back in his throat, stuck up there somewhere—he can't
get it out. Doesn't want to make any noise. Everett returns to
the living room to chat, and Lawrence tries just to clear his
throat very quietly.

Laurie was sitting now at the round white table in my kitchen
as the sky turned royal-blue with the beginnings of dawn.

"So, it might be the imposition that scares me more than
hurting you," he said. "People never know what the other one
really feels."

"Well, I never know," I said, taking everything, as usual,
personally. "Or even feel. Except when I'm drugged one way or
another so that it doesn't count."

"I don't mean you personally, or only you," he said, putting
a little whiskey, a little cinnamon, in his coffee. "Hey, let's
always have heavy cream, to whip, for Irish coffee."

"I'll remember. Let's." The implication of Us.

"I think," he said, "that the trouble is I can't make you my
prey. Even symbolically."

Shades were down on his eyes. Some people need privacy
when they have just returned from their own pasts.

"Laurie, don't let me ever use you." I held his hand. "Do you
really think your stepmother knew what was going on?"

"She'd have had to. It wasn't that often, but I felt somehow it was kind of authorized by her, and even if it wasn't, I felt if I made a fuss it would have caused more trouble than the cock-sucking."

"Oh, if I was Sybil I'd tear back there and haunt them! Did you have anyone except that stepmother?"

"Grandparents—but they were pretty old by then. They were my father's parents . . . and some aunts. But that was it."

"Experts and authorities would probably have said, 'There goes his sex life.' "

He sipped from his coffee—a drink of some kind, I see, is always with him like a shadow; perhaps as much a part of his character as his smile, or his silence. "Nothing happens like that. There was nothing there that would turn me off women. And it wasn't a great introduction to homosexuality as a way of life."

I put my head on his shoulder—his skin was so fragrant, mildly astringent. I wondered if drinking gave it that scent. It was very pleasant, like fine, pale Scotch. "I'm beginning to see that a person could take just anything out of your childhood and make a case for permanent fucking up. Just from that."

"You can't let things be excuses," he said. "And it's a logical step in getting information about your sexuality. You start with yourself, go on to someone with a similar frame of reference, compare notes. Every kid knows that data you get from talking and books isn't so reliable."

It was getting light now; out over the canyon the world looked pale-olive, cream-colored and lilac. I felt, rather than heard, the sounds of early-Sunday people in other houses—flushing running water and setting up coffee to perk. "Now," I told him, "I've got this Sunday-morning show to do, so let me put you back to bed where I can find you easily when I come home."

"No, you let me walk you to your car . . . I'll be here."

I closed the car door and opened the top. He leaned down and kissed me, then went inside.

I started the car.

Then turned it off and ran inside to see if he was still there.

Although the format of my show was telephone-talk (sometimes known as two-way or fistfight radio), I had studio guests whose good fortune it was to be able to speak with actual radio listeners.

"Only one call, one question to a customer, remember—I know your voices. You will be caught! Your tennis shoes confiscated before your very ears."

"Linda Goodman," I said, "is the author of the new astrology best seller, *Linda Goodman's Sun Signs,* and she comes to us from New York City, so I would suggest you have one of your more articulate representatives call up today . . ."

When everyone in Los Angeles had finished asking Linda if Scorpio could make it with Virgo (Name your favorite combination; there's always a way to say yes) and the show was done, I told them all to go home and wash out their flags with soap. And I went with Linda for coffee.

I asked her about karma. I explained, talking very fast, about Laurie. His mother. Geminis don't believe in such things except when they are of Southern California abstraction, and wackers anyway.

"Well," she said. "Of course, the most common thing happens just about every day. You know, when you're walking and you suddenly catch someone's eyes—there's something there, but you've no need to stop? Supposedly that's a karmic situation you've worked out."

We stood like gypsies in the May Company department store speaking of karma.

"What," I asked, as we tried on belts with clattering gold coins, "about karmic duels, or relationships that aren't resolved, and you just keep coming back at each other for centuries until you work it out. Well, if a mother dies when the baby is little, wouldn't she come next as grandchild helping that son when he is in his old age? Can lovers be mothers, and so on? I mean, can karma cross taboos?"

"That's possible," Linda said, seeing how two belts would look.

"So it would be the force of the feelings, not the structure, that can set it in motion?" I like to speak of myths as if they were real.

"You might say that," she smiled wryly, "you might say anything. No one really knows."

"I just feel, or want to feel, that maybe his mother had to get back to care for him—I don't know why she picked me to come back as, though."

"It also could be." she said, looking at me closely, "that you want to mean everything to him."

"I suppose. And why would it have taken her soul a day to get to L.A. even then?"

"The packing," Linda said. "She would need several changes of clothes in order to be you, I think. And Geminis never can decide what to bring with them."

"It's nonsense, isn't it?" I said.

"Not," she said, "if it's what you believe. It's a very protective idea. Is he a Libra?"

"Yes."

"I thought so. They are lovable men. And they need to be cared for." She bought two chain belts. One for me, one for her, and she pulled out of her purse a royal-blue medallion covered with golden stars.

"In case—for luck," she said.

What does she see in her stars? What comes through so strong that she doesn't even need her ephemeris to see I may need luck?

On the way home I picked up some figs and heavy cream.

I looked at my children like this sometimes. They are like breathing peaches. His cheeks are just as rosy in sleep. The difference is I have unlimited touching permits with him. I lay down beside him now. He automatically kissed or hugged me when I touched him. He must be accustomed to being loved in his sleep—he avoids awakening with little tender offerings. A thousand women must have loved him. I could not imagine a woman passing him on the street without touching him, as you would touch a lovely cat.

Still he slept. He had spoken before of being a night person. I was, too. But also a day person. Such universality is the speed freak's prerogative. So I lashed out at my novel. It quivered, terrified, in its corner, as I thrust at a page here, a paragraph there. Then I read over the good, finished parts to reassure myself I should work on it again next week, next month, three weeks from a full moon on Tuesday.

I stared him awake. I had begun to feel like the dwarfs with Snow White there in the glass coffin. It was beautiful, but after a while you wanted to do something with it.

He ate his figs and cream. "Did you ever find out what fig means?" I asked him.

"What do you think?"

"Oh, they look like breasts, like balls, or open, like—I mean, the obvious . . ." Words I could write, even technical words I often used on the radio to distress the listeners I could not say to a real person. "I guess they look like everything sexual."

"*Fica* means 'cunt' in Italian."

"Well, that's what I really thought, actually. You eat figs like you eat me like you really love to."

"Well, I do. Chicks have all these funny ideas."

"That we've mostly gotten from men," I said, quietly.

"From crazy men with phobic mothers. Come to bed with me."

"The children will be home soon."

I must not do too much of that: putting off parts of our lives "Because the children . . ." Usually, I think, it translates, even in marriages where both are the real parents, as "The children come first." Because of their newness to the world, their vulnerability, they do. But Laurie seemed to be as vulnerable as a child, and, as children make allowances for their more fragile siblings, so I hoped they would understand. He was the sick child you always hear in the night, even when the child has not cried out.

Sybil. I am probably her. Reborn. To take care of him. I set her picture up on the dresser we were sharing. I looked at her and then back at myself.

The children's birthday party was to start at two. Laurie would take Wright's group riding. Emily's younger people would have a folk singer to entertain them.

I went to do my radio show early—then, because I had promised (and would not miss any chance to seem important), I spoke briefly on the steps of City Hall at a war-protest rally.

I had just finished speaking when suddenly a solid little elderly woman with a slightly askew wig, several badges and American flags bristling about on her dusty-rose sweater, and carrying a large black purse stuffed with literature, caromed up the steps like a shot of a cannon ball run backwards.

"I knew I'd find you here, you dirty Commie hippie bitch," she screeched and swung back her purse, smacking it hard into my face. "You're unfit to be with decent people!" and she added, scurrying off, "Intellectual!"

My nose was bleeding, eyes unclear, the light in my head seemed fractured, but at that moment I felt terrific. "Intellectual" —the TV news had picked it up, would probably run it.

Intellectual: the curse of the California psychotic—who defines decency by violence.

When I came home, Wright and Emily were playing with a puppy. "What is it?"

"Half mule, half coyote," said Wright.

"No," Laurie said, laughing, "half shepherd, half collie."

"But we already have the cats," I said to Laurie, who was sliding into the kitchen for a drink—for both of us. Pink lemonade and vodka. Happy Birthday.

"Well, they're more Emily's style; Wright doesn't see much use in those cats for catching balls. When you're small, everyone seems so much bigger than you are. They yell at you and complain." Laurie usually spoke in captions, except when he'd had a few drinks. Even when this increase in w.p.m. was apparent, he was selective. He was no risk to his insecurity.

His eyes looked earnest. But they were always a bit wan before 3 P.M., as though it took some time for the circulation to get to them, to turn the aqua to blue. "With a dog—you can take a little heat off, bossing him around, you see what I mean? I think it's a reasonable idea, and I should give him something special —he feels a bit usurped."

What did drinking mean or matter really?

I drank, but except for the floor naps it had absolutely no effect on me, just cooled down the speed. Did I seem to talk too much? I have always talked too much.

In liquor ads and certain literary legends it's implied there's something sexy about a man who can hold his liquor, really belt them down, drink all night and never show it; man with the hollow leg. A cocky kind of thing. But, I thought, *macho* is not Lawrence's drinking style. He drinks like Elizabeth Barrett Browning coughs. A subtle romantic clue, a hint that something else was gravely wrong. "Pay attention," he was saying when he lifted the glass.

So, as Laurie said, "We have this puppy."

Emily made him a bed. "He's gorgeous," she exclaimed, giving me full information on his shots, dietary requirements and biographical details. "And he must have an egg now and then for his coat . . ."

"We're calling him Jasper-the-Dog," Wright said, "so he understands he's not one of the cats."

In the same manner as the children arriving at two for the party could not wait to see the new dog, so my friends, dropping off their children, could not wait to see the new man. Before he took Wright's group out riding, Laurie met some of the adults who would be returning later to have some informal supper before taking their kids back home. These parties are like relay races.

Laurie chugged off in his little Renault car with the boys, and with Jasper-the-Dog, who already had a look of constant anxiety.

Inside, Emily's group was singing rounds and madrigals with this boy from a Renaissance fair, and some of my friends stayed to help me cook so the supper could be ready before midnight.

In Hollywood, suburb that it is, the more vital the business contact, the more casual must seem its maintenance. Where better but at the children's party? Even on the semantic fringes of the Industry, where, like dust, the writers and the journalists live, the birthday-party custom prevails. Here, however, the conversation is primarily of politics, to remind ourselves we are not really California people.

It is the children who are most poorly served by this birth-day-party convention. The children of successful Hollywood people have faces as old and long as the snake coffins from the Egyptian Sixth Dynasty, worn out by watching their parents get there. Or stay there. I looked at this one child, the seven-year-old daughter who had been invited because her father was the host of a talk show I wanted to get on. I felt predatory. I had been that child once.

The party was shifting into the adult phase as Lawrence walked in the front door, carrying Jasper over his shoulder, muddy, with at least two boys clinging to his slacks; those shiny slacks now additionally graced by a rip in the knee. He nodded in his way, briefly, and with the puppy (blinking and looking even less happy about the crowd than Laurie was) still curved around his shoulder like a large epaulet, he fixed himself a drink.

In a sense the party did not begin until Pola arrived. No: Pola swept in with a brace of electric exclamations. Kisses going off into the air. All rusty crepe and silk head wrappings, odd colors and increments of ivory and tortoise; her husband, Paul, the producer, swirled in just beyond. Pompous, pretentious, daz-zling: love as a design for social impact. I had told Laurie she was one of my Fame women. I wanted to watch Laurie watch-ing Pola. I wanted her to see I had my own prince. In spite of all the costumes, the stories, the plumed cavalier hats, the boots and the cloaks I had put on to amuse her, to Pola I was of interest because I was Jill-the-Daughter (as Jasper is Jasper-the-Dog: so I would know I am not one of the real cats), invited to parties as the rather old child of prestige and power.

"Where is the new lover," she whispered, and she looked at Laurie. Did I need her approval before I could be in love? Is that why I couldn't wait until they had talked to him and dis-covered how brilliant he is? Suddenly I thought, I should have gotten him some kind of thing to wear, a leather jerkin sort of. He can wear clothes so fantastically. And—his slacks. He needs to have bell-bottom jeans. Yes. Next week . . . I squinted at

Laurie, trying to see him from Pola's point of view. He does not know I have terrible values. Pola will tell me what I am really doing with him.

And later only Pola and Paul remained. They seemed more subdued than usual. Although they usually looked at each other a lot, very much the way professional ballroom dancers do, to be sure the incandescent charm is turned on, tonight was different.

"Jill, my pet—another triumph. What you really need is your own private court so you could arrange the most incredible fetes. Don't you agree, Paul?"

Paul turned to Lawrence. "What is it you do, Larry? Did Jill tell me you're an engineer? We hope you also have a family fortune somewhere. You can see you'll need it." He was teasing; mean.

"I'm a mathematician." Laurie watched them carefully. I couldn't tell what he was thinking, but his lithe hands were swiftening around some matchbooks as though they were playing cards. He added, "It's different. But you know that."

"You'll have to forgive Paul, Larry, it's just that we do adore Jill."

"Pola, it's 'Lawrence' really. I mean, you can see he's more of a Lawrence than a Larry," I said. No. She couldn't see. He was not the kind of date that was like a new dress: subject to approval. Could I be having a conviction of my own, flying in the face of an arbiter's opinion? "Incredible!," as Pola would say. All this disapproval added a new dimension to wanting him. Was it just rebellion?

"What Pola means," said Paul, "is you have to ask us, of course, before we'll share her. We always like to look over her men to see if they also appeal to us; if not, I'm afraid . . ." He turned out his hands, signifying emptiness.

"Well," Lawrence said, frowning slightly, "I'd like to think about whether you appeal to me, I guess, too." This was a game that he didn't like.

"Amazing!" Pola flashed her megacarat smile at Paul, who nodded. Lawrence had won that hand.

He stood up, stretching, but not a lazy stretch—the stretch you hope will get rid of tension.

"I'm going to get some brandy. Be right back . . . do you need cigarettes, anything?" Lawrence had offered the brandy originally in little lovely glasses. While we were sipping ours, he had been refilling his tumbler with the rest of the brandy bottle.

I watched him go, then I yelled at them, "You're really being awful. This isn't his style." They had been fonder of a former lover's sleek cool. Or had it been his success?

Laurie doesn't enjoy poses. I wonder if I will miss the fantasies we had articulated together. Fantasies we knew would have been shattered in the acting out. (That's what we had used as the excuse.) Perhaps the private consideration of fantasies could be as exciting as the verbal sharing.

"Darlin', he's not your style," Paul said to me, flicking an ash from his Sherman cigarette.

"Yes, pet," Pola added, her hand on my arm. Her touch made me wonder if what I had just thought about the consideration of fantasies could be true. "You have class," she said. "Don't throw that away on a wounded sparrow. Wait for someone who can take care of you." Pola looked quickly at Paul. She is like my mother: every opinion is co-signed. Perhaps that is why this feeling of defiance was so familiar.

"But I'd be screaming my eyes out in the meantime. And I also think I love him. Your values are all mixed up, you know. They are alluring values, but they're all mixed up!"

Paul leaned forward, his absinthe-green eyes sincerely concerned. "I think, sweetheart, that he has a drinking problem."

"Yes," Pola added, her hand stroking my arm (can I count on that consolation, can I get a guarantee?) "He drinks too much."

"Lawrence is just anxious," I said, "and I need him, I need

him. You don't know how good it is to feel haired skin next to you at night when you wake up."

It was mentioned after a while that Lawrence had not returned.

"He likes," I said, "a late midnight stroll. And he cannot feel you would be missing him."

As they stood in the door to leave, all aubergine and sienna—an Art Nouveau frieze, I felt that it was Pola and Paul who were out of phase. As though the situation had been reversed: I had checked them out with Laurie. And he had clearly made his statement, "They simply won't do." Yes. It is Laurie who belongs now. After they left, I ran to the little covey of bars down the street to look for him.

It was a variation of the turtle-shell game: to find Laurie in these bars added adventure to the business of everyday living. In which one would he be this time? There were three, which made it perfect. I could look in one, then run fast to see if he was at the next one before he could switch.

In months to come the local bartenders would only have to hear the door opening, and without looking up they would say, "He left about five minutes ago."

"And, yes?" He grinned when I found him on this night after Pola and Paul had left. And he said, "How are things? I was coming right back." He thought he'd been gone for just the wink of an eye or so.

"They're gone." But one anxiety had lingered on. "Do you drink too much?"

"Probably," he said. Smiling. Looking quite crisp.

"You never seem drunk."

"Some people don't. My grandfather drank a quart of Scotch a day, except during Prohibition, and he lived to be eighty."

"Maybe it was the recess during Prohibition that pulled him together so he could start again. More likely, I guess it is that pioneer sort of strength—that's what I love about you. You're Johnny Tremaine, strolling through our sturdiest history since the Revolution. I'm sorry, I really got mad at them. At Pola and Paul."

He kissed me. "It's just a game, I guess. But not my style." Laurie considered Pola and Paul. "The games people like to play represent mostly frustration," he said. So he understood such things.

I wondered when, or if, I could explain to him about the dark-haired women and what it was, actually, that I felt there was to explain. "Maybe, for some people, the most effective pornography is frustration. Everything happens slowly, slowly. People, faceless, doing things, then just when it begins to work, they cut. Like Pola and Paul. They fade out. I love that frustration. It is like movie stars. Possession would be disillusion."

"The secret, then," said Lawrence, "of being a film star is knowing when to fade. Legions of Cheshire cats—just their smiles remain."

"Will you vanish someday, too, leaving just your smile?"

How can I make him stay? And . . . would that be risking disillusion?

My lawyer called the next morning to say her husband said he heard me mention on the air that I was living with someone.

"So?" I said.

"So," she says, "if Berenger wants to make trouble he can."

"But he won't—we told him he can drop alimony just as though we're married."

"Look, do what you want. But the problem—and you know it—is not money. It's the children. And if it ever got to a large court battle . . . some of those California judges . . . I don't have to tell you."

"California psychotics—the cradle of our empire's morality. Okay. I hear you."

An hour later I was asked to resign from the PTA.

"It's not me—God knows," said the one who called. "But your politics are so controversial."

Then Berenger's Pat called to say they hoped the children liked their gifts, and to say she had seen me on TV. Being hit.

Then she said these things:

One: She and Berenger had gotten married.

"Congratulations," I said. And, "That was quick."

Two: "Aren't you scared one of those crazy people might hurt the children? You never know what people like that will do, and you've taken some very controversial positions."

I waited until after dinner to tell Laurie all this news. It was too lovely a supper, eating like a family with a dog and two cats. After Laurie and I settled the children, we walked down to the bars by the sea for an after-dinner drink. He sipped on his negroni. (He doesn't have a real drinking problem, I decided. A lush doesn't have the elegance to order drinks with fancy names. I, for instance, fond of pink squirrels and champagne cocktails, could not be considered a lush.)

I started with the PTA. "See, Laurie, the status mother is not inventive or famous or even very creative, except with making cakes look like lambs."

"I wouldn't have wanted that."

"Probably not. You were more into cats."

"True. But not as cakes."

"Well," I said, staring at the countertop, melting ice looking like crystalline blood on the red Formica. A PTA mother's blood would run ruby clear crystalline like that, like Jell-O.

We ordered more drinks.

He said, "But Wright and Emily talk about the things you do with great excitement."

"It's a defense they use to pretend being different is better. Compensation for the lunches I bring in to school late, after the lunch bell has rung. The breakfasts they make because I've been up all night working . . ." I just sighed.

"Well?" He kissed me on the forehead, imitating my sigh, adding a laugh.

"Well . . ." I sighed again, and smoothed at my bangs. "I have to tell you. It's all part of a chain of events that have just made me terrified of losing the kids. You don't understand the California Conservative morality: never mind what you are really doing or saying as long as it looks proper on the outside and you aren't really having any fun. It's Rafferty, Reagan—Nixon may have invented it, but he lost his temper. Oh, you've been away too long, Laurie. Well, I almost married someone with that kind of head . . . I mentioned George earlier, you know, how he demonstrated his sense of humor by putting a plate of fettucini on my head."

"That was not exactly secret," Laurie said.

"No. But he stood up and held my chair, you see, when I came back from the ladies' room after washing my hair. Clowns are all California psychos."

"Darling, what are you really worried about?"

I put my arms around his neck, holding tight. In a fast, whispering voice I told him my worst stories, and about how George had once said I was a depraved degenerate. "I've been dirty such a long, long time. I'm Mrs. Macbeth. I can't get clean."

"*Lady* Macbeth—they haven't gone off with your title yet. Nobody will hurt our kids or you now." He held my chin and stared hard, to imprint what he was saying. "It's all right now. You're going to make it."

"Our kids." This is a nice man. How do I know if I love

him, or if I just need someone to hang on to, to keep me from falling all the way down?

"Laurie, what do I do? About everything. Us living together. Is it rebellion? Is it a problem?"

"It may have been rebellion, partly," he said. "But it's not a problem."

"What do you mean?" I knew damn well.

"We'll get married. That's no problem."

"People will find out." I was pretending to be very surprised, and to protest what we both knew I would want from the beginning and for none of the reasons I had given, but simply because I still believed it's easier to keep a person if you're married . . . no matter what I said I believed. "I mean, I've taken a stand on that, you know. In public."

"And gotten hit in the head for it. Actually, no one has to know, except the people who have to know."

"You sound like me."

"So I might as well marry you. Actually"—he kissed my forehead—"another way to look at the whole thing is that if this piece of paper doesn't matter, then why does the issue of not-having-it have to be as big a deal to us as having-it is to other people." How wonderful of him to pretend that he didn't know I adored the idea. He was letting me have my fantasy —if I had to.

"Well," I said, grinning. The closet square-creep that never quite closes the closet door, so everyone knows she is there, anyway. "Just so long as you don't tell, I'd really love to marry you. I mean, I really would like it a lot. To be Mrs. You."

"Mrs. Robinson. You have a ready-made theme song . . ."

"Coo, coo, ca-choo, Mrs. Robinson. And I've got this old necklace we can trade in for a ring."

We walked back home from the bar, touching arms, hips, shoulders, getting as close as you could and still walk, and sometimes stopping just to feel each other.

We walked slower, throwing laughs off into the dark like

pieces of clothing you don't need, when the skin feels like it belongs next to you.

Shortly after we were married, we came home from the bars one night to discover four human shapes strewn about on the floor. Prodding quilts and sleeping bags, we discovered my friend Brooke and her three children.

"Dennis: Impossible!" she said sleepily, referring to her husband. "I paid your sitter and sent her home. I figured with me here it was okay. God knows how long we'll be here."

"Of course!" I was enchanted. Stay a month, six months. Perfect distraction from writing. And Brooke was the kind of beautiful one wanted to have around to look at.

Like Laurie. In the morning I watched him oversleeping. So beautiful. I went out of our room, then, closing the door quietly, to get the kids ready for school.

I saw Brooke in two moods. Semiconscious with depression. Or bracing, with sort of English Upper-Class Great Good Cheer.

That's what we had this morning. Bracing. She had made breakfast for everyone, bounding around the kitchen like a deer. "Well, why isn't he up? Doesn't he have to get to work? My God, he might as well be Dennis."

"It's the same kind of animal," I said. "Charming." I really liked her then-husband—Dennis Hopper, actor, artist—gifted with rage. When they were fighting I would not take sides. I shared a lot of memories with Brooke—we had known each other since we were four—and yet somehow I identified more with Dennis. Jordan was like Dennis.

"But he shouldn't be late, should he?" asked Brooke, who had been brought up partly in the East; the current hip laissez-faire was, to her, only a sort of aesthetic overlay. The bones, the background and the breeding were still there. And Brooke had no room for the utensils of self-destruction the rest of us collected with such enthusiasm. She had grown up in an emotional minefield, she did not need to set off nickel firecrackers for excitement.

I padded to our room and wakened Laurie gently, sitting on the bed and watching him as he rushed languidly, which is his unique ability. He cut his chin shaving; then, spangled with white stars of Kleenex, he went through the kitchen to the door leading to the garage, quietly smiling hello/goodbye at the assembled children.

"Breakfast? My God, you must have something," said Brooke.

Laurie stopped and nodded, taking a piece of bacon she handed him. "Crisp," he said. What he meant, I could tell, was "Noisy." Brooke didn't understand about the head and how it feels in the morning. Dennis, into nonverbal expression then, had not been able to explain.

"Mmmm," said Laurie. An idea had occurred to him. He got out the vodka and some lime ice from the freezer and whipped it up in the blender. Brooke laughed, such a merry laugh of total disapproval: drinking in the morning. I took a Dexedrine and shrugged as I looked at her, as if such a thing would never enter my mind . . . and I was longing for a drink, to break up the fuzz.

I went out with Laurie to the car and kissed him, taking off the Kleenex bits. "Lose your looks, you know, and it's all over."

We laughed. I hated to let go of him.

After I had taken Emily and Wright to school and Brooke had returned from taking her children, we talked about the men. About Dennis and ending things. And about Laurie and beginnings.

"You have such an aptitude for extravagance," she said, "I don't know why you keep finding poor ones."

"But he's not poor . . . really. I mean, he pays the rent. Landlord has been ecstatic . . ." ("Isn't that nice," Landlord had beamed when he discovered Lawrence was a mathematician. Soaring visions of prompt rent payments on checks that always cleared had sent him into a whirlwind of improvements and heartwarming gestures of good will.)

"But it's not money," I added, "it's partly that I don't know much about him. That he is like a suspense story. And what I do find out is always different . . .

"You have seen," I said, "that he does not eat breakfast. Well, he actually eats only dinner or an occasional club sandwich. And he doesn't like to be watched when he eats. He has no 'god' guilts. And no family, so we can concentrate those conflicts on mine, which demands center stage in any case.

"On occasion when he does watch the sports games on television, he doesn't shout. And he would actually rather make love, which is a very unusual quality in a man today.

"Playing sports? He said he had pretended to play golf in the Air Force so he could nap under the nice trees at the edge of the course. 'They don't give a person much rest in the service,' he told me. He doesn't seem to notice what he wears."

"That," Brooke chortled, "is obvious . . ."

"Only that it should be soft and not noticeable to him, or to anyone else either. But," I added, "it's enough there's one person with the taste of a drag queen in the house.

"He has hitchhiked almost everywhere and so he reads road maps for nostalgia, the way other people look at old family albums. I don't think he has ever written a letter, but something tells me he can write . . . and that someday he will write a great American novel with a lot of heavy, quiet clout. He doesn't like to make phone calls. Although he called the radio show when I had the late shift the night before we were to be married, and he asked me to marry him. Right on the air, just as though he was a real listener. And I said yes. There is some show business to him. Or maybe it is that he is romantic, and that's hard to recognize these days. To believe in. What can I tell you, Brooke, except that he is perfect and he has made my life something I am glad to be having for once . . .

"We were lying on the beach at sundown the other night, all alone, in the peachy light, on the cool sand, and we were just lying there close to each other in our clothes, and he was smiling at me. We were touching hands and looking at each other and there were finally tears in our eyes and we just held on to each other, patting each other's hair and back, and— Just a minute, I'll get the door."

Landlord. Standing disconsolate with a check in his hand.

"This check's no good, Jill."

"Laurie's check?"

He nodded his head.

I froze. "Put it through again."

"I did," he said. "Twice."

"Well, okay, I'll take care of it." I was burning with shame. He went away.

"So, as I was saying," I said to Brooke, "things have never been more terrific."

"Since we're staying here anyway, let me take care of it . . . he can pay me back."

"No," I said, "I can handle it. I'll just get this *Cosmo* rewrite done faster."

"Except what if they ask for another rewrite? Come on, it's no problem."

For so many years I had been saying "I can't afford" and accepting things from her. "I know it's just a mistake. I'll call him."

I hardly ever called him at his office. Somehow, I was always pleasantly surprised to find him actually there. Or anywhere predictable.

Money. There is a subtle thing that happens: once an affair

becomes a marriage, money moves in, too, and makes trouble.

He came right home, even though I hadn't suggested such a move, chugging up the driveway in his Renault. He had a gift-wrapped bottle of lovely Châtauneuf-du-Pape and another check. From another bank.

"Is it good?" I asked.

"French—'63" he said. Brooke laughed, in spite of the outraged-oldest-and-best-friend hauteur she was affecting.

"I meant the check."

"I know. Of course it's good."

"Why," I demanded, "since you are such a math person, can't you keep track of how much money you have? Jesus, if you have two accounts that's even more important!" Two accounts. To give one an illusion of wheeling-dealing.

Money. He didn't seem to care about property. But he cared a lot about the money itself. Not the things it can buy, because they tie you down. But the cash that lets you out and keeps you free.

I think one thing he was proud of, felt secure about, was that he could usually figure out how to get his money. When his father had moved from Santa Barbara into the house near San Diego, the room that was to be his had been lined with racing forms. The house was only a short walking distance from the Del Mar race track and when Lawrence wasn't reading, counting artichokes, mowing neighborhood lawns or avoiding Everett, he was at the track playing the horses.

"When I was a kid," he had said, "I always had money. A couple of hundred dollars on me all the time. And in New York there was always a poker game to get in. I won seven thousand dollars one night. The guy let me win—it turned out. I thought he was just playing badly. But he knew he was going to kill himself the next day. It was kind of a legacy. I didn't have to work for a year . . . But I wasn't married."

I've got to get more work or get that book done, I thought. I don't want him to feel married in that kind of way.

Money. Pride goes with it always. It was easier for him to give Landlord a check than to say he didn't have enough money. He meant to have enough money by the time the check went through, and what he required from his self-image was that he would somehow have "eeled" some money into the account just in time.

"Eel," he said, "is what they used to call me in the Village. 'The Eel.' "

He is essence of hip. Imagine me. Having him.

"Laurie. Please don't be bugged . . . but is this check now, that we give Landlord now with this wine, really cool?"

"It will be. I'm getting paid tomorrow and I'll deposit the bread right away, so it's fine. Fine." It was an invasion of his cool. Being forced to go into such details.

If Brooke had not been there, I doubt if he would have gone back to work. After he had his vodka and tonic.

"Does he drink all the time?" she asked.

"Not really. He's an original, like Dennis, and I don't care what he does like that. He's the only man who's ever really liked being with me. It's easy for you to say; you're beautiful, you can make demands . . . you really don't understand. If he was sober enough to see me, Brooke, he'd leave."

"Since you have embarked on your favorite complaint, I won't bother to argue—you've practiced all the answers anyway. You like to think you're ugly, for some obscure reason. Six months ago, if memory serves, you were crying that you needed someone with money to help with the bills. That is a serious problem and I think he's going to make it worse."

"Well, I was desperate."

"This is only the beginning. I know. I recognize the lack of responsibility from five miles away."

"Oh, Brooke. Responsibility really—I love him, that's what matters." Brooke seemed to think responsibility was a lovable quality.

Hardly a turn-on, I would say.

We had news for each other:

"It is incongruous," Laurie announced one night on his arrival home from work (and a bar, I think. Like a wagon train, he stops at water holes on his journeys; just in case there might not be another one), "for me to be working on a system for new killing devices and bombs, during the week. And, on weekends, helping in the antiwar movement."

He seemed to be trying to say and not to say something at the same time.

"Yes. I think so," I said, "but everything supports the war directly, indirectly. There's very little difference . . ."

"I disagree," he said, "and so I quit my job today, in protest."

"That's great. I was going to ask you to take a vacation anyway—*Cosmo* called. They wanted to send me to Esalen—the sensitivity farm with all the nude baths and stuff—to do an article. And I suggested we should both write about it. You can write, you look like you can, and so—well, I talked finally to Helen herself . . ."

And she had said, after a long thinking silence, "You are such a romantic darlingskin. Well, I suppose, although they're going to kill me for spending so much, that this can be a lovely honeymoon for you both . . . so, we'll send you as a couple."

When, after dinner, we dropped in on Mike and Karen, and Laurie reported he'd quit his job, Mike said (half smile), "Cut out the crap, Larry, at least with me. It wasn't a protest, you were just bored . . ." Laurie looked wounded. He didn't give

Mike an argument. Actually, I thought, he should have found another job before he quit—but I knew, without testing, not to criticize.

I scheduled our Esalen excursion to coincide with Nannie's vacation from her job so she could stay with Wright and Emily. And I arranged to switch a couple of shows with the all-night moderator so I wouldn't be giving up any income.

The all-night shows were long and quiet, and even the eccentric calls had a mellow quality. "That," Laurie said, "is because they are night people. And we are different. There is a conspiracy against us. You know—the way the system is designed we are even discouraged from voting. Polls are closing as the confirmed night person is getting up . . ."

"That's it," I said. "You'll do the show with me! As a campaigner for equal rights for night people . . ." I would have expected at least a mild argument, but his eyes lit up . . . he is not so shy.

"I'll have an organization they can write to . . . N.I.G.H.T., for Nothing Interesting's Gonna Happen Tomorrow." He stayed up all that night (the only civilized time to work) planning his protest for night people.

"You know," he said, "night people never cause trouble. You don't find confirmed night people running armies, turning you down at the post office because you didn't wrap the package right, or even getting drunk. It's the occasional day person who gets out too late that causes trouble at bars."

We did the show together. Signed off at 5 A.M. and started off for Esalen. It is an especially good hour in California, this predawn. The birds get up noisily, then quiet down. The sky space lightens like a stripper slowly revealing its vast dimensions. We heard the ocean slurping from time to time as we drove up Highway 1.

Here and there, kids were hitchhiking. I sat close to him. Time, stop now, I thought—let this be it for us.

We were looking for lunch late in the morning and I said, "I should have packed a picnic, some lovely cold chicken . . ."

"Oh, I'm much happier without the lovely cold chicken," he said.

A series of half-empty dinner plates flashed before my eyes. "You don't eat chicken? Why didn't you tell me?"

"Well, you see that I never do."

"But I never pulled it together as a generic chicken rejection. You hate it."

He made his characteristic sound of ambivalence which, if you understand music, is best described, according to a composer we know, as a minor third down, from E to C ("When he's really on the fence, it extends all the way down to a perfect fourth").

"We raised chickens when I was a kid . . . during the war people did that. So I've had a lot of chickens. They're not interesting animals."

"You mean you had to eat the ones you knew? And see them killed and all that?"

"Well, I had to kill them. There wasn't anyone else, you know."

"I should have known."

"How could you know?"

"It fits with the childhood. Was it with an ax?"

"Wringing necks, mostly."

"Somehow more personal?"

"Well, you have to see that you can't get involved with a chicken. They're the stupidest, dirtiest . . . The real point about not eating them is I just got bored with chicken as a thing to eat."

"That's not as heartrending as having a chicken-slaughtering trauma. But you were always so accommodating with all these things. Didn't you say 'No' ever? You went along with everything, it seems. You do that now a little. Like not telling me you hate chicken. Are you just Stoic?"

"No. Not really. Sometimes it's not important."

I didn't think that was it. It was more as if he expected things to go badly. As though that was what he deserved. Part, perhaps, of a dedication to a terrible guilt. Such guilt, I thought, might be tied in with the way he froze at any criticism.

I remembered how he had been when my parents came out for our wedding. He sat so straight that his hair looked cut up higher on his neck. My father gave him a check as a wedding gift—to buy a new suit. And Laurie looked so terribly embarrassed, not by the gift so much as the implication of criticism. Around certain people, older men, generally, or men who seemed older, I suppose, because of their success, Laurie seemed to expect criticism, and that made him, I began to see, almost awkward. Ashes spilled. A drink would almost tip over, barely caught in time.

"Laurie," I said, as we cruised past Santa Barbara, where he began his life, "was your father very critical?"

It is 1944:

Laurie feels the Santa Ana wind in the air. And he feels the apprehension coiling up, turning everything stark and still. Laurie's father, Matthew Robinson II, is always on edge when the Santa Ana wind is blowing. It's as if he has a score to settle with the wind, and the wind comes by like a bully to needle him about it now and then.

Lawrence is in the living room; it is late day. He is playing chess with his father, who is having more of his fierce stomach pains. Laurie knows not to mention seeing a doctor. His father does not have much use for doctors, and less, Laurie suspects, for his health. Matt has found a diversion from the pain: a hook for his temper: he sees a space in the bookshelf.

"Where's my copy of *Moby Dick?* What did you do with it?"

Lawrence is on his feet fast. "Oh, the book's outside. I'll get it."

"Outside! With a dust storm building up faster than hell?"

Matt punches in at his own stomach with a rage that could apply to the pain or to his son.

"Dad, I'm getting it."

"You do that. You just do that." Matt moves his ashtray now slightly to the left. Gasps, then takes a deep swallow of liquor from his glass and sets it down in precisely the same spot.

Lawrence knows that this anger goes back to Sybil, and that is a subject which is not discussed, although Lawrence feels that his father knows when he has been looking at Sybil's pictures. He is so careful to put them back always just the way they have been lying in Matt's cupboard behind the shirts. His mother belongs solely to his father's orderly memory. No idle mention of her, no dinner-table reminiscence is permitted to violate private thoughts and moments. He is sure, from his mother's smile in the pictures, that she had a sense of humor.

And from a picture or two of his father with her, when he was just a baby, Lawrence is certain his father, too, had humor then.

He is standing now, holding *Moby Dick*. Standing there, to hand it to his father.

"What are you giving it to me for?" Matthew snaps. "Put it away." The pain is lighting up his eyes.

It is getting late now, even in the cycle of his father's normal drinking day; near the time when the subject of Lawrence's carelessness comes up. Lawrence assumes his father's hostility started with his birth. If he hadn't been born, maybe if he hadn't weighed ten pounds, or if he had at least been born right (whatever that meant), Sybil wouldn't have needed the "female repairs" as Alma had called them, and she wouldn't have been sick ever after he was born, and she wouldn't, of course, have died so young. Alma had not had to explain it, although Lawrence had asked. His father had implied as much once, talking on the phone with his aunt.

That is why his father is so angry with him all the time. The small wrong things he occasionally does shouldn't warrant the kind of anger Matthew is able to sustain. For, it seems to Lawrence, his father is not a completely unreasonable man.

"He died the next day, I think it was," Laurie said, as the waitress brought us vodka and tonic and club sandwiches. "Something burst. You see, he wanted to die. There was a wake. His drinking buddies all came over the next couple of days. We played cards. And my aunts came out to see me sometimes."

He shook his head and downed his vodka. "So that was my father."

So that was the criticism. And that was the guilt.

"You had the feeling that everything you touched went wrong."

"Yes. I suppose so."

"You think you hurt things—and you have such beautiful hands. I thought I really did hurt things, too, and that's why I was given such ugly hands."

"You have nice hands. Busy hands."

"No." I shook my head. Shoved hands into my lap. "My mother has that facial paralysis, you know. I used to practice her expression. I thought, when I was a child, that it was stylish. Haughty. Father caught me. He picked me up and sat me down on the breakfast table and held my hands down with his. 'Don't you ever hurt your mother,' he said. He explained how she had fallen when she was a child. So I told the children at school the next day that my mother's father had thrown her down the stairs. It was such a cruel thing to do."

"You may have been making your own father the villain for catching you."

Typical destruction. I realized, as usual, I was using Laurie's ear. "This started out to be your turn. I'm sorry. You understand my parents," I said, accusing. "You think I should work it out with them?"

"Probably."

ESALEN:

Her hips were flat, going on down straight to long, lean legs dangling in the steaming water. She was laughing and splashing water in our faces as if she were sitting in sunlight on the edge of a real swimming pool and not in olive-green moonlight on the edge of a sulfurous vat carved out of a deep slit in a Big Sur cliff like the iris of a squinting eye spying. "Like a World War Two pillbox," I murmured to Lawrence, who seemed to be quite enjoying himself as he sat immersed to his neck three or four miles across the square vat, as the stoned crow flies.

"How can they remind you of something you couldn't possibly have seen?" he asked, querulously, for him.

"You know how I feel about the past. That it is there to visit," I said. "I've told you that. Find an empty moment when you can slip away—and you can go back. So I've just come back from a pillbox and this is how it looked before it exploded. I got out in time, I hope you noticed that."

An hour and a half later he answered me, which wasn't fair, considering he had something to do, what with that lean-hipped girl diving under the water all the time to play with him. I was just sitting there with this odd young man next to me with the haircut of a boxer dog and the peace symbol around his neck. He kept asking me about the time, or had I misunderstood that as well?

I tried to keep track of the misunderstandings so far, but with the grass and the wine it was hard enough to keep track of what that girl was doing to Laurie. Staying under water as long as she could showed unusual depth, and unusual women interested him. I'm not possessive. I would not have minded an ordinary person.

It was freezing when we climbed out of the rough, square vats. The towels we'd brought were like dishrags, wet and chilly. We wrapped on our robes and walked, it seemed, ten or eight miles up a stony path on the edge of a cliff overlooking a fierce ocean. Bushes clawed at us. Stars moved eerily, yellow as bug lights.

I was not loving when we came to our room, redwood as it was nevertheless, with the paper cupful of wildflowers I had picked and placed on the desk. Marking out my territory.

"Do you like her better?"

"Who?"

"The girl with the long hips and the lean hair."

"Listen, it's okay for me to talk to someone."

"I know it's okay."

"But you jump right into the middle when I do."

"If you're talking to just someone, no. But you never do talk to someone, so when you're talking to anyone for a while, I know that it's not just someone. If you know what I mean. Normally, you do not talk. And I said one thing down there."

"No, you really did a lot of talking and people come there to be quiet."

"I guess that's just the way I am."

"No. I don't think it's just the way you are. I can't accept that like that—if I did, I think it would mean I don't care. That's why I have to think about why you were like that. You hate water?"

"Yes, I hate water. I really do. Scalding, sulfur water with strange people in it saying stupid things . . . I hate all of that."

We were lying in bed now, holding each other with an odd

mixture of terror at an edge of hostility in our feelings and bone-deep chills from the climb up the hill.

"And I get paranoid on marijuana. You could say she was not getting at you underwater and I would believe it. You could tell me she did not answer me when I talked to her, and walked away, flipping her towel at me to make me colder as she left. I would believe that."

"Well, she wasn't playing with me under the water. The only one who was, was you when you came over and sat next to me."

"Could we *not* fight?"

"We're not fighting. I'm trying to figure this out. I love you . . . I've just never seen that you were possessive like that, and if that's it, I think it's interesting to think about. But I don't think it was just possessiveness."

"I don't want to talk about it." I got up and stalked to the window and looked out at the sea. "I don't want to learn how to touch stupid people I loathe and don't know . . ."

"I think," he said, "you're testing me. You always react to anything new with fear—I think you're excited—but you're afraid I'll think it's square or something. You have to show me right away that you feel the same way you're sure I'm going to."

"I hate feelings! I'd rather talk about dresses even!"

I punched the wall. It hurt.

The difference between us: he knows what he feels but won't reveal his feelings. I act out feelings constantly but they may have nothing to do with what I really feel.

Whatever that is.

Our sensitivity to each other is not infallible, we'll make mistakes and read each other wrong. This frightens me. I wonder if I can learn to identify what I feel. So we will not get each other wrong. Ever.

His footsteps on the floor came lightly, slowly, nearer, and he put his arms around me. "Come to bed . . . we'll see how it is tomorrow."

He would amuse himself by being unpredictable.

But I was not amused to find that he was not next to me in bed when I woke up the next morning. I tore down the hill, late for the morning class in Elementary Touching; there he was with that same girl, palm-dancing across the wide green grass plateau that overlooked the world and all the rest of Big Sur. Tall as gazelles they were, guiding each other, eyes closed, only by the touch of the palms.

"Teaches trust," said our leader, Taylor, handing me over to Short Hair, the young man from the night before.

We were lurching around. Taylor came over. "No," he pointed out, "Watch that couple out there—they've got it just right."

And we all looked at that lovely tall couple, the fair-haired man and the graceful girl with the long dark hair fairly floating along the edge of the lawn. How terrible if they tripped and she went flying out over the cliff. I was rewarded for the generous thought by tripping myself.

"Taylor," I said, "I'm sure you know I'm here as a reporter only. Well, I've been wondering, where do you draw the line when it comes to how much Joy? Or what kind? And do people ever break up over one of them having a lot of Joy?"

"Who can say?" he answered with the sweet smile of the profitably pure. "That which is strong becomes stronger. The opposite also holds true. What happens, happens."

Laurie and I were now in our room.

"She has beautiful breasts," I said. Leading.

"So do you," he said. Led. "It bothers her, I think, that she's alone. There's something resigned about her . . . I was trying to show I understood. So we bored each other for a while."

"Oh." I was nipping at my fingernails. He took both my hands and held them to keep them still. I pulled away and stood by the window. "Don't hold me. I'm all raveled—I think it's cutting down on the speed too fast, maybe. I want something. I don't know what. I feel tied up. I want to scream."

"Why don't you write it down?"

"Writing is not therapy. It's my work, you know."

"I know, but you feel better when you work." He held out his arms. It was easier to be held after all. Easier to hang on to the feelings of tension and jealousy because they were so familiar. Easier than getting into the strange new territory of thinking about my feelings. Much easier than writing about Esalen with the confident chattiness required by the article I had come there to write.

As I fell asleep I was aware that he had gone to sit by the window, to watch the sea and the moon and to drink the Scotch we had bought.

The evening of the following day there was a Gestalt session. One person sat in what was referred to as the "hot seat" and explained what she/he considered a serious conflict to the entire group, sitting around in a circle. With mild hints from the leader, the subject decided how best to act out the problem, sometimes by playing the various roles involved in the conflict, at other times addressing her/his remarks or actions to individual members in the group. The more violent and hostile the feelings you expressed the more "beautiful" you were.

I thought that perhaps Lawrence could exercise some of his hostilities—he must have angers somewhere. And then, perhaps, he would not drink quite so much. If he could just cut it down here and there . . .

The present subject, or victim, was a very angry man, raging about various injustices. He seemed suddenly to be addressing me. "And you," he screamed, stamping on pillows that had been provided, "are a coward. The only time you talk is when your husband is around."

He turned next to Lawrence, not snarling. "You don't even show up. So I don't have any hostility toward you yet." There was disappointment in his voice.

Lawrence just sat watching. Paler, perhaps, than usual, under the eyes. I softly suggested he might take the stand. He was always wan and a bit unsteady until he had a drink. The way

I was before the early speed. With booze, though, it was not a good sign. (Addicts are quite on to the dangers. It's just that one always exempts one's own thing.)

"What for?"

"Well . . . nothing. I just thought you might have some things you could say here."

He just looked at me rather curiously. Almost blank. Was this how he looked when he was insulted? There were so many feelings that remained unseen.

Well, screw it. So it's corny and he'll think I'm square. I'm dying to go up there. Just to see. And there is also this powerful inability I have to resist being the center of attention.

I took my place. They were on to me right away. They knew I was a fraud; that I had no important conflicts. I could tell by their boredom, their hidden glares. I had nothing to say. I shrugged and just looked at the leader.

"I don't know why I'm here now," I said, grinning.

"How do you feel?" he asked.

"Well, I think I feel . . ." I just looked at my hands. Such a fraud.

"Don't think. Feel."

"I can't. Do you mean—well, my arms feel cold?"

"Wave them around." I did. And I laughed. Now they were all watching.

"No," the leader continued, "just let your arms go."

I thought of something: "I can't do that. I'm not free. I feel like I've been watching everything, and with contempt too. I think I'm being honest now, but I'm not even sure about that . . ." I would not stop talking.

"Go around the circle," he said when he could get a word or so in, "and let each person know how you feel, but without words."

"That's impossible. I really don't feel anything toward these people. I mean toward you. All of you. That sounds so awful, but I can't relate without words, and you use so few words . . ."

"Shhh," Taylor said. "Go around."

"I have to?"

He nodded.

They seemed to be baby birds waiting to be fed. How anxious everyone else is, as I am, for someone else's reaction. I could not look at Lawrence.

The group was heavily into hugging all the time. They liked that, so I hugged a couple of the matronly women, one of the priests. Then there was this woman with a Southern accent who spoke of the various locks she needed on her doors back home, who clearly set her hair every morning of her life. I shook her hand. Someone else . . . I just walk by. I knew there was a hurt expression, but it had to be.

Then.

Then Elly. The girl. I sort of lunged forward and pulled her hair, and as I stood back, my fingertips still on her long, soft hair, we just stared at each other, eyes going into each other, and my arms reached out; my hands just kept on moving down from her hair, and they kept moving down, to her breasts, stroking them, coming around them from all sides, enclosing them, feeling nipples through her soft shirt, like little lights burning into my palms. And then, only with the resistance of breaking off from a magnetic field, my hands moved from that heavy softness down to her slim waist.

There was the feeling. I was acting out what I felt, before I even knew what it was. Or reasoned around, in forty ways, why I should not express it.

But Taylor kept saying, "Just go with the feeling." Where could I go with this? And when?

I fled to Laurie, sitting so silent in the circle like all the others, and he wrapped his arms twice around me, it seemed, and he had tears in his eyes. Put back those feelings, I thought, slam that lid back down.

After the Gestalt thing broke up, everyone hugged and cried. Everyone was "really beautiful," everyone said.

I told Elly I'd like to maybe take a walk in the morning.

"Well, I'm going into town tomorrow," she said. "Maybe we'll talk after dinner."

"Yes," I said. "Perhaps you can come over."

Laurie and I went to our room.

"Well," I said. "Okay, I always wanted to be homosexual—to be accepted. It's partly the life style. Or just style I feel more comfortable with. Especially gay men. Actually I don't know any gay women to be close to. But when I see them anywhere they have this look of knowing, of being in on things. A look of something happening. If you hadn't come along—if there weren't children, I think I'd go there . . . if I knew where, that is."

"I guess a thing you have in common with homosexuals," he said, "and I haven't thought about this too much before, but it occurs to me that you haven't resolved your relationship with your parents, either. I think that's why homosexuals I've known seem younger, and hang on to artifacts that remind them of their childhoods. I just thought about that right now, so I may not be right."

"Nobody's resolved any relationships with parents, God, Laurie!" I said. "And if they claim they have, it's because they haven't really thought about it. I don't want to talk about parents, however. What I want to talk about is what happens to us if I get involved with a woman."

How adult that sounds, I thought. Facing up to it, at last. I was staring at the paper cup full of orange California poppies that are illegal to pick. They had closed up for the night. Hiding the good part, like a woman. Yes, I want her.

"I think you have to see how it is. I think you should have, a long time ago." He shrugged. "I think you should have known that was possible."

"It's strange—I never thought my body was unattractive for men, but I thought it would be for another girl. I think I never got really thin when I was young because I would have had to take that step. Such a coward."

"No." He opened his arms for me to come to be held. "Not

really." He was thinking, "Yes really"? Or was he thinking . . . ?

"What are you thinking?" I asked. Coming to lie across his chest with a pounce he has not anticipated.

"Why you don't stop talking about it? And as they say, go with the feeling."

"Okay." I was a little angry. I sat up and turned to look at my reflection in the sliding door across from the bed. Or was it that fear-feeling I get when I have to make up my own mind about something? Or was it something else? Yes: that to him it would not be as important if it was a woman.

"Laurie, would you be mad if I slept with another man?"

"I would be sad." He got up and sat behind me, his legs around mine, holding me like a soft-sculpture chair. "Because you have had a lot of experience there and picked me, evidently after a lot of consideration . . . but I don't think I would be jealous."

"Well, what if I got the experiences with women, and then fell more in love with one of them than with you?"

"I think I have to take that chance. But we have a closeness that is unusual and special, and I suppose I don't feel it could be seriously threatened." He leaned back to reach for his drink. Then he sat on the edge of the bed, looking up, thinking carefully about what he was going to say.

(Yes, Laurie, be careful, I thought. One husband simply laughed at me when I told him this hip playwright had made a pass at me. "Jealous?" he said. "Hell, men just don't see you like that." Such crows I served for him to eat. Crow after crow after . . .)

"I think," said Laurie, "we are very different from a lot of couples."

"Yes. She's beast; he's beauty. Lovely beauty," I teased him, lying on his lap for a moment, my hands stroking his chin. It was incredible to have such a creature in your room to look at any time.

"You're lovely and sunny and young—stop fishing. The difference, I was going to say, is that you may occasionally need to have adventures, as you call them, and that could be a problem if I was possessive. And I don't need to have adventures, fortunately, because you are possessive."

"Pulling her hair? No. That was not possessive. Lust is such an unusual feeling for me, it often comes out mixed up." I was going to say it comes out as violence, but he hates violence . . .

He said, "I don't think lust is such an unusual feeling for you. I just think you've made it a pretend game, even in sex—that way you don't lose control; you feel less vulnerable. But you do lose touch with what really turns you on."

I posed for him, for myself in the window—dark mirror— and flipped my hair about. "Laurie, do I look really younger today, up here, or is it just the way I act?"

"You look younger. Especially when you're happy, when you're not tired . . . or speeding too much."

I leaned over him. "I love when you tell me things you think about me, about how I am—that shows you watch me. I do demand attention like a child. Maybe that's the part of me that is homosexual. Although that seems like such a contradiction because to live like that you have to be so independent and able to face up to a lot of bullshit, I think. And give up things . . . Do you think I am basically straight homosexual, that I've just adapted—except for you—because of conditioning?"

"No, I don't think you're basically any one thing." We were now lying in bed. It was a conversation between two cigarettes. "I think you have to learn that you really are all the many different things you pretend to be, and that that's okay. There doesn't have to be a one you—it wouldn't be a you."

"Oh," I said. "That's more acceptance than I can handle."

His breathing sounded asleep. I put out his cigarette and kissed him.

"Are you sleeping?" I whispered.

"Yes," he said.

Let him be, I said to myself.

WORDS:

GAY: The irony of that word. Some gay. Any of us.

LUST: How does one inept body deal with the various lusts and anti-lusts of all these suddenly acceptable personalities? And what do we do with the personality who demands that sex-lust be combined only with love—who, every time she acts on that feeling he has called lust, either falls in love or gets a disease?

SEX: Enlightened sensuality, they say at Esalen, is good for sex. And sex is healthy. But Taylor explains that these feelings you are feeling should nevertheless not be confused with sex. However, what is sex to me if not confusion—and confusion but a lure I rush to?

LOVE: Yes. That. How much confusion can love afford? Especially when love is a gentle man who's already had a lot of confusion. Does he balance this account better than his checks? And will he warn me when he's running out? (before he does.)
Love is: a gentle man. Yes. That will do. For today. Tomorrow . . .

The next morning we had the famous bath thing: Everyone in the group took turns being It, being soaped and splashed off with buckets of water by all the others. It was supposed to teach trust. We detested it. I cried at my turn. Laurie tensed his muscles at his.

I whispered, "Relax, darling, it's okay."

He said (eyes closed against the soaping hoard), "I am relaxed!" His arms were frozen stiff at his sides.

A woman was taking more time with him than I thought was necessary to wash a cock. I finally plunged around through the water and pushed her away. "That's enough!" I yelled.

"Okay. I am possessive," I muttered to him. "Conceded."

After the bath, the group divided up into teams of three for kind of relay rubbings on the massage tables in the sun, on the very edge of the stone plateau—the natural balcony, really, that runs around the outside of the bath cave. There were five tables placed along there, so fifteen people were taking turns, two massaging one. Unpossessive as I am, I clutched Laurie like a koala bear. I also looked around to see if Elly had by some chance come back early. An ideal third person to complete our turn. However, we selected a shy young man to be with us. I knew, as we had our turns, that I would take this exercise for a sexual fantasy.

The men were both aroused during all the variations: Laurie and I massaging, the other man and I working on Laurie, and both on me. I felt a lust that peaked to anger. "Do not confuse sex with sensuality"? How to separate the two?

If "sex is healthy," and one is to "go with the feeling," then why this incompletion, here?

We thanked each other, and glossy with clove-scented massage oil, we slid apart. How lucky I was to have Laurie—fast as skating on cold cream, we were in our room.

"Lawrence," I said when I awakened him later in the afternoon, with some orange juice and vodka and some cheese, "we've having a little party tonight. Could we go into town and pick up some things?"

"Grapes? To peel?"

"Don't tease. I don't know about the whole thing, but I'd like to see what happens. Or feel what happens, I mean."

Elly dropped by later than we'd expected, with a young man who seemed to be sort of a fixture around the place. When I was fifteen I would have thought he was handsome. Although I hadn't expected her to bring anyone, it seemed inappropriate to express preferences. Everyone was to be loved.

"I'm so exhausted," she said, lying against the pillows. "I was practically not going to come, but Jim really was dying for a joint, so here we are." Elly was sexier, I thought, like certain film stars, where there was no sound.

Lawrence was quietly tapping tobacco out of regular cigarettes and filling them with marijuana while Jim sat watching gloomily.

Did I really say, "Well, we'll be glad to give you a joint to take with you, Jim"? That was not loving.

"Thanks, I'll keep it for later."

"Actually, I did want to speak to Elly . . ." I sort of waved my hands in some inexpressive, ineffective way.

"Go ahead!" He smiled charmingly.

Elly sighed, from the pillows, "I'm just staying a little while, anyhow. I had this really weird dream this afternoon. What a trip!"

Jim, staring at Laurie, said, "I have a cigarette machine."

Laurie nodded. He didn't have to look so formally amused, as though he were hosting a child's birthday party.

"Why don't you go get it," I snapped at Jim.

Even Laurie seemed farther and farther away. Elly's legs were so sleek and tan under her long white cotton Mexican skirt. I reached out and touched her hip lightly as if testing a stove.

"Home," Jim said—ages later, it seemed, "is in Minnesota. Home. Is where the cigarette machine is."

". . . and where the heart is, don't forget," I said.

"You know"—he looked at me with that glazed look men get when they're longing—"I've been wanting to touch your hair for ages. May I touch your wife's hair?"

"Well, that's up to her, I think," said Laurie.

"No," I said. "I don't like being touched."

Jim seemed to think that was terribly funny.

I looked back at Elly.

"I just want to think about this dream," she said dreamily. "It was all about my ex-husband, and about loving, about life, about me."

"Those are all beautiful things," I said in the Esalen vernacular. "Except, perhaps, the ex-husband. I can't say about him."

"Oh, he's a beautiful person too."

Of course. I looked at Laurie. He was reading. He was sitting on the floor with a drink; even stoned, I noticed that (or did I just *know* it?). Reading.

"Is there anyone who isn't beautiful?" I tried to say it softly, not to interfere with the reflective gaze of dopiness so easily converted to a lustrous sensuality if you squinted a little, as an artist would, to get a sense of the composition.

"If you love everyone," I said quietly, "it makes some of them feel less special." She was falling asleep. That was not terrific. "Tell me about your dream, Elly. What about you and loving . . ."

"Oh, everything. Just everything."

Jim said (Jim was still there? I had forgotten him in my concentration on the way the skirt swoops across her lap. And dips in. There.), "I had a dream the other night about building a house and when I finish I am stuck on the roof, no ladder, see—what is that?"

"It means perhaps you should jump off."

Elly's hair: It seemed as if I had been pulling my hand back and reaching it out for ages.

"I've been wondering," she said, "if this dream means I should get back with my husband. Or get a job."

I didn't want to hear about these problems. "Well, do you love your husband?" I asked, anyway. Almost automatically.

She sat up a bit. "Oh, yes. It's not that. It's just he's into different things. But we love each other very much. That's not the problem."

"It seems to me there isn't any problem, then." I looked over at Laurie. Our chaperone was looking over his book at me and grinning. Having had one of the last of the real gut-level hostile divorces, I could not understand the friendly ones. But then, you have to have started in passion for love to turn to hate like mine had. It has to have been unreasonable to start with.

"But," I added, "you probably, as Taylor always says, should go with the feeling. Just let what happens happen." I shrugged. Helpless. Partly because I realized through the haze that Jim had taken off his shoes and socks and was now standing up and working on his other clothes.

"Let's all make it," he said cheerfully, only moments after I had figured out that's what he was getting ready for. Or moments before, possibly. It's hard enough to set things in time as it is.

He looked at Lawrence, who, I realized, was watching now from the other side of the room. Had time gone by? Jim said, "Your wife has a fabulous body. I was digging her in the baths."

I didn't think making appraisals was part of it. It was different for everyone to be easy about nudity in the baths. I had picked up the Esalen paradoxy. The sex/sensuality confusion.

I had also picked up Jim's hands upon my hips.

Elly, oblivious, was still puzzling. "But on the other hand, I'm not sure if my husband ever really understood love."

I could have told her it has baffled experts . . .

Laurie stood up, stretching. "Hey, man," he said to Jim, "I think going to bed sounds just fine. And it's been fun, but we're splitting tomorrow, early. So we'll see you around . . ."

"But I did want to talk to Elly about a dream she mentioned, you know," I said wistfully.

"Oh, I love you," she said, "you're beautiful people . . ."

The orgy put on its shoes and went home.

It was generous of Laurie not to laugh until I did. At first I just sat on the bed, swinging my legs.

"Rats," I said. "A Stella Dallas orgy."

We started, then, to laugh together. "They did all show up," he says. "So it's not a classic Stella Dallas situation."

"It's somehow worse when a woman rejects you. I mean me. It's like animals throwing the bad ones out of the litter or the herd or whatever."

"It's not that. You can't just set things up. We've talked about that." He refilled his glass. Again.

"Well, now I know, at least, how men feel when they make passes. But it's different."

"How different?"

"Just different. I don't want to discuss the whole thing." I took a sip from his glass. How strong his drinks were now. Laurie knew I would discuss it. Things I can't possibly talk about generally receive quite as full coverage as things I can't wait to tell you about. The comment is a disclaimer: this is something I don't know much about, or haven't given any thought to.

"Well. Maybe it isn't different. I wanted to use her as a symbolic someone. That's not fair . . . And something else . . ."

He was sitting on the edge of the bed. I pushed him down and held his shoulders, rumpling his hair. "You lie, Yankee dog!" I said. "You are possessive. Look how you didn't like him touching me!"

"You didn't like him either," he said. "And even if it had worked—with her, I think it would have been pretty grim. The people ought to start out liking each other."

"I do like her."

"You don't. She's boring."

"Well. I make my own fantasies, anyway . . ."

He was lying on the bed. It was true that even the consideration of unsatisfactory sexual options had turned us on.

"I wonder," I whispered, thinking over my collection of fantasies, "how to get enough of you. To be everywhere on you at once . . ."

We chewed the remains of the last grass cigarette. The last drink from the jug of red wine, chased by Laurie with a beer, and by me with a quarter speed. Just to make sure the marijuana would not put me out while we were making love.

The grass took effect. I drifted into today's fantasy—Take One:

Hands working perfectly together, Laurie and I are massaging the young man, chest side up with clove-scented oil. Smiling at each other, watching his expression deepen as our hands move over his abdomen and then sweep up and back down his hips, working now onto his thighs. Silently, we are all alone now, the three of us, on the stone balcony, the wind blows over the mountains behind us, but the warm sun flows down. It is so still. I stand behind his head, leaning over, watching Laurie's hands as I rub the young man's jaw . . . as he reaches up to hold my breasts, and I hold down his arms, just as Laurie helps me turn him over and places his hands on the man's buttocks, and leans toward him, moving up between his legs . . .

I shut off the fantasy and sat up. Why was it going that way?

Laurie pulled me down again gently. "Are you okay?"

"Yes. Just something . . ."

"What?"

"Nothing."

It is the same again. With Laurie lying on the table. Handcuffed. Other sordid details well up from a magma of destruction. Go with my feelings and you arrive at chaos and pain.

I sat up again. "I told you. Grass makes me paranoid. I keep having images. Horrible, horrible things."

"Let's just rest . . ."

"Oh, Laurie, healthy sex doesn't work for me. I want the dark side. Raw. Seamy. With seams, garters, torn stockings, little whips and handcuffs. There should be no confusion that it's sex, not therapy. Sex, fucking, eating . . . I want to get in all the places. I want it all over me. When the lust gets out, it's only mean. That's why I confuse it with anger. It is anger."

He was holding me. My arms were wired like springs.

"I've got to get off. It's like a fire running through me. You don't know how it feels. If sex is clean, it is not sexy."

"Here now," he said, kissing me gently, "let's try. Let's see if we can't . . ." He was tired; he had had a lot to drink. And then there was my screaming and bolting at the wrong times. I would have been very bugged with me. Perhaps the drinking softens my hard edges for him. Perhaps, to like me, a person has to be drunk.

So he held me as he dozed, and I tried to go with the feeling, my own feeling, my own hand.

Fantasy: Take Two.

I let my mind go back to the terrace on the cliff. I am on the table in the sun. Laurie and the young man rub me gently, taking turns, then order me in firm and gentle voices to relax. "No," Laurie says. "Now, those neck muscles are tight, now let go, there. Just let go." I am assured that there is all the time in the world. That they have nothing else to do for the entire rest of their lives but to stand in the sun touching me.

Then: Elly is in the fantasy. Weightless, and she is astride my chest. An exquisitely enameled terra-cotta boat she presents to me, a marvelous complexity to explore. I'm sailing off—Her hair is fair like mine.

Cut. Sit up.

"Laurie?"

"Yes?"

"Nothing." My attention transferred to the walls, where, high up, just at the juncture of the ceiling to the wall, where one used to find wallpaper borders, I see a parade of Wac nurses. Marching around the room, truncated, chopped off from the waist up. They are circling in. I am to be punished.

"Laurie. We must get out. I have to get out of our room for a while. I have to run around."

He got up, put on his robe, took his cigarettes. I was already waiting by the door. In the dark, feeling out pebbles with anxious soles and toes, we walked down the hill, down the path, past the dark cabins. We went through the eerie green entrance to the bath caves, an artificial light shining somewhere with a false turquoise note. Soft, out beyond. The sound only of the water lapping, the waves. A couple laughing very quietly. I pulled him along by the hand. I would teach my fantasies to behave. I led Laurie to one of the tables and he lay down, too tired to be puzzled or annoyed.

When I came back with the clove-scented oil to massage him, he was asleep. But he was smiling. His robe was open. I would give him an exquisitely detailed loving. His cock was sleeping; in the steel-gray light of earliest morning, I could see the trails etched along the mauve-rose flesh. I could read his cock, tell his fortune, but the significance of the paths I traced with my breath, with my fingertips, had not been established, and as he stretched, awakening, the paths changed, swelled and disappeared. So now I concentrated on how pointed my tongue could be—like a dancer, curving to precision, twirling with the lightest steps just so barely inside the tiny sly smile on the now gleeful face.

I am not so dangerous. He trusts me.

A feeling of pride. A thing I could do: I felt how the strong root came up whipping around, it seemed, from his spine, filled with the backbone that made him so straight. Sweeping down hard to its source, I could run my fingers along like trilling up and down an octave. Such a bubbling of extravagant appreciation—an exuberance—this was a song I'd rather play. His sighs a better song to hear. So much easier to love him than to be loved.

I think I have been mistaken about fantasies. If one acts them out, then they can be controlled. That is the point. Then you do not have to go with the feelings, for that is where the danger is.

I fell asleep on the massage table next to Laurie's. Carcasses side by side on trays, wiped out.

I dreamed: I am on a stage. It is the stage of a huge musical theater. Through the glare of the footlights I perceive that the theater is packed with people. I'm doing an incredible high-stepping dance; a fast cakewalk to the gorgeous sound of a huge, throttle-out band; wearing a Gay Nineties gown of fine white net, sewn with fringes, pearls and lace. My hair is piled high and draped with swinging strands and loops of pearls. A cheering audience. A curtain call. People whisper, "It's a smash hit!" "She's a huge new star!" "We never knew!"

I'm opening my arms wide, motioning them to keep on, blowing kisses, crying out, "Don't stop—don't ever stop! That's right, that's what I want! Yes, yes! That's just fine, fine, fine. Thank you, I love you . . . this is just it, just it! Just perfect!"

I hear a voice whisper in my ear as I'm catching the roses flying at me through the footlights, "You really ought to let your father take a bow, Jill." And I say, "Fine, but only for a moment, you know. Just a moment. This is my act." And I see him, in the backstage shadows, in the wings, dusting off his stars. Silver stars appliqued on a royal-blue smoking jacket.

It was a soft, gray, still dawn. The water lapped in the tubs. Even the steam seemed chilled, stilled. Shadows of pines marched solemnly through the fog; an army moving out of a Chinese watercolor. And Laurie slept.

Fame. It's the thing and not the woman I get off on.

There's your lust.

Get your act together.

I didn't want to go home to where I knew how hard it was. To where I feared I couldn't. So we drove on north to San Francisco.

And while I was putting flowers in my hair because that was what everyone was wearing there, I was thinking that love might be two other things:

1. When he allows you to act out your fantasies.

2. And when you reject the fantasies that do him harm. And I can count the contradictions on the fingers of two terrible hands.

But we did come home.

Laurie got another job. "It is different," he said, "primarily because I am driving in another direction to get there."

And it was another month or so when Landlord stood upon the front porch woefully holding bounced checks in his hand.

"Two months, Jill. I'm sorry."

"You're sorry!" My voice went up. "I'm hysterical. I will kill!" I was not being supportive to my husband. "I'm sure it's just an oversight."

Landlord and I had known each other too long: there are no oversights. Just no funds.

"Well, I'll do what I can."

"You have him call me tonight . . ."

When Laurie came home from work he looked very pale. Very frightened. Very young. For a minute.

"Look. I have never even asked you how much you earn. I won't be a nosy real wife. But when it's rent, which really counts, you should keep things straight. And this time, Laurie, I don't know what to do. I mean, two months' rent! Jesus Christ, where the hell is it going?"

"It goes. It just goes, you know. I'll go get some money."

"It's eight-thirty at night—what do you mean, go get some money?"

"What I said. Now don't you fret."

I tried to work on the rewrite of the Esalen piece. I knew just by the sound of things around four-thirty in the morning that he wasn't coming home.

Karen said, the next morning, "Of course he's coming back. He's probably in Gardena. He played poker too late, so he's going straight to the office."

"I wish you had told me all this."

"I did. You didn't hear."

"I heard. I didn't care. Difference. I suppose."

By eleven-thirty I decided I had to call his office. Maybe he was there. I had been to the other office once, and gotten lost in the maze of cubicles. It seemed too anonymous for him.

Laurie had said, "It's depressing enough so that we should both not have to go there." He seemed to feel the same way about the people.

"Shouldn't I," I'd asked, "do a few of those executive-wife things?"

"I'm not an executive."

"Well, the upward mobility striving exercises. Dinners."

"I'm not sure about whether I'm striving. If I decide to, I'll let you know."

"Fine . . . because I don't want you to think I don't know how or anything."

The secretary who answered the phone now said, "Oh. Mr. Robinson. Yes—well, he won't be in today. He called in sick. You might reach him at home."

I said I would try that. Yes, I thought I had his home number, I said.

I went over to face Landlord later in the afternoon. "I feel awful. But I know he's out there somewhere trying . . ."

He looked puzzled. "Well, it's all right. Larry was over an hour ago. He paid me in full. Cash. And we had a couple of drinks. He sure can put it away. But I'm surprised—"

I did not wait to hear what he was surprised about. I dashed back to the house, through the front door. Laurie was standing in the kitchen. Calmly arranging long-stemmed red roses in a glass pitcher.

"Where have you been?" I said, pawing at him as Jasper pawed at me. (Pawing order indicating eminence of household gods.)

"I got the money. That was all." Innocence accosted.

"I was worried. And listen, don't leave me all night like that . . . you could have called. Something."

"I love you . . ." He lifted me into the air, kissing my neck and shoulders.

"That's what my mother says to change the subject." I looked at him. He was not to be resisted. "Those are nice roses. I love them. I love you. You make me crazy . . ."

How do you freeze destruction so that it stands still in its tracks? You don't.

These were odd, queasy times—the California primary in 1968 promised a lot. We really did feel we were just on the edge of achieving a change. Such anxious energy—not to mention the flashy wheel spinning of two really parallel camps trying to create a conflict. The unbalanced really get nauseated at the prospect of change. Get violent. Get destructive. Get crazy.

On the night of the primary election, I had gone up to Senator McCarthy's suite at the Hilton Hotel, hoping to get a special interview that I could use for my show. Since I was not in the press union, I had to have the interview recorded by one

.he official station newspeople. Al, top newsman at the station
., and a friend, had done the taping for me, after he got his
rview for the regular news spot. We had just left McCarthy's
room when we all heard a scream from his room, "My God, my
God—Bobby's been shot."

Al, whom I'd always been nagging about getting to share
coverage of a big story, grabbed my arm. "Come, come with me
—we'll get over to the hospital where they'll take him."

Lawrence was somewhere in the defeat celebration downstairs, somewhere, perhaps in the VIP bar.

"But Larry's down there—I should at least get a message to
him."

"There's no time, come or not. Up to you," Al said as I ran
through the hotel beside him . . . newsmen were running in all
directions now. "You always said you wanted to be in on a big
one. Jesus, I hope those bastards haven't killed him! Come on
now."

I was running as fast as I could through hotel hallways.
Everyone else was, too. Even just regular people. Running, just
to feel less bewildered and helpless. I had visions of pandemon-
ium in the streets. We must have a national apocalypse.

I looked to the future: I saw Lawrence in 1992—some time
to come—pushing his shell-shocked way through mobs of the
panic-stricken, then through hospitals of victims shot in the
Insurrection. The Beverly Hilton lobby filled with victims lying side by side as he, older now, and quite gray, walked
through the rows of the injured and dying, a bottle of whiskey
in one hand, a picture of me in the other, to show people; he
would stop them, his beautiful hands purple with frostbite, the
cuffs of the ragged sweater pulled over to warm them. (War
changes climate.)

"Have you ever seen this woman—my wife? We were separated the Night of the Third Assassination and I've been
searching for her these many years. Do you want a drink?"

Now; again. 1968. Al roars through death-still streets on two

wheels to the hospital, through red lights. We never saw
policeman—there were no people running out in the streets
thought of the hotels where they would still be running like
in mazes until they could get into the safety of their cars where
the panic would be contained in parking lots. And the tragedy
itself would be contained in a place where you could drive by.
Another sight to see. Or you could stay home and watch it on
your small screen. There is no need to panic. And you will miss
none of the excitement.

The ambulance was backed up to the first hospital door. And
through the ambulance window I could see Ethel Kennedy.
And as a camera might, in a movie, all my awareness, all my
feelings zoomed right in to her face. For an instant I could feel
her scream start from my gut.

She roared with horror and fury at the crowd immobilizing
the ambulance which stood there like a beast caught in a trap,
its red eyes flashing with frustration.

That anger must make him live.

There were screams: "Let them out!"

How do you get your love so strong? How do you electrocute
destruction so it stands stark still in its tracks? I clenched my
fists to pull for her.

When, at the second hospital, Al had established tie lines
with the station through a local phone, he asked someone to try
to find the "Resident hippie's" husband. "Check bars around the
Hilton," he said, winking. "Tell him she's with me."

Another newsman, who considered me "a pain in the ass,"
said, "He'll never find you, you know. He'll never get near the
hospital now without a press pass. You oughta go home. I sure
as hell wouldn't want my wife hanging around here all night."

I was afraid that Laurie might (any second, as I turned
around) slip out of my life. I needed to test my fears. That's
aside from the curiosity—always wanting to be in the middle,
even if it is horrible.

"This is my job," I said.

"You're not a reporter; the station could lose its license if they put you on with hard news, who the hell are you kidding?"

"I have to be here. It's something else . . . and as a newsman, you wouldn't go home just because you couldn't get on the air. Jesus, Al, tell him to get off my back."

"You're telling him—" He was busy. What I needed to tell them and wanted not to was that I had to seem to matter somewhere. Even if I had stayed, and had gone to look for Laurie, I had no way of knowing he would have been there for me to find. Wright and Emily were with Karen and Mike's kids at their house—a sleep-over election-night party.

"Maybe I could do one interview, actually, Al, just so Larry would hear it and know I was here."

Al shook his head. The other man yelled at me, "Hey, I'll run you out sure as hell if you don't cut it out now. We'll get canned if you get on the air."

"I could do the woman's angle—what Ethel is wearing, the food that's being sent in. A little number on whether Jackie will show up . . . that would be nice." Eat it, I thought.

All through the night the Eastern journalists stood like Druids watching the hospital. And I thought, as I spoke with the ones I knew who had been traveling with McCarthy, that my eyes are darting about like a gossip columnist's. I would have explained I was looking for my husband, but it seemed insensitive to be looking for a perfectly well husband when a woman's husband is up there dying and that is why we are here.

Except: I'm not so sure of his wellness.

But that is a distraction: Listen, love, you got to share me.

I should explain now the game of Careers: a board game. Before the game starts, you must decide what you want to emphasize in your life plan. You split up the 90 optimum points among Fame, Happiness and Money points. Most people go for about 30 each, although a surprising number I've known split it up between Money and Happiness.

I've always gone 90 for Fame. You get that, I figured, and

you get all the access you need to pick up the money and happiness you want.

Oh, yes? Look at the limousines now snaking into the hospital garage. Reconsider that point breakdown. Think how happiness is symbolized in the game by a heart: happiness/love. Not the inevitable combination.

Frank Mankiewicz came out of the hospital. He looked khaki. A reporter, astride another's shoulders, yelled into the night, "Have Joe and Rose been notified?"

"Mr. and Mrs. Kennedy have been notified."

"What was their reaction?"

Frank said, fast, "How would you react if your second son was shot in the head?"

Fame. Love. And Money.

So much for the game of Careers.

You do know when someone you love is somewhere around, getting closer. It was near dawn when I saw him: Laurie, evading the police barriers, leaping over a rooftop onto a fire escape. A regular Fairbanks.

"I was so scared you wouldn't find me."

"Where else would you be?"

"It's terrible, isn't it" I said.

"Yes"—he looked around—"McCarthy said, remember, he was afraid of making it an issue of bad guys against good guys. Do you think anyone has a beer?"

As soon as I could get to a phone the next morning, I called the children at Karen and Mike's. Karen was just getting everyone ready for school.

The children had wanted to come: "Did you see him . . . the blood and everything?"

"Are his children there?" Emily asked.

"Three of them are coming soon," I said. Every time I thought of their children I started to cry. I wasn't sure exactly why. I was only sure it was probably for the wrong reason. I told Karen I might have to stay around there—who knows for how long.

"No problem. They'll sleep over again if necessary. Keep me posted."

I called the children with bulletins during the evening. Nothing they hadn't already seen on TV. But I made it sound new so they would feel I had to be there—that it was not a matter of choice that we were not home.

Laurie and I were sitting on a step outside the newly established press headquarters. Laurie, having no press pass, had earlier, nevertheless, borrowed a walkie-talkie, and looking tweedy and busy, strolled out of the barriers with an official nod at the police, returning with vodka, orange juice and doughnuts in considerable quantities. Especially the vodka.

We had talked the night before about what Laurie referred to as a national trouble.

"Some of the trouble," I told him quietly, "is people like me. When I said 'It's terrible' the other night, I was exhilarated. I don't really hate all this action. Now, that's what is terrible. I call it involvement. It may be lurid curiosity. And then I yell at you for not showing up at peace marches—when maybe I'm only going, hoping for the confrontation."

"You're being too cynical. I think showing up is your way of validating your commitments—whatever, and it's cool, but it's not my way."

"I guess with us, then, involvement is that one of us watches and the other one stays home and thinks about why it's happening. Some involvement."

"True," he said.

"True," I muttered. "True. You always say 'True'." I looked at him, sitting there as newspeople, police and campaign workers moved about with the hustle, the sound of people who have some purpose.

"The big Truth Watch," I said. "If you watch long enough, do you think you'll find it?"

I was probably attacking him because I wasn't important enough to be doing anything productive, taking it out on him because he wasn't important either. If he'd been important, it might have rubbed off. One would think I'd learned how that goes.

"Not exactly," he said. "Truth seekers aren't aware of how certain they are that they will not find it. The truth."

"But you are aware, of course," I said (snapped). I was angry because he didn't seem so interested in my observation either. I was angry that I did not see him as perfect any more.

"Yes."

Yes. He just sat, drinking slowly but steadily. Watching. Bullets—booze. See how the good men go. And we cry as we can. I poured some of his vodka into my orange juice and sat beside him, frowning.

But I never could sit for long. In my system's battle between the knock-out effect of booze and the speed energy, speed won because the speed input was higher.

So I ran around taping interviews which I would not, of course, be permitted to use on my show.

By 9:20 A.M. Jesus Saves had been by with handout hats. By 10:15 "Pray for Bobby" bumper stickers were being passed out. A poker game was on in the press pavilion . . . the vodka, shared to be sure, was gone. Lawrence was thirsty.

"Did you call your office?" I asked him.

"Sure, sure."

"Is it okay . . . I mean, did they understand?"

It seemed obvious that a company would not concern itself over attendance records of the brilliant, particularly sensitive employee. You don't rattle brains.

"You're sure?" I added, being not so sure after all. He had not been there very long, after all. Or does brilliance give instant seniority? I doubt it.

"Half the office is out anyway, it's cool. Listen, since you can get in and out easily, would you get us some beer?"

He moved away from the table at least to hand me money, and with his arm around my shoulder walked me to the door of the press pavilion. "What's the matter?"

"A presidential candidate is dying and I have to feed your problem."

"What problem? I don't understand."

"Booze . . ."

"Hey, I love you, don't be mad at me, please, darling. We have to hang together. That's where we have to be involved . . ."

"Oh, I'm not mad. Just crashing, probably. I'm on to my last Dex. I'll have to get more, somehow."

I looked back at him; he was pale. Probably needed sleep. On the way to get his beer, I decided to call the L.A. *Free Press* to see if they would like a story on the hustlers, the crowd people who hang around at emergencies.

What do they do on their days off? And what is it they think they really feel? It is a Southern California profession. Requires good weather. Like most outdoor work.

I am a Southern Californian.

Several newspeople suddenly rushed by. "McCarthy's here," someone whispered to me. I was off the phone, running to the hospital. "Keep back!" the police shouted as McCarthy, tall, silver, moved through the mob. A newsman asked, "Will this give you a better shot at the nomination, Gene, or do you think . . . ?" McCarthy's face, his eyes, were flash-frozen. "You son of a bitch," he said.

I focused in as I had with Ethel Kennedy: These are feeling models. McCarthy: This is how rage looks.

And how it looks when everything is all over. When you know pragmatically that there is no case for hope. About anything. Some of the sharper saints may have had that look on office calls to the Inquisition.

Ethel Kennedy: The love that is tied up with rage is what must count. "Love" doesn't seem to be the right word. It's written on too many ashtrays, sold on too many loony records, desalinated by too many Esalen disciples. There is no word. There is just that expression. It's an expression I would feel on my face like the wind.

I had to go get Laurie's beer, and when I passed Frank Mankiewicz coming out of the hospital, walking by fast, looking like hell, he paused and hung an arm around my shoulder. "Yes?" I asked. "Off the record," he said. And he just shook his head. It could not be: you could not love so hard, want so hard and not have it be all right.

Love is the big lie. Here's what love is: powerless. I would have to tell Karen I figured it out.

Here's power: having your own radio show and getting to say exactly what you think.

"We'll not have commercials today," I announced as I signaled my engineer to fade out my theme song, "The Eve of Destruction." "We're sponsored now by the National Rifle Association, the CIA and the FBI—the people who make history happen live, so to speak, on your own home screen.

"You've been unappreciative, however, my friends. You ask: Why is it only the Good Guys who get shot? Perhaps you should look at it this way. Perhaps the assassins feel our empire is an oppressive parent and the Reverend King; and those Kennedys are the favorite siblings.

"We, the assassins, must kill these favorite siblings. We are the silent, corner children; unloved, the self-hating. We must punish that parent by killing the favorite child. But you don't understand: you're only killing the Symbols. Your real rivals, the powerful ones the empire adores and spoils, you've never seen. You cannot kill their corporations."

I sat at the controls, the desk like a pilot's board, a cockpit panel (where, as it usually goes, only cock may sit), and through the window before me, the engineer held up a card, shook his head: "No Incendiary Comments!" He was grinning.

I said, "Put out that match, folks! Now, let's keep that hate mail coming. Hate gives some of us this fantastic sense of identity. Aren't our bad guys more alluring, and, watch now, they're enduring, they have more staying power, and if not that, then what else, I ask you, is of value in this land? America, home of the . . . land of the vastest, coast-to-coast, sea-to-shining-sea masochistic-rape-assassination fantasy. Fantastic! Let's put it on the market!

"Display it!" I told my listeners. "And now—we have a message from your Outlaw Boutiques, opening today in your local department stores. Be first in your area. See this exciting innovation!" I described the latest wonder of contemporary merchandising: "You will see a tall man, with the handsome smile of a mannequin, standing in the corner; he wears a sky-blue satin cowboy hat to match his sexy cool eyes. And he holds his gun . . . so appealingly. My dear, it is to be the rage! For only a dollar-fifty service charge, you too can get caught shoplifting. Surprise hubby, come home with a real bullet wound. You too can be shot . . . be-someone, be-loved. For charge-account customers this exclusive new service is free. Just come in and get yours . . . no shoplift necessary. Listen, I'm just trying this out—we'll run it through the copy department again.

"I've been talking about love. And how to fix it all up. You don't want to hear that."

The engineer was joined by some of the news editors. I had my audience, cheering with the cheers of those who watch girls fuck᾿ donkeys. The pointing, the madness in the eyes, the tumescent charm of woman-out-of-control. But I had them . . . running around in there. I had the reins, I whipped them on. They twisted knobs. I made this one jump with a tape into the slot as I pushed the button on my controls for a howling-sound sound effect . . . now fire engines, and perhaps the wolves. Yes.

Now the bugles. They were turning, clicking, clipping tapes in there, tied up in the shiny brown cords like slaves. To my right a producer was bringing in a guest. To pounce on for the direct attack. They waved anxiously through the thick glass. My eyes narrowed and gleamed.

And I leaned back in the chair regally, as I'd seen the Big Men do. I fooled around with the mike. Then, rubbing it up and down, to the glee of the engineers, I leaned forward, seductively, addressing myself to the listeners, as I imagined enraged conservatives, the fainting liberals.

I saw, in my mind, the Conservative in his dark room where only his white socks stand out, his ham radio and his collection of *National Geographics*, yellow like stacked lynx eyes against the wall. His pure-white nylon socks with clocks running up the sides. The prototype California conservative caller who whispers of the lewd effects of LSD, of the Communist plot behind the doll that has a penis. I said the word on the air. I told Conservative, as he clutched himself in terror, that he too has tasted the governor's jelly beans, and I have heard about that. I know all these things. It is not only he that is Ever Alert. I, too, have my methods. I told him, whispering, that the raspberry jelly bean is Red. And that, quick, for his last glass of water before the fluoridation comes in and overnight he will turn Chinese!

I spoke to him of boys with swaying long hair and women going braless. And he was fainting, and of men going undrafted in the Swedish sun, and he fell to the floor, whipping himself with birch sticks. "I know how to get you, Conservative, in your room . . . to see you clinging to the phone, strangling it with both hands as you scrawl a note with your stub, your stub," I said, "to get that perverted, filthy Commie whore bitch off the air . . . to get her off, get her off. You want to know a secret? She can't get off."

I had learned well how to get them to call. The switchboard was filled with calls now—a beast with fifteen flashing red eyes.

Or I could add, "I don't think anyone has the right to shoot a person for burglary. Human life has more value than private property." And that starting gate would swing up, the phones light up and the hate bolt out thundering like horses.

Perhaps a flip through the file box for the quote to pin their arguments like moths to a board. Should I, today, resist the shout, the punching off of their phone lines, a graceless end to their calls? I rather like hitting the moth with a hammer after it has been pinned. No. Today comes on hammers.

I am a knight. They are coming up to joust. I will kill them with buttons. Punch them out and off.

The power I felt on the air, and the power I have often used, is the power of the small mind which must feel and see the opponent conquered and so go down. The power satisfaction of the personnel director, a sergeant, and plow driver of mules. And it is true, for often when my show was done, I would say, "That should hold them. That should keep them back." And I had said, too, before many shows, "This will teach them." And I had mused, as I have driven to the station, often, "In what fashion shall I alarm them this day?" Today I felt an excellence to my anger, for it is valid. I was responding, this day, to assassination.

I executed the swirls, the leaps and the dives of conversation, using words like flashing skate blades; it was like being in the Ice Follies. A star at last. I dashed about the edges before whipping in for the final spin, the denouement of controversy, the sudden attack: "You put down that grape. Don't you know there's a strike on!"

"It is not so much the theory of assassination," I said, "as the specific applications I object to.

"Yes, I do approve of capital punishment." (And I knew the liberals would put down their pottery and rage to the phones.)

"Yes, we must have a government of the elite. We have not educated you well enough to vote properly. 'A government of artists, intellectuals, scientists.'

". . . Send in your votes now, please, so we can confiscate them before the morning." I have Them there to terrorize.

They were my Congregation of Theys to rise and fall at my command. I could scream back with torrents of accusations. I listened other times in silence. Or barricaded myself behind facts. Facts made them melt like the Witch. They did not know what to expect.

"Timing," I had told Laurie once. "You sketch a show in your head; it gets, each one, a composition of its own. Such a lift and a swing it had today—such a ring. It was involvement."

Hands flew, chewed-at fingers punching out buttons. I drove Them. I directed Them. And I shut Them off.

And thirty seconds after I went off the air to the murderous lilt of that theme song, I was fired.

I was coming down fast now from speed, from no sleep. So my eyes filled with tears. (Jordan, who was running the show, does not cry.)

I must not cry. But the tears came flooding down.

"You're terminated," the station manager had said. I felt my fingers were being taken away, as well as the switchboard for punching up my calls.

"Listen, you're irreverent, you're funny and brilliant, but you can't play with emotions at a time like this. I warned you before."

"I wasn't being funny. I was angry."

"You can't let it show like that. You have to be angry within FCC regulations. Thirty-five minutes with no station breaks, no spots. Those incendiary monologues!"

"Thirty-five minutes? Oh, I did the weather. I always do the weather."

"Check the log yourself."

"Am I ruined in radio forever? The end of a person's career? Bright future smashed?"

He fooled with important papers and wished me luck.

"We'll have to leave town," I told Laurie. "It feels like being shot."

"Like sympathetic labor pains," Laurie said dryly except for the fresh wet drink in his hand.

"You really can't understand. Being someone doesn't matter to you. Oh, I don't mean that; I mean, being famous."

"I know, but maybe being famous only goes so far—maybe there's a point where you do protest."

"But," I screamed, "I didn't do that! I'm never really involved, remember, we said that, we agreed: we never really, really care." I thought about that for a moment. "Anyway, I'm no use off the air. Groups and organizations will start calling in five minutes and tell me not to come places—you'll see. Jesus, Laurie, you're always finding these nice subconscious reasons for all my worst things. I think it's just that I'm crazy."

"You and a certain craziness are not incompatible. But it's the guilt that makes you unhappy."

"Oh, don't be so cool and rational. You'll be sorry when we eat home alone every night and the phone never rings and I have nothing to tell you about because no one talks to me. I mean, this is dirt failure, right down there, all the whole way. You don't know about failing."

"Listen, I'll hate it because you hate it. But it's not going to happen that way. And last week you said you were a failure because you didn't have your own TV show . . . so, it's relative."

I knew he'd remember that. Which was why I had added all the material about it being a real failure this time.

I stood out on the porch, looking at the paper. "And they'll all laugh. They love it when someone fucks up—then they'll forget and it will be all over." I hurled the paper over the fence. "That's me. Yesterday's news. And now . . ."

"You'll get another, better job. I believe in you. I love you. Now, sit, rest, here's a nice Scotch. I'm getting some cigarettes at the corner. When I come back we're going to the movies and we'll make a new plan."

He licked my mouth, then held me tight and kissed me, kissed me. I cried and cried.

"Hush, now." He kissed my eyes, then put the tears back into my mouth with his tender tongue. "When I come back, I have a better idea," he whispered, husky, playful. "We'll fuck . . ."

People always think of that first when someone dies. It was a good idea, except he didn't come back.

When I called his office the next morning, on the razor edge of hysteria, the voice said, "We don't seem to have any Lawrence Robinson listed, but I'll connect you with Personnel." Click, click, click. "Is that Mr. Lawrence Robinson whom you were making the inquiry about, madam? I'm sorry, Mr. Robinson is no longer with us. I'm afraid he was suspended ten days ago."

What I was thinking about, the line I could cut out of my throat with dull shears was, "You don't know about failing." I realized what I had learned about Laurie was he knew more about failing than I would ever learn. He knew very little that wasn't somehow about failing.

I heard the footsteps soft on the driveway about five-thirty the next morning. Quickly I ran into the living room and threw myself down on the floor so he would know how I had cried myself to sleep right there on the rug.

I waited. Arms wrapped around head so he could not see by my expression that I was not asleep. Maybe he knew that I wasn't sleeping and he was waiting out there, walking around in circles, in the carport for me to come out like an adult and greet him. Maybe he felt too guilty to come in. Perhaps something had become of the car and he did not know how to tell me. He might have misplaced it. That problem was not without precedent.

I was getting angry, fingers twitching at the ultramarine woolen tufts. I imagined him out there in the thin gray dawn, just walking around, smoking, looking as though he were thinking of butterflies, flying them like kites, in and out of floating mathematical hieroglyphics and parallelograms.

I padded to the window and peered out. It was not Laurie. It was a working person in coveralls with badges and shorn hair. He was looking at a clipboard and writing things. Then he stooped, as if looking under the network of tricycles, bikes and toys in the carport. He shook his head, dazed. Continued writing.

I tore out there. Flannel nightgown in full sail, Jasper-the-Dog loping sleepily behind me, awakened finally by the slide of the glass door.

"What are you doing? Jasper, stay right here." The dog glared at the man from a safe distance, preferring always the security of bed: under, on or in.

"Are you a Mrs. Jill Robinson? Owner of a '65 Mustang, license—"

I screeched, "What have you done with him?" (Noting to Jordan, proudly, that I meant Laurie, not Mustang. A person, not even a perfect person, taking precedence over a thing.) The man side-stepped my attack neatly; lucky he hadn't married such a bitch.

"I have an order here to pick up said vehicle." He shoved the repossession notice at me and demanded that I produce said vehicle, or "The bank will be forced to take action."

"What would you call this if not action?" I said. "Sneaking up here before dawn to steal my car, trespassing, disturbing a family in the home."

Of course, it was a problem with payments.

I arched my voice, made it wear family pearls. "If there was a financial oversight, I don't understand why you people didn't call my business manager."

"Look, lady . . ." According to this "Repossess" order he had here, we had been delinquent for four months. When Laurie's old Renault had died, he'd insisted on taking over Mustang's payments. Laurie's cool astonished me: the last weekend he'd put a small deposit on a new Karmann Ghia. Why that, instead of making the payments on the car we had?

"If you don't leave, I'll call the police." There was new force in my voice from anger at Laurie. This vicious man, waking me by making his footsteps sound like Laurie's and bringing only more rotten news.

Wright was next to me now, hair on end like animal ears on alert. I put my arm around him and continued, "Listen, in two minutes I'm calling the A.C.L.U., the Peace Action Council . . ."

Emily was standing in the wings, rubbing her eyes, wanting breakfast.

"Mom," said Wright, an embarrassed grin sliding on his face.
". . . and by tomorrow morning all the activists in town will have closed their accounts and withdrawn all their money." I could imagine Laurie's reaction: smiling, he would say, "Taking everything into consideration, not an imposing threat."

The man was writing. "Ma'am, if you'll cooperate and tell me where I can locate the vehicle?"

"Probably in Central America. My husband, the archaeologist, has taken it out digging. But keep in touch!"

The children and I padded back into the house; everyone into my bed.

The cats arranged themselves on the pillows, tails and fur puffed like flounces. Jasper-the-Dog hid himself under the bed, lying on his side with his four trim, light-tan paws sticking out. He never hid very successfully. He assumed if he couldn't see us, then we couldn't see him. For some reason, Jasper was under the impression he was my dog. Possibly because we were both manic-depressives, either cutting up loudly or sulking.

Wright said, "Poor Mom." I didn't want to be "poor Mom." I wanted to be Large Capable Supportive Mom. What are these children to think of themselves, I wondered, if this, Failed Heap, is the mother?

Emily anxiously fingered the eyelet border on my flannel nightgown, finding a "place," as she had called the folds in the bindings of her security blanket where she could burrow a couple of fingers. "He'll come back this afternoon," she said. "He's just off having a wee nap."

Emily had picked up Nannie's comforting manner and some-times her dialect. I tried to remember if this was Nannie's free day. Perhaps she would be with the children after school. I needed to spend the day on job interviews.

Such fantasies I once had about a patron/husband bearing tokens—fresh violets, jewels in snap-clasped leather boxes. Alter-ego Jordan despised that fantasy. He/she believed in tough experience as the literary source.

"Research, you coward," said Jordan, glaring at the TV the

children turned on for a pre-school fix, although I reminded them that TV rots the brain. It is something like alcohol. And patron/husbands. Since I know all these things about what rots and softens the brain, why was I having this vodka and orange juice to chase the pre-breakfast speed?

Speed. Singing through me like silver wheels of a fine German bike striking through iced streets. I got on and rode it to the typewriter, where I turned out one résumé for advertising agencies, one for TV production work, and then three biographies, composed more like press releases than résumés. One for comedy, another, very sober, for straight news editing, production and commentary; and another for women's show producers, emphasizing how cheerful, sweet and helpful I can be to have around your house, on your small TV screen every morning.

Flying now, I tore through boxes of tapes and photographs from interviews, tryouts and auditions. I put each photograph with the biography it most resembled, in mood or costume, and slipped it in each immaculate manila folder, with a copy of my various concepts and outlines for television talk shows, all these ideal vehicles for me.

The biography folders I would deliver myself, which reminded me of the car situation. I took a deep breath. Friends would help. It would work out. (Catch the optimism here, watch how it goes . . .)

Fingers walked through the Yellow Pages and made a list of all the phone numbers of advertising agencies that hadn't already said: "You're too old to start as a junior copywriter. Too inexperienced to be a real copywriter. You don't have a college degree."

Made another list of public relations agencies who hadn't already turned me down because: "Considering your father's position in the community, it wouldn't look right to put you in a mediocre job. You want to be famous and would only resent our clients." Sabotage. They feared sabotage. And: "You don't have a college degree."

I did now. Have a college degree. It comes with being thirty. You automatically put a B.A. down and the name of a college large enough to have lost records. B.A., UCLA. 1958. This manic preparation seemed necessary in order to make it, but it rarely occurred to me that all this racing and dashing, and the amounts of speed required to do it, would probably have to continue when Fame arrived. Just to keep it going.

When Laurie and I were lying on the beach, close to each other, talking of words and faces and of how we felt about each other, and being so slow and easy, then it would occur to me that I might not have the metabolism for Fame.

Both, what about having both the Fame and the Happiness points, I wondered as the morning and the speed eased away; children off to school, all my folders of résumés and biographies neatly organized. I stared at the list of phone numbers. What if the TV people, the program directors, have all heard that I've been fired.

The operative concept in Hollywood is that everyone knows when you're bad, but when you're good, no one has ever even heard of you.

By midmorning I was on my third spansule, but nothing brings you so far up as the first pill of a new day.

Karen knows about tone of voice. "He didn't come home last night," she said when I called.

"Helpless," I sobbed, "I have destroyed everything again."

"I'll be right over."

She came. She looked at the manila folders. "Some helpless."

"But I can't call anyone . . . and there's no money."

"First, we go to Unemployment." She was fixing coffee.

"I'm not sure if I want to take their chairty. Fired for cause, I'm not entitled." They were patronizing me by saying it was a format change on the record. I resented it, I told Karen, because they obviously thought I couldn't get another job. "And," I added, "what if I'm seen?"

"The best people I know are in the Santa Monica Unemployment line. On Thursday morning it's so chic you have to call for a reservation. Never mind will you be seen, start thinking what you should wear. Snob! And with two kids you can't afford pride, anyway."

"Karen, I love you." I hugged her. "Oh, Karen, what does Laurie do when he needs someone? Or doesn't he?"

"He drinks. Possibly because he's afraid to admit if he needs someone she may not be there anyway. He's afraid he might be misled. But I'm just guessing. I don't really know."

I thought Karen knew. I would have to think about it more. Later. I felt a bit fragile suddenly.

"Karen, you don't think he's crashed somewhere—dead or hurt in the car over a cliff—"

"He's not. And you know that. You know he's nursing one hell of a hangover in some motel. By himself. And he feels lousy. You told me yourself . . . Now, I'm calling this old friend over at KTTV, he's the new program director, so he'll be making some changes."

Her friend, we shall call him Mel, could see me in the afternoon. After I registered for unemployment.

Karen talked to me while I pulled myself together. Mountain red wine on the rocks, and the midafternoon spansule—a kind of business expense, deductible from the addiction tax.

"What are you drinking for? You never drink." Close friends attributed most of my misbehavior to speed. They rarely noticed my drinking because I never talked about it. And it seemed that I always talked about everything that I was doing or taking.

"Nothing. I don't. It's just a little wine."

By the time Karen had driven me into Hollywood to the TV studio, the mood had lifted again and I was fantasizing about my new television show. The reviews. The picture in *Vogue*, celebrity guests.

We drove east on Sunset Boulevard past the ancient woman in the canvas shoes with the bunions cut out and the mauve tulle kerchief. Witch of Hollywood she was, forced by her low birth to sell maps to homes of the famous and never invited to their parties, so she had placed the Curse of Failure upon the Second Generation.

"Break the spell, Witch," I said to myself as we sped past where she stood on the ivy-covered hillside, "and when I'm famous and living in that Tudor *palazzo* up there, I'll invite you to all my private screenings and caviar cookouts."

"What are you doing?" Karen said.

"Nothing. I just thought this might be more together-looking." Anyone who changes clothes as much as I do learns to be good at doing it in cars. Off came the red turtleneck from under the bright-green suit. On with the silky white shirt. Chains and beads had to be realigned.

"Do I have enough on?"

We were passing through Hollywood now. I was much more conscious, it seemed, these past few months of how many bars there were. How many liquor stores. How many flashing signs —"Cocktails."

"I think, Karen, really, that Laurie may be tired of his work. When I get the TV show I think he should be on it. With his wit and looks, we'd be divine. I'll suggest that to this Mel right away."

"Just do your interview, Jill," Karen said as she parked the car in the studio lot, "and relax about Larry. Let's at least pull him together before he becomes a star. Fame is tough enough for the very sane."

I handed the program director my manila folders and went into my best routines, adding shape to my punch lines and credits with swooping gestures of the terrible hands.

"And," I said, "instead of the static kind of staging there is on most talk shows, I'd want more action. There's that whole video part of the medium. The moderator should move around."

I considered getting up, to show him what I meant.

"Interesting," he said, punching a buzzer, moving papers.

"I met Karen a few years ago. You know, isn't that awful, I can't remember her husband's name."

"Mike," I said. Briskly: "And now for my next idea, even more controversial. You have, say—"

"Goddamn, excuse me." He was pushing buttons furiously on an intercom. "My girl must have fallen in, I asked her to bring my coffee on her way back. Jesus—now, where were we?"

"Nowhere." I laughed quickly. And went on talking fast. "You see. I also feel strongly that—"

"I have a question," he said (my bangs fairly straightened with delight at his sudden enthusiasm). "What's your Old Man up to these days?"

"Oh, well, he's just terrific, which brings up my other fantastic idea: 'Second Generation,' famous people and their kids. I mean, everyone wants to be successful, but is it such a good thing in a parent? Success—"

"See," I said, running down fast now, "I would love TV to get into problem solving, in relationships—more. And to block commercials so you can talk."

He put down his pipe. "Listen, we're wasting each others' time. We're looking for a bubble-headed, bubble-ass button-nose blonde who will do exactly what we tell her. I could make you feel good, have you come back a few times, but, baby, they'll take one look at that profile of yours and it's Goodbye-Charlie."

"Or Goodbye-Jill, so to speak. Well, I get the message."

My nose. I'd forgotten almost.

This was hardly a new experience. Usually they said I was too distinguished.

"You're too smart for me to hand you any bullshit," he said.

But it would have made it easier, at least a little hope— until Laurie came back.

"Perhaps if something, a job, in production comes up . . . I've had some experience in that, too."

"Yes. Well. Production crews—that's out of my ball park."

As I had started edging toward the door just to show how

marvelously I move and everything, I tripped; my purse flew open, scattering jewelry and gum wrappers and broken cigarettes, bottles of pills and unopened bills all over the office.

"I can see," he said, "how well you move."

Distraction is required: I will have my nose done. The excuse is that it will make it easier to get TV jobs. The second night after Laurie had not returned I made a list of his possible reactions:

1. He will be happier when he looks at me.
2. If I am prettier, will he worry more that if he does run away, another man might come along more readily, so he'd better cool it?
3. Jealousy is not his style. I do not think.
4. And insecurity would hardly keep him from running away.
5. If I feel more confident about myself, he won't feel so pressured to reassure me all the time.
6. And he won't have to escape for "breathers."
7. Will he think it's a pretty shallow reaction? Nadia would not have done something so banal. She would have had her legs amputated, perhaps, to show her pique.

No. Nadia would not have gotten her head trapped like this.

Love is not a head trip, I thought, it's a trap. And in either case, if this is how it seems to always be, it is a fixation, a hangup. And I have enough hooks in me already. I hate it!

. . .

I put the pillows in a row so that they formed more the shape of a tall person, and I sniffed hard to catch traces of the fragrance of Laurie's hair and body left on the sheets. Even when he was dead drunk, he was clean. There was very little to smell except a cologne-like trace that represented what he drank. Not what he was.

Jasper-the-Dog walked by the bed, I could see his tail waving in the dark and hear his licentious breathing. He looked over the bed at me wondering if I was ready yet to give up on Laurie and settle down with someone who was truly devoted. I patted him and asked him if he would lie down in his customary place under the bed, which he did. With heartbreaking sighs. I was going to tell him self-pity is not attractive. But if I talked to him, he would jump up beside me, pretending he had misunderstood.

I must have fallen asleep.

"Jill!"

I heard Laurie call me. Instantly I was wide awake. I looked at the clock: 4:30. But I didn't see him. I went for the light and an instant later the phone rang. I grabbed the receiver. "Darling"—his voice over the phone.

"But I just heard you call me. Your voice woke me up before the phone. It does work . . . with us. ESP. What am I talking about! Where the hell are you? I want you . . ."

Be careful. Don't frighten him away. He sounds fuzzy. Yes, he sounds like people do when they are drunk.

"Laurie, I love you." I spoke very slowly, in my gentlest voice. "Laurie, everything is really great. Please forgive me for carrying on. I've got some fantastic leads for new jobs. And a wonderful surprise to tell you about—I mean, everything is going to be so much better. So come home so I can kiss you."

"Well, I am. I am. I was just calling to say I'll be right home and to tell you that so you could get yourself ready and we can go to the movies, although it's a little late. But maybe you'd like a nice steak; we can drive into town, to Kelly's."

It doesn't seem wise to tell him it is four in the morning, or to do or say anything contradictory. I feel as though I must pull him along home, like pulling a ship through the Panama Canal by a piece of thread I've got tied around my teeth.

"Laurie, can I come and meet you. I'll call a cab. We all miss you. Would you feel more comfortable if I just come where you are, to just hold you?"

I don't want, God, for him to think I'm prying. I don't want him to think he has to hide next time somewhere different or worse. At least he is safe, I assume, where he is.

"No. No. I'm on my way," he said. "You get ready now . . . I love you, darling. I'll see you in just a few minutes." He was also trying to convince himself that he was on his way. I knew he wanted to come home.

But the phone clicked off. And although I did get up and dress, very slowly, I knew he was not coming. Not tonight.

The children were silent the next morning. They knew I was compensating—that is why I was up before they were, making rafts of bacon, their favorite soft-boiled eggs—peeled—and chopped with too much butter. None of us talked during breakfast. Not one word—hush—in case it should mask the tinny gasp of the Mustang beginning the ascent up the driveway into the compound.

No. He is not coming today either.

I will call Nannie to find out when she can stay with the kids.

Then I will call *Cosmo* to see if Helen can use an article about a girl who cuts off her nose to spite . . .

To spite nothing—only because it's probably less destructive than cutting off her hands and surely just as distracting.

Children and magazine assignments accounted for, a couple of days later I checked in at the hospital. After the first day, which was a misery that, if revealed, would cause me to be run over by plastic surgeons, Brooke picked me up and drove me to her house, where I collapsed onto her elegant bed. The children, she reported, were well and quite relieved that they would not have to see me in what they were smart enough to know must be very lousy shape. I did not ask about Laurie. I did not think he had come back. Or called. I was trusting the ESP now. Hearing his voice that other night, before the phone rang, had been the proof.

So had knowing he wasn't coming back yet when he did call. But that wasn't just ESP. I had also heard the uncertainty in his voice.

Brooke insisted I sleep in her room, newly done after Dennis' departure, and she would sleep in the guest room. I couldn't breathe or see; I was coming down, under all these downers, from months of speed, and was forbidden to talk for a week. God must be a woman; only a woman could hate herself so as to have created me in her image.

I had no idea of the time or of how much time had passed when I heard the Mustang coming up Brooke's driveway.

"Laurie," I tried to shriek, realizing I might be undoing my face. It was Laurie; I staggered to the window and saw the moonlight gleaming on our beautiful navy-blue Mustang. Tears were coming down, melting bandages, melting plastic. I didn't care. I ran down the stairs.

Brooke was at the door. Locking it. Standing in front of it, I was trapped again in a Hollywood house. I could not get to what I wanted. Everything I loved was outside of here.

"No, no . . ." Screams seemed muffled in my head. I pulled at Brooke, clinging to her nightgown, pointing frantically at the door. She gestured back at me; then furiously remembered it was only I who could not talk.

"Now, just stop getting hysterical," she said. "He can't just come here in the middle of the night. You've had a serious operation . . ."

Laurie was now banging on the door from the other side. Brooke shouted through the door, "Jill is forbidden to talk. And

I am far too furious at what you've done to her to speak to you tonight. You simply must go away and give her a chance to recover!"

More pounding. His voice, "Darling, I love you."

Brooke said to me, "He's drunk." Then, through the door, "Look. You've taken her car, left her without money, practically gotten her evicted. Now go."

I would not have spoken to Jasper-the-Dog in such a way. I stared at her with what would have been total disbelief if it was not for the fact that my eyes were swollen almost shut— God, I'd forgotten!

He must not see me this way!

Vanity the motive, I called, weakly, "Laurie, darling. I'm fine. Just go back to the kids . . . they need to see you. And come get me tomorrow, really. Please . . "

I wanted to touch him. There was silence on the other side of the door. I wasn't strong enough to argue or think or even to stand up. I slumped all the way down, and with great difficulty, Brooke helped me back upstairs. I remembered at some point hearing the car start and then leave, and feeling I was never going to see him again.

The stupid vanity.

Brooke tried to explain that everything was all for my own good. I tried to say that was what everyone says when they want you to do something you hate, but my mouth was swollen shut now. I could not think too clearly. I might be a failure. And Laurie, too. But that didn't mean it was a further sign of failure that we wanted each other. It could be, I thought, the first positive sign of a climbing back. In mental hospitals they watch to see when patients begin to notice and care for the others . . . it is considered a sign of progress.

Unless he had just run away again. Tears ran down around the bandages. Then I just kind of fell out of awareness.

Sounds came through . . .

The early-morning birds.

No.

I heard the tapping now at my window.

I saw Laurie clinging to the heavy wisteria vines leading up to the second story and I ran to the French windows, threw them open and let him in. He was shaved and clean, except for leaves and lavender blossoms from the vines. But I thought, sadly, his expression seemed slightly askew. I tried to see if he looked more traditionally drunk. He had some very battered roses stuffed in his pocket. He took them out and handed them to me with a card. "*A nose is a rose is a nose. Love, Laurie.*"

I must not cry any more. Or even talk. He knew about that. He said, "Don't talk . . ." He told me he had been home much earlier and the children had told him everything. Emily, he said, had explained all the rules. He also said softly and very evenly that he had given Nannie some money. And that he wanted me to make a list of what we owed. I did not ask where the money came from. Gardena, I assumed.

He lay down beside me on the bed, dipping his fingers into the bowl of ice that Brooke had left there before, and slipping bits of ice into my mouth.

He had left the car up the street, he said, and walked back through the garden. He wasn't even mad at Brooke. "After all," he said, "it's not easy to understand how I am. But I do love you. I have missed you, and"—he kissed the top of my matted head—"I'm glad you finally did this. It seemed such an obvious thing for you to want to do for yourself." He shook his head in his perplexed fashion. His expression was a little less askew; maybe it had been my vision that was askew.

"But I thought you loved me for me?"

"I do, but loving you is seeing who you want to be, too—and wanting to help you be that."

Who, I wondered, does he want to be?

He did have the one possible reaction to the nose thing I hadn't even considered.

I wrote now on the pad Brooke had left for me near the

bed: *"Do you think I don't understand you? I think sometimes I don't. Is that why you go away?"*

"No, I think you do," he said, smiling. How good his hands felt on me. "Even when you don't follow through on what you understand, I know you do, anyway, if that's clear. I think we understand each other very well. It's our own selves sometimes we get confused about . . ."

"Laurie," I wrote, wondering if the timing was very good, but realizing there would be no good timing for this suggestion, *"would it help for you to go to an analyst, perhaps? Do you hate that idea?"*

"That's fair," he said. "I'll talk to Mike and Karen; they'll know someone reasonable. I guess it's time."

I just held his hand tight.

Things, I thought, for someone feeling swollen and bashed in, someone broke and unemployed, in love with a trespassing, unemployed, drunk person, were looking up. It seemed, then, however, that there could be no other possible direction.

November days can be the most beautiful in Southern California; there is a subtlety to our seasons, and the winters are deeply cool and sunny with that sweep of sky and space that makes you always want to return.

It was the afternoon of Laurie's weekly visit to the analyst. I had dropped him off—by agreement, Laurie didn't get to take the car anywhere. Mike was afraid he felt trapped, but Laurie said he didn't mind; he never liked to drive, and it's an interesting challenge to try to get around on buses in L.A.

The phone rang when I was about to leave the house to do an underground FM radio show I was moderating every day. I had total editorial freedom. Everything was free. Including me. But the station was listener-subscribed, and being me, I would pay to go on the radio if they had to transmit through my bones —just to be on.

Now I said snappily "Yes?" into the phone.

"Is Mr. Robinson in?" An unfamiliar male voice: a creditor. An employer Laurie was doing—or not—free-lance work for. A principal from one of the adult-education math courses he taught when he showed up. An acquaintance perhaps from the casinos of lovely Gardena.

"No, Mr. Robinson is out of the country on a business venture. May I help you? This is Mr. Robinson's administrative assistant speaking."

"Oh, I was under the impression this was his residential number."

"No." I put a little huff, a little snap into my voice now. "Please, could you state your business? There are other calls coming in."

"Well, yes . . . just tell Mr. Robinson to please call Dr. Bromberg when he returns."

"Dr. Bromberg! But he's with you now!" Of course. Simply because I always dropped Laurie off at the doctor's building did not mean (even if I did see him go inside) that he actually was seeing the doctor. He could so calmly stroll out another door and just slip into a nearby bar to have a quick drink.

"No, Mr. Robinson is not here now. Is this Mrs. Robinson?"

"Yes!" The cool gave way. "He never does come, does he? Oh, I'm sorry about that other thing—creditors, you know . . ."

Yes. Dr. Bromberg would know. I did not want to ask if Laurie had actually paid him. Laurie had assured me he had.

"How much does he owe you—never mind. Look, when was

the last time he came?" I could tell by the tone of the doctor's listening that he was one of the analysts who has no patience for crazy people.

"Dr. Bromberg, is he a serious alcoholic—or is it just a drinking problem? Or none of the above?" I was running on.

"My dear woman, I only saw your husband three times, one of which he was forty minutes late. One, twenty. The third time he was—well, let's say he was never less than twenty minutes late." Dr. Bromberg sounded like a personnel adviser: "His sense of responsibility in regard . . . to the matter of my fee . . . indicates . . ."

I could not listen. I felt a personal embarrassment, as though I had not paid the doctor—as though I had been late. The doctor was speaking . . .

". . . as to your husband's condition, I'm afraid we were unable to establish any lines of communication."

"He didn't say why he was there?"

"Perhaps, Mrs. Robinson I should point out that in most instances, unless there is strong motivation on the patient's own part, there will be a severe resistance to therapy."

He thought I was forcing Laurie into something.
Which I was.

"Laurie did you feel forced to go into therapy?" I asked him when he met me at the radio station only two hours after I'd gone off the air, two hours after he said he would be there. "Is that why you haven't been going?"

I was trying to appear very calm, very cool, as I packed up the daily collection of pamphlets left in my mailbox at the station; the requests for replays of certain interviews; the articulate fan letters . . . such an ideal job if it only paid.

Laurie looked quite puzzled. I thought he was puzzled mainly because I was not hysterical.

"Well," he said, "I'm sorry, darling. Dr. Bromberg and I had nothing to say to each other."

I looked at him. I couldn't stand having to be in control all the time. I couldn't stand the position he was in. How docile he was, moving through our lives like a beautiful sleepwalker.

Of course he suggested, "Let's go have a couple of drinks somewhere quiet to talk about it." I was trying not to drink all day because I had a column, a book review and a small article to write that night, which was not an impossible problem if I started before midnight. Just one, though, would help me unwind.

"Do you have bread?" I asked him. "I only have enough to pick up some stuff at the market before the kids come home from school."

"Sure, I've got some getting-around bread."

And from where he was getting it I didn't know. He always had just enough to—exactly—get around. We'd both have been doing OK if we actually did the work we had been assigned to do. I kept not writing the articles because I felt I should have been working on the book, and not working on the book because of guilt about the articles. I felt it was pretty much the same with his free-lance electronics work. No matter what the specific work is, I suspect the production hangups are similar.

Look how we match, so neatly lined up at the bar.

"Oh, Laurie." I popped the pre-dinner cocktail spansule, moving right into the big-league milligrams again. The occasional articles I saw in the paper about amphetamine dangers, the possibility of more stringent controls, sent me into rages. And terror. Why didn't they crack down on rapists. War. If they spent all that energy on cancer, they could cure it. What I do to my body is my business. I am not a child.

Yes. People mess with children's bodies too much, too. How free I'd be if they'd left me alone when I was small. Doctors pay up: write me my prescriptions. To be taken as needed.

Laurie had been telling me now, in six various ways, how open he was. "Haven't you noticed I'm revealing myself more? I do talk when I feel comfortable with someone."

"Laurie, if you've haven't been going to this shrink and you didn't even tell me—that is not exactly open. You're too brilliant and you matter too much. It makes a difference if you're well. I'm the same if I am or if I'm not."

"I don't think that's true. No . . ." He knew, of course, that if he started talking to me about myself, most of the time I wouldn't turn the subject back to him. Lately I couldn't get him to talk about himself, and when he did he'd do this repetitious number. It was as though when he looked at himself he felt dizzy.

"Listen, Laurie. Maybe there's some other doctor you'd like better." Mike had felt the real problem would be to find a doctor Laurie would not be able to outsmart. Laurie looked into his pockets for his lighter. Gone. I got matches from the bar.

"I went to a psychotherapist before," he said, "in New York. I'm not that crazy that I don't know I'm a prime candidate." Seventh variation: "When I discovered I wouldn't say to him anything I wouldn't say to anyone else, I stopped."

He smiled and kissed me. While I was busy liking the kiss I was not to notice he had flicked his index finger deftly to order another drink.

"Possibly . . ." he continued, sipping his drink, and becoming more animated and slightly less listless as usual, at this stage of the late afternoon. Later in the evening the listlessness would return. I ran the same schedule on speed. Substitute tearfulness, edginess for the listlessness. We had to mesh our doses to get anywhere . . . "Possibly," he repeated now, "the only thing I got out of this experience, these experiences, with all these shrinks, was realizing that."

He nodded. His way. The firm period at the end of what he felt was an important statement of his position.

"I'm lost," I said.

"Well," he said (eighth variation), "I believe I should tell everybody everything that I am aware of, but because some of the world cannot handle that candor, I have to pull a little of it back from everyone."

"The misunderstood silver genius— Jesus, Laurie, that's the

kind of thing I say. Not you. It's you who can't handle that candor! You haven't said a candorous thing to yourself in months —and don't just dare tell me that's not a word. I know it. I'm angry. I guess, at you. And I don't like that happening, either."

"That's interesting." Only he said it "Inneresting."

"Stop it!" I thought I was going to cry. "I hate it when you slur. And it's not interesting. Laurie. We're fucking up." What started out so good was slipping by. Lovers leap hand in hand.

"Another Scotch and soda . . ." We'd take the kids down to Ted's for cheeseburgers later.

Christmas Eve: Berenger and wife, Pat, were having a party. The children were to be there, to spend the holiday. Laurie and I took them over.

Emily whirled joyously in the lovely pink satin-and-lace gown they had bought for her. We watched and had a Christmas-eve cocktail with them. They brought Wright into the garden to show him their new pure-bred shepherd dogs. Dogs of a size and ferocity that would have turned Jasper's hair white. Wright said "Wow!" Laurie drank slowly there. I watched every sip. Easy because I sat almost on him. My ankles crossed like irons around his legs to keep myself from rushing Pat and tearing out her throat. Who can compete with such stability? So endearing to children.

We had to run because Laurie had picked up a little Christmas-eve job at the gay bar down our street. You didn't have to be in the union there to bartend, mainly because you couldn't get into the union if you were gay.

I dropped Laurie off at the bar and said I'd feed Jasper-the-Dog and his cats, and be right back with a sandwich or something for him to eat.

"No . . ." he said. Something else was happening.

"You are not being open again," I reminded him as I promised to whenever he thought he was explaining something.

"I think it's going to be pretty busy, you know. Why don't you snuggle by the fire, all cozy in your nice flannel . . ."

"Laurie, I can't handle it if you take one of your vacations over Christmas. If you don't really have the job—just tell me."

I was terrified that he would go away again.

"No, it's not what you think. The manager just said they don't like chicks in there."

"Oh. Okay. No problem." I smiled and kissed him, extravagantly relieved that there was a real reason. And there was something sensible I could do about it. Trusting as I am, I went home and put on my drag: shoved my hair into the old tweed cap. Pulled on a pair of George's old jeans. The Beatles sweat shirt. Large hiking boots. And the old knit muffler, wrapping it around the chin after some jaw shadowing with a little dark powder. Large black sunglasses—passable.

The handsome bartender down at the bar said his name was Larry when I asked.

I said, "You look more like Laurie to me."

"I have a friend I live with who calls me that . . ."

He handed me a drink, then whipped some whiskey sours down the bar to a couple of people. I muttered into my beer. "So how was your year?"

"Year of the sloth," he said. Grinning. Spearing onions. "Not a great year for bread, but I've been happy."

"Well—who, I ask you, can live on bread alone?"

"True. True . . ." He swizzled up a couple of rum and Cokes. "It's a good idea to leave some things incomplete—easier than starting the New Year with nothing in mind."

I agreed, "Oh,—yes, like looking at a blank piece of paper. I'm a writer, so I understand—and a famous radio personality in case you haven't recognized my beautiful voice."

"I was sure I'd heard it somewhere," he said.

Near the holidays there's a tendency to sum up all the recent failures. You call it a list of resolutions, a reminder not to fuck up the same things next year.

"How would you like to write an encyclopedia of under-achievement with me?"

"We could call it 'Failing up,' " he said, slicing limes.

I said, "And we could show how well we know the subject by not writing it."

I was, by now, so far behind on the book, on magazine articles, that I was not able to walk near my typewriter without a guilt so heavy that I had to run away. It was like a force field. So strong. It was easier to spend all day at the radio station "working out ideas."

Laurie sloshed some glasses swiftly in and out of water, setting them on a folded cloth to dry. He must feel the guilt, but he never talked about it. He'd been given writing assignments by an editor on the L.A. *Times*—pieces to try to work into a possible column on new technology in business.

"Listen," Laurie said, and he looked serious, "about writing . . . you've got a perfectly good father to compete with."

"I know. But you are good. That's all . . ."

"I'm not sure. I've been thinking that it might be California. Somehow work always seems more serious in New York. I always felt that way, even before I had lived there."

"We could move there, I suppose." Although I hadn't the vaguest idea how.

"It was just something I thought about." I wondered if that had to do with Nadia. If her success sort of got him going. No. Clearly—or he wouldn't have come out here—maybe he was really a writer. It would explain some of the craziness.

He was turning out lights now. I took off my cap and shook

out my hair. "Laurie, I wonder which kind of failure we have: are we afraid of success, or are we not successful because we are so frightened that if we really try, we might fail, and it's easier to fail without trying? If you know what I mean."

"It sounds," he said, "like something I once talked to this friend I live with about. The Chrysanthemum Problem, see . . ."

He lifted his hands to describe it, grinning.

"Oh, yes," I said, "I know something about that."

"Christmas present," he said, handing me a bronze plastic candleholder, one of the ones scattered about the bar for decoration. It held a red candle and had a sprig of plastic holly attached.

When we got home and when Jasper-the-Dog had been settled with his Christmas bone and the cats were stoned enough on their catnip grass, we lit the candle and made love by its light. I felt as if we were brothers. There was a lot of clasping of hands, and my thighs felt like a match for his in strength. Our arms grasped each other. It was a match. A pairing.

As people, we shared the same kind of problems, and even if the problem was failure, it made us more to each other than lovers.

I have such a nightmare—I dream he has gone.

It is too dangerous to sleep. I stay up and make a list of projects and how long it would take me to finish them if I started tomorrow.

Except tomorrow is Christmas and who works on Christmas? Day after tomorrow.

The book is not on the list.

When Laurie was not occupied teaching, bartending or getting money in Gardena, he would drop by and be a guest on my *Free Lunch* radio show. This wasn't very often. But he had a nice, relaxed style, a good easygoing voice, and so when a Monday-night spot became available, the program director offered Laurie his own radio show.

With his customary cool, Laurie said, "Fine, fine. A reasonable idea, I guess." And he put together his own format. Generally not arranging for guests until about five o'clock on Monday afternoon.

Worst come to worst, he could always go the rounds of the Montecito Hotel, Chateau Marmont, the Raincheck, Jay's or Barney's Beanery, and come up with a night person who wanted to talk on the radio.

From the opening of his theme song, "My Time of Day," the phones would start ringing (when the call-in system was working) and his show was extremely popular. The listeners seemed to appreciate the fact that he often was late: an authentic night person. They were also enchanted to discover a call-in talk show hosted by someone who permitted the callers to do just about all of the talking.

Karen listened one night and said he was the only silent radio moderator she'd ever heard. Or not heard.

He called his show *Watchman*—the title came from "Watchman, What of the Night," a chapter from the novel *Nightwood*.

Laurie had recorded parts of the book, on a tape to be played on the "highly unlikely" chance he might not show up. "For emergencies," he said. And he would be sure to let them know. When it was just a problem of lateness, the engineer played records—music about the night.

We were through the cool, foggy spring, and May moved on to June. Laurie had not missed a show yet.

I had paid off Mustang. A feeling of accomplishment in no way compromised by the other debts.

Only by the dead weight of the still-unfinished novel.

Many years before, my father had helped to organize a summer camp. I called and asked him if Emily and Wright could go there this summer; he made the arrangements and paid what fees were involved.

So summer lay ahead free and empty. We would lie together every night like animals. And during the day I could finish the book. I divided days into pages, pages into days. There would be time. My radio show would be a lunch break.

But I was crying as we drove the children to camp. Sniffling as we helped them get settled. "Don't pay any attention," I said. "This is called guilt mongering. You're not to notice."

One thing to let them know at least I'm aware of what I am doing. Better thing just not to do it.

I think I was really crying because now there was no excuse for not finishing the book.

I should have known I could always count on Laurie.

We walked back to the car after leaving the children. It was a long dusty road. The pepper trees hung low in the dry hot air. I grabbed his arms so hard and said slowly and firmly, "Now. If you go away while they are gone, if you leave me all alone, that will be the end and this is something I really mean."

I stared at him so hard. I wanted him to feel this need I had for him to stay. To feel it like a kiss of silver burned into his head. Had Sybil given him such a kiss before she died? So he would remember what she meant. It had not worked.

"You can run away in the fall if you have to do it, just to remember how energetic I am when I am completely hysterical. But not now."

Most inappropriate suspicions. Paranoia, clearly.

"Listen, how much speed have you had today?" he asked. Innocence accused. Virtue attacked.

"Oh, I guess too much. I mean, more than the usual too much. You're right. I'm reacting as usual to the wrong things. Over-reacting to leaving the kids. Misplacing the feelings." I covered him with kisses and laughs to apologize.

We drove back along the Coast Highway and had dinner at the Boathouse on the Santa Monica pier. After his third stinger, which was to be thought of, Laurie always said to me reassuringly, as the day person's third cup of coffee (I sometimes think the distinction night person/day person is a cover story for drinker/nondrinker), he dropped me at home while he went off to do his show.

I put the radio near the typewriter and started typing a few things the way a musician tunes up. There never had been a bill for this new typewriter Laurie had rented for me when mine broke down. Could he have given the rental people the wrong address? Surely . . .

One cat lay next to the typewriter and batted at the carriage as it came toward her. The other cat, J.C. (Jasper's Cat), was stretched out on Jasper's back. He slept across my feet so I couldn't get away without him.

I thought Jasper-the-Dog and I had this similar problem. He also hated being left alone. I couldn't tell him he didn't quite make it for me as total companionship. I felt loneliness come over me like a cramp. There was no breathing in the house. I had nothing to type. Hands crunched together, buried in the pit of my lap. The speed was racing too fast for me to write about the fear, and the feeling, in case a character should need to borrow it for a scene. I was shivering so that Jasper opened his eyes and sighed at what he realized was his inadequacy. I got as many of the animals as would let me into my arms and I buried myself in them, crying.

I put on the radio. There was dead air. Perhaps the transmitter was broken again. No. Came on now canned Mahler. Then the theme. Then dead air again. He could be bringing in his beer and coffee.

It was now five minutes past his air time and when I heard the voice I knew it was not a live Laurie but the tape that was on—his voice, reading from *Nightwood*:

". . . for in the girl it is the prince, and in the boy it is the girl that makes a prince a prince—and not a man . . ."

"Go Down, Matthew"—was the chapter. I went to the phone. Dialed the station.

The tape went on. *"They are our answer to what our grandmothers were told love was and what it never came to be . . ."*

"Where is he?" I screamed to the night engineer.

"Oh, yeah, Jill, hi—he said he couldn't make it. Something came up."

". . . When a long lie comes up, sometimes it is a beauty; when it drops into dissolution, in drugs and drink, into disease and death, it has at once a singular and terrible attraction."

I threw the radio on the floor. It kept on. Stupidly I had to bend to turn it off.

Go down, Jill.

He couldn't stand it, of course. The pressure of my needs.

He was gone. And, of course, with the car. I should never have let him drive it again. I knew he'd do this. He can't do it. And I can't live with this.

I thought for a moment that he had plotted it all. That he had planned to play *Nightwood*. It's also a story about someone who can't stay—leaves people longing, leaves a son, too. He is a male Robin Vote. This prince seems to be such a prince precisely because he is a prince—and not the ordinary man, I thought. That was his own message. He made such a cool goodbye. And he didn't have to face the children.

Oh, I will love no more of these princes.

Of course, the princes in *Nightwood* were girls: "The girl lost, what is she but the prince found."

I am going to find me a lost girl for my lover. A grief of a different color. Perhaps I will visit Nadia. She had written once, to Laurie. Such a direct letter. She was subletting a friend's loft in New York. Another photographer. She will teach me how to be independent.

No. I will not find Nadia, because she will think I am an idiot. Lawrence has said that California, like TV, rots the brain.

I was up all night planning and thinking, and the busyness made it possible to spend less of that time listening and hoping and wishing for him to come home and crying because I knew with all the feelings I had that he was not.

He had not taken his pictures, his packets of childhood letters. I would take them. Then he would have to find me. That was not true. He had a box of things he had left with Nadia. That was why she had written. And he had not answered her letter. Perhaps that would give me a reason to call her.

No. If he is to find me at all, it must not be because he has to. Are there many other women each holding bits of his past? Like archaelogical ages we are. With fossils from him.

So I took his pictures and packed them in a canvas bag with jeans, a smock, my favorite hate mail from listeners, and the notes, the timelines, the incomplete manuscript of the novel. I packed up the typewriter in its case.

I would buy a ticket by bouncing a check.

I called the good friends who had been so patient with so many scenes. Psychodramas. Adventures. Rapes and escapes. This time I seemed to sound rational or together. No one tried, for one thing, to talk me out of leaving. And it's very convincing when you call at three in the morning without apologizing. Who is awake enough to give you an argument? No one. Except Laurie. And I thought I was doing what he wanted me to. Leaving him. Which was why I was so angry. My friends felt, I thought, that I would not come back. I didn't think so, either.

Berenger and Pat said they would send the children, when camp was over. They did not ask any questions. There was not even an "I told you so," possibly because they were half asleep. And I spoke to my lawyer, who said she would see that there would be no problems. They could come right to where I would be living in New York. I called Nannie, who was accustomed to being awakened by children in the night. She said this was the best thing for the children. "Leaving him" is what she meant. She wanted to believe my parents would help, would straighten me out.

By five o'clock. I had arranged for the neighbors in the compound to care for Jasper-the-Dog and the cats until I could send for them. I had put everything I wanted in piles which my friends would help me pack in boxes later in the morning. These they would arrange to have put in storage. Someone else would see that the furniture I didn't want to store was sold or sent to the Salvation Army.

It was so definitive that I was not feeling sad. I had taken so much speed that I couldn't tell.

Before I went to the airport, Karen drove me to the AFTRA credit union and I borrowed money on Mustang, giving them the pink slip. I gave her money for the initial storage payment. She gave it back to me. "We owe you a wedding present," she says. "Now don't cry. That was my very dry wit."

"They'll find the car," I said. "He'll come back sometime. I hope someone else is living there by then. I hope he feels how I would feel to see that: someone strange living in my house and everything of mine gone.

"He'll probably feel relieved," Karen said, "that you have made a decision. For both of you. Something he can't do. We'll keep his things for him and when we see him, which we probably will, we'll try to get him into Synanon. He needs something like that . . . It wouldn't have hurt either of you," she said, looking at me. Appraising. "You're back on the junk really good now. I can't even see the pupils of your eyes today. And you've been losing ten pounds a week, it looks like."

"Hipbones," I said. Pleased. "Tell me I look gaunt and haggard."

"You do. It's not attractive, either. You should stay here, on second thought, and go into Synanon. You wouldn't be a square either, if that middle-class concept offends you. To look at you, you could go right in as a dope fiend."

"Karen, stop with Synanon! You know we've talked about that."

Laurie and I (I would have to stop that! Funny—I'd never had that kind of rapport. To stop taking for granted with anyone before) had felt that most of the Synanon games for squares, which was what you went to when you lived out, were designed for people having trouble as couples. I think we said, "In that way we are enormously sane."

Oh, of course.

What we did not say, and what I'm not really certain we even felt, was the fear that perhaps if one got well, or was able to really "see" the other, that well person would say, "What do I need this for? This maniac is mugging my life."

We couldn't think of anyone who had changed much, or gone into therapy (mutually exclusive activities, it also seemed), who had remained with the same partner. What we may have feared, I used to think, was that neither of us was strong enough to run away as long as we were both on our junk, our booze.

Laurie had once said, acknowledging, even obliquely, that he might have a problem, "People never get themselves together at the same time, and few people are patient enough to stay around waiting for the other one to shape up.

"That," he went on, "isn't even a good idea if they do; it's easy to turn it into the alcoholic-nurse syndrome."

'A frightening thought," I said, ordering another drink myself. "Perish that thought!"

We were having this discussion—like most—at a bar, of course. Is leaving each other, I wondered, considered the well-person thing to do?

If so, I thought now, being driven to the airport to leave Laurie, I am well. Well. I said to myself, gulping down a little half-meth before Karen looked back at me.

"You know he'll ask me where you are," Karen said.

"Say you don't now. I can't handle finding him, or him finding me, because it won't change. I mean it." She would probably tell him, I thought. But this way I am not asking her to, so it is really running away.

And I didn't want him to find me. That's why I didn't even leave a note.

Or much of a note.

On the glass door. In case he returned, by some chance, before I had really left, which would technically have been his game.

I would have stayed if he had come, say, while I was out collecting boxes for the china and stuff. The note just said: *"Goodbye, Laurie. I love you too much to love you, which is known as the Lawrence-Jill Problem. Something like the Chrysanthemum Problem . . ."*

Jordan got on the plane, fingers snapping, speed gum cracking, eyes covered with the black shades against the prism flashes that went through like painful shards now and then. Sunlight too bright was Jordan's rationale. Jill knew it was too much speed. But Jill could not get on that plane. Jill knew she might die. No. Correct that: would die.

And she did not want to go, after all.

That's why Jordan handled it for her. Strapping on the seat belt. Clenching and unclenching hands around the amulets, rubbing the picture of this lovely woman in the thirties dress with the small blond baby in her arms. Putting the picture of the woman back into her bag with the other papers. Giving a kick to the stolen typewriter under the seat. To be sure it was there.

A little something, Jordan thought, opening the spansule, to be sure we get off. Pouring the beads straight down her throat. Shifting about like a zoot-suit hipster in her seat. The jets roared. We were all taking off, and before the ground was gone, Jordan was lifting. "Hah!" she snickered. "Premature elevation . . ." She roared with laughter.

Once the plane settled back, Jill leaned against the seat and looked down as the plane crossed back from the takeoff that went out over the pale Pacific and crossed over L.A. before heading east. Floating over the beaches, the highways, the house with the window like a ship's prow, she was weeping. "Goodbye, sweet prince."

And she thought: Not much of a decision when it wasn't really me who did the leaving. She got out her papers and her brightly colored pens and started the letter she would write straight across the country:

"Darling Laurie . . .

"Jesus, I don't even know where to mail this . . ."

PART TWO

New York

Flying away from him was enough for one day, so instead of doing anything else brave, I tramped right off the plane and ran—ran to the nearest phone booth and called my parents collect in their Connecticut summer house.

My father suggested I spend the night in his city apartment and come to the country the next day. He arranged for me to rent a car. The closer I came to his territory, the more helpful he would become. And the guiltier I would feel about being alive. How much more successful and lovable I would seem if I died.

On the way to pick up my suitcase and typewriter, I saw another phone booth. It glistened at me.

I remembered the name of Nadia's friend—the one with the loft—and I looked up the phone number in the book knowing/hoping it would not be there. It was. I would not have a dime. I did. She would not be in. She was—but the phone, thank God, was busy. I walked away to get my suitcase. The phone, perhaps, would be out of order when I came back.

Picked up the suitcase. The typewriter (portable guilt). The phone rang. Once, twice. I swallowed. I could not breathe. What would I say? I hung up quickly as I heard the phone being picked up and I ran to get my suitcase, knowing she was laughing, knowing she had figured it could only in the entire world have been "that woman, what-was-her-name, who Larry picked up." Or better/worse, she knew nothing of me and would have coldly said, "Yes . . . what is it you want?" Famous people don't care for people just calling up. The fact that I like it when people just call up always reminds me that I'm not famous, on the off-chance I have forgotten.

I could not say just anything to Nadia.

Perhaps, tonight in my father's library, there would be a book that has some good quote in it—something I could refer to so she could, at first, think I was smart.

When I walked into my parent's apartment again, the sense of their neatness and propriety overwhelmed me. I wanted to be four or five with hair like spun gold. I wanted to walk through the wisteria arbor of our old house; to see my father tan and laughing, wearing frontier outfits made by the studio to look like Howard Keel's. And to see my mother in her slim-waisted mechanic's overalls painting pictures of movie stars in costumes. I remembered two childhoods: the one in the sunny photographs I looked at now and the one I spent sitting in my window seat watching the limousine going down the driveway with my parents' two heads turned, talking only to each other in the back seat.

I was so anxious about seeing them that I couldn't sleep. The feeling was like coming upon an old storybook. You want to love it with that same young consciousness. It seemed so irrelevant to call Nadia, as though independence had been a stranger's idea.

I hadn't seen this Eastern countryside, and as I drove in the rented car over the freeways named turnpikes, the sky became a tiny canopy over tight brown towns with the church steeple and the factory whistle. Soap-opera country. The green is Crayola-green. The trees were shaped like the trees in workbooks when you were learning to match the picture with the word, or fill it in with the proper color.

Going to my parents, I was speeding back into a formal childhood. I expected to see black letters perfectly formed under each

object: TREE; HOUSE; SERVICE STATION; GIRL; BOY; MAN; LADY.
And to make the childhood more familiar, I couldn't breathe. The green shimmered. The sky had perimeters. The sky was a hot silk tent tied down over aphid-green fields and trees.

In the West, the trees are gray-green; sage-green.

In the West, the sky is so vast that it is not hard to believe that you are on a planet spinning through space. You could believe there are limitless options. A way out.

In the West, existence is external.

In the East, I could see, you go inside. Locked in here, inside your head. This tight silk sky coming down and this suffocating green dipping down like a womb of hot lettuce, sucking you up inside to keep you there until it considers you full-made.

I wanted to go back home. Speed didn't seem very fast, in the East.

My parents' summer house was painted night-sky blue with starlight trim. A telescope stood on a small balcony outside a room where a restless white curtain tried to get some action from the cockteasing Connecticut breeze. Was this telescope, I wondered, so my father could see his favorite stars? Perhaps it would be better not to ask. His favorite stars had burned out, falling in a hot, sharp crescent. Out of sight. Perhaps that was why he had come here. Not to watch.

"Seen any good movies?" I said to my father as I lugged the suitcase over the front step, into the living room filled with autographed pictures of everybody. My father is the only person I know who, having had much experience of life, still believes in movie stars, politicians and God.

"We came here to rest and to work," he reminded me. "Am I glad to see you?" he was asking himself and not actually aloud, but his expression was clear enough for me to read/hear: Was I there to be pleasant or to torment them, to remind them that I had discovered they were not perfect? Was I going to be amusing or psychotic? A clue, please.

He hugged me. I still love him. Over his shoulder my mother had picked up on that and greeted me, eye to eye with wisdom, like a rival: "You've been cutting pieces out of your hair."

Do mothers and daughters—do we—treat each other as rivals, or more like spurned lovers who, meeting after many years, cannot remember who was the spurnee and who did the spurning?

"No," I said, "I've cut out chunks. Torn them out with my bare hands. You can even see the spaces."

She looked closely now and said, "They did a good job on your nose. You can't even tell it was done. You know, you were always so scared of having that. Jill has always hated doctors," she pointed out to my father. "Yes, I know," he said patiently. I was thinking of reminding her that she had not wanted me to have my nose done. But now I could not remember if that was true.

He was working on a new play. I saw the neat pages spread across his writing table. I picked up a page and looked at it. "Racy," I said.

"Yes, I was sure you'd appreciate it," he answered. He had this understanding of how it was with us now that I was trying to see him outside of being in his shadow. Some of our talks had the trippy rhythm of people snapping fingers on a zoot-suit corner: the gamey, competitive chatter of the cockmongers —men shiny with success—the casual one-liners they throw back and forth with the easy grace of champion ballplayers.

We sat in the study. They would not ask about Lawrence. They knew it would be only a matter of time before I would bring up the subject, and why should they give me the opportunity to snap, "I don't want to discuss it"? Which is what would have happened if they had brought the subject up first.

I assumed we would go through these rituals for a day. Of being cool. Showing off our latest accomplishments. Discussing politics. We might sulk through dinner.

"It's very green here," I said. We all sat and stared into the view, as though we were looking at a green fire dancing. The leaves, open to suggestion, gave off yellow and blue sparks in the sunlight. My father was angry because I was giving him no clues that would make it easier for him to be helpful. I sat waiting, in silence, watching him hunt for the trouble.

I distracted him. I attacked my mother. "Why aren't you painting?" I demanded.

"I have painted. I will. When I'm ready."

Father said, "Have you been up to your mother's studio? It has a lovely view. A beautiful studio . . ."

Silence. They had such privacy here. I felt left out.

We had an early, very quiet supper. Then my mother went to her News Watch. It was as though she had a contract with Walter Cronkite.

Father and I talked about politics. Shaking our heads over the catechism we recited of the latest enormities. It was a game we played like Scrabble to show how well we got along. We were pretending to be talking to each other.

Before I went to sleep my mother called me in. "Please," she said softly, "don't ask me about painting. I don't work when your father is not working well. It isn't fair."

"I don't believe it—that's such a cop-out!" I tried, whenever I could remember, to use slang around my mother because she detests it.

"Now, don't raise your voice—he'll hear . . ."

I went right to my father, who was writing in his study. I stood in a slouch with hands in the pockets of the jeans I wore because he hates women in pants (the effort I went to for them), and I said, "Do you know why Mother is not painting . . ." And I told him.

"That's ridiculous." He shook his head. Got up and went into her room. I wolfed down a spansule and trotted along behind.

The door closed. I listened.

"You're not painting because you're lazy!"

"No. Now don't get so angry. She shouldn't have told you."

"She didn't have to. I built a beautiful studio for you, it cost a fortune . . . and you haven't gone up there for a month!"

"Because I can only work with my music on, and the last time I was up there, you made me turn it off."

"I asked you to turn the records down. I was trying to work."

"If you'd built a door onto the studio, I could play my music as loud as I want to . . ."

No. I ran outside and sat on a bench under a tree.

It was hot even at night.

I hadn't meant for them to argue. But they interpreted each other to me all the time, and the picture was never the same. What one said about the other was not what I saw.

Was it the illusion they loved? Or was it the illusion I thought I saw, and the person each told me about was the real one?

Did it really matter?

Yes. The truth could give clues—to who was in my head dragging all the furniture around so I couldn't get a feeling for the place. It also told me when I thought about it, much later, that they had these very private definitions, the only one of which I knew for sure is that love is a totally private environment. I am only, ever, to see shadows, and as I said, what I see may be wrong.

Love: what my parents make of it is obscure. But it is a real thing. It has endurance as one tangible quality. I just guess at others.

Endurance. Perhaps that is the mystery. Their love is not obscure. Endurance, I should say, is what makes it seem obsolete.

Father came outside and sat on the bench beside me. Quietly he asked, "Is Lawrence away on business?"

"No. Sometimes he must go off alone. He doesn't want to be controlled," I said. Swallowing, swallowing. Father could always make me cry, it was part of the breaking-down process of the resistance to his allure. Once I have cried I can be a promising child again and therefore know my failure more keenly, as well as his justifiable astonishment that I never could go so far as to say, "But I know you meant well."

But I didn't cry this time. I went forward to try something new. I simply said this time, "Things aren't easy. But I love him." He leaned back a bit, folding his hands behind his head assuming his softest expression, the expression of the storyteller. I felt my shoulders loosen and my breathing came easier; he's found me, we have a way to be comfortable with each other again. I hated having to look hard at him. Would it mellow in time to reality? I had liked the child part, the unqualified adoration. Did we have to discontinue that subscription?

He said, "Of all the many things I've done I suppose that the most satisfying, and the most frustrating, has been writing. And the hardest thing a writer has to do, when a character begins to come to life, is to keep it from running away with the story. To keep the plot moving forward. Your mother is like a romantic character from a novel." He paused. He was being cautious. "Lawrence, too—I think. That's part of their charm for us. But when you marry a heroine or a hero you must be aware that you have to maintain a structure. Do you see, Jill?"

"Yes. I will think about that. I will."

My father had come halfway with something new: he had not done the fatherly half of the game, which would have been to say something like, "We warned you about that guy." He had accepted (more than I had) that Laurie was a permanent fixture. Or as permanent as something liquid could be . . . hard to contain, I mean, and liable to evaporate if placed on strong heat for any amount of time . . .

I stayed there a week.

During the day I typed letters to Laurie. Of just his name. Or lists of ways to make love to him. Or ways to kill him so he would not be able to go away. To kill him and carve him and eat him up and then kill myself. Dying happily with him inside of me, unable to leave. I wrote letters to made-up bars and poker places asking if they had seen this tall man with the look of a poet. And I wrote letters to the kids from Laurie and me about the fine time we were having in Connecticut on vacation.

At night, when my parents were asleep, I called Los Angeles. The reports all said that no one had seen Laurie. I kept gasping air, swallowing hungrily, fighting with insects and all that green for breath. Missing him crowded in on me, and I'd go off into a town nearby "to mail some letters . . ." (to have a drink or two, and see if there was a sort of friendly doctor anyone knew. Speed was running low. And it didn't look as though there was a connection in the entire state.) If I had been gone for forty minutes or more, I would call my parents to ask if everything was okay, meaning, "Did he call?"

"No calls," Father would say. I felt they were discussing what to do with me.

During the midmorning speed highs, I could work. This meant I would call my book editor in the city to say I would make the deadline next year. Since it had already been three years with this book, he sounded skeptical. I wanted him to sound convinced so I would believe myself too.

And I called Helen, who heard my entire latest installment before she could say hello. But she listened. I heard her listening.

"Jill, dear," she breathed, "you know some men are like sable coats. A gorgeous luxury. I think," she whispered, in such thoughtful, intimate consideration, "that a girl has to *want* to work very hard for that sable coat, or she must carefully ask herself, 'Can *I* afford a sable coat?' "

Romantic hero. Sable coat. I was concerned about affording speed so I could write the article I was going to try to sell her. And when I was into my wheeling-dealing self, I thought of bread first and Laurie second.

"That is useful. I will think about that." I had an idea . . . "Do you have a job for me on the magazine? Anything?" I asked her. A salary would be so secure.

It never occurs to occupational fuck-ups that offers of employment will not follow hard on the heels of revelations of our latest madcap adventures. We do not make ourselves enticing investments.

I think the world allows one conventional failure before handing you the albatross suit.

So, no job—but Helen switched me over to her articles editor, who said she had a little three-hundred-word number available for someone to write on why nice guys make lousy lovers.

"I'll have it tomorrow," I said. "And Helen says she'll get me a check fast, so hold it for me. I'll be in the city around one."

Nice guys do make lousy lovers but are better than lousy guys because at least they come home. And a real sable coat may require a big initial investment, but you can keep it in your closet and it's there to sleep in if you want, every night.

A week. I had given myself a week to be where he could find me. To be where he would assume I would go.

So I told my parents I was going into New York to stay with a friend who was an editor on a magazine. (And who was away, I knew, on Fire Island, but I would find somewhere.) Hoping it was not a lie, they nevertheless could not help me pack quickly enough.

I wrote the *Cosmo* piece and then I took four Coricidins to provide a little nap so I wouldn't just lie there speed-dreaming of him.

Then, very late, the night before I had planned to go, I heard the car. Father was up before me, switching on the outside lights.

Listen, my father doesn't know this character, this hero. He picks his own entrances. Such timing. Such style.

A long black Cadillac limousine pulled up through the hot green shrubbery, hot and green even at night. The lights flicked off, the Rent-a-Chauffeur, his cap slightly askew, got out and opened the rear door. Leaner, drunk, but mine, the passenger Laurie emerged. We ran to each other. Running for so long until I reached him, I saw us from every angle. When you've seen enough movies, your whole life becomes its own fiction. You don't know what is real—he felt so real.

He came, he came, he came! His arms came around me and held me tight, lifting me into the air. Kissing, kissing. "I love you, I love you!" A second later I was screaming, pounding his back, "Don't do this to me, I can't stand it again! I'll kill you."

"Hush," my father said. "Now, let's go inside. Lawrence, have you any luggage?"

"No, no," he said, peeling bills off a wad of cash and handing them to the chauffeur.

"How much was that?" I whispered.

"It was cool—I just didn't want your father to think I'm a loser."

"A hundred dollars, I'll bet," I said.

Father shook hands. "Nice to see you, Lawrence, old boy." He slapped Laurie lightly on one shoulder and entered into a formal man-to-man dialogue, appropriate for conversing with sons-in-law, New Hollywood executives and other young men he wasn't too impressed by. Even in Cadillac limousines.

"When did you get in town?"

"Oh, a couple of days ago," Laurie said. "I had some contacts I wanted to make in the city." He turned to me. "And I played a little poker."

"Did okay, I gather?"

"Fine, fine."

My father asked Laurie if he would like some coffee.

"That would be great. Thank you." My father went to turn on the hot water. Laurie looked around—looking, I knew, for something to drink.

"No," I told him, "there's just coffee. For now." He nodded and came over to me, leaning over and kissing my neck, and then lightly greeting my breasts under the white cotton Mexican nightgown.

"I never wanted to see you again," I said. I wanted to feel his thighs, his long legs around me.

"I understand." He understood what I said, as well as what I wanted and how I could mean both at once. That is what you don't trade for a steady income or a real sable coat. I thought it was the legs—it is the understanding that comes through.

"Well," said my father, coming back in with the coffee "How long did it take you to get out here? Which way did he bring you?"

"Oh, about two hours. We stopped for—"

"—a couple of drinks." My father smiled benevolently. "That chauffeur looked like an old comic drunk. Or else he was doing a hell of a good routine."

"I don't think," I said, "that drinking is a good subject for comedy. Laughter is a form of approval, and if people stopped laughing at drunks, or at comedians pretending to be drunk— I mean, you don't think comics who do cripples are funny."

"Jill"—my father stopped my tirade—"no one is laughing."

Laurie sat there, holding his coffee mug by its waist as one would a glass, moving it a bit, pretending to hear the comforting sound of ice cubes.

Was I mad because he did not instantly sweep me off to bed —because he was being considerate to my father? How shrewdly he had sized up the priorities. You are what you wear and what you drive. Of course, Father would require immediate reassurance and Laurie was being so earnest, so witty and so very sober, unless one knew that he never talked except when pie-eyed.

Father, he seemed to assume, did not know this. Drunks, like liars, believe the longer you talk, the more sincerely you nod your head, gesture and look right in the other person's eyes (or as close as you can make it), the more convincing you are.

Father had on his polite expression. His hands were folded in his lap. The knuckles were blue-white.

As for me—well, Laurie knew that could be handled later. The delicate touches earlier had told me that. Later would come soon. Small talk gone, Father went to his room. Laurie and I went up to the guest room. He had, I noticed, both his suitcases. Picked them up from Karen, I gathered.

We sat on one of the twin beds in the guest room and held each other.

"I'm sorry," I said. "I just panicked."

"Hell, no," he said, kissing my eyes. "It was a brilliant idea to move to New York. Your head was rotting out there anyway. Our heads, I mean. You were becoming suburban. New York will be good for your work. More action."

"I just don't know about the kids and New York," I said. "I've never seen children there. I don't know how to do that."

"We'll work it out. Don't you fret. We'll make it seem like an adventure."

"What will we do?"

"We have the whole summer to work it out, and I've already talked to an old friend of mine . . . yesterday. He's still with the company Mike and I worked for. He doesn't think there will be any trouble getting installed again."

"A job. For you!"

"Yes."

"Mike said you liked it there."

I asked Laurie gently, "Could you go back? Really?"

"I wasn't fired, if that's what you mean." He looked hurt. Such implications! "I think it will be cool."

"I know you weren't fired. It was about your first wife. I know. Karen told me once what happened," I said, clutching my arms around him while he stroked my orange hair. He made it feel like beautiful hair. "It must have been unbearable."

"It wasn't unbearable, but I did go a little crazy at the time. Actually, she smothered me. I was her creation. And when I became more successful, it was difficult. I wouldn't play the same role. But she was a remarkable woman. I just couldn't be what she needed me to be."

Later his body curved around me so neatly. What if he hadn't found me? What if I never felt this body again? No matter what he does, or where he goes . . . I couldn't give this up.

I remember: I could almost hear Karen's voice as we sat in her living room sometime after he had come to stay with me. I had asked her about his other marriages. What she did know she told me.

"We were all in New York. Mike and Larry were working together. Barbara had a good job—more status than Larry. She had a fine quick sense of humor and a lot of drive and energy. And that's always attractive to Larry. Soon they were working together, and they were married. Barbara was a perfect wife for him. He was never late for work. They had an apartment in the Village. On Saturdays they would look at pictures; he has an infallible eye. I would say he was very happy."

I could see, now, for myself, how it must have been. I pictured Laurie, lying smiling on a bed. There are fine graphics arranged infallibly on the wall. He has one arm over a strong-looking tawny woman with neat dark hair. She looks at the clock and dashes out of bed, squeezes oranges, grinds coffee and brings it all to him on a teak tray.

I could hear Karen's voice again: "Larry started working with a guy named Asher; Barbara worked in the same office. Asher, being unmarried, was the buddy who comes home to share dinner, to play a game of Go . . .

"Then Mike left the company and Larry followed, probably to escape this cottage-industry closeness. When the new company decided to send him to Rome and Paris to train people there, Larry asked Asher to be sure to look in on Barbara to see that she was all right.

"Larry decided to surprise Barbara. He returned from Europe late one night. Asher was with Barbara. Now, don't look like that," Karen had said. "Nothing like that should be a surprise if you've been listening. It had been fine for Barbara when he was dependent, but then he became more immersed in his work . . .

"Remember how Larry always says 'Anything worth doing is worth overdoing'? Barbara was capable of sharing work and goals, but he wasn't expected to exceed certain unconscious limitations.

"He came to us and sat on the couch, and cried for almost three days."

I remembered that when Karen told me, we had both looked over at her couch. And transferred it back to New York. And I saw him with his head in his hands.

I wondered now, thinking about it, how Barbara's side of the story would go.

The next morning I got out of the twin bed where we had made love with no sounds. Like adolescents necking. And I started putting away the clothes he had dropped on the floor. "What are you doing?" he murmured from sleep.

"Neatness counts. Here. Sleep a bit. It's early." I pulled the covers up around his shoulders, tucking them in tightly. Neat. And he couldn't get away so fast.

I wished we had been borne away to Death in the night. Anywhere but where I would have to go downstairs now and confront my father. I thought I could hear his dismay even up here in our room. Was Laurie only another symbol of my determination to create trouble?

"Well, quite an arrival," my father said, laughing. Then a quick look at the watch. "What does he like for breakfast?"

The laugh put me immediately on guard. "I don't know. Nothing. Anything. And he should be able to sleep. He's tired." Who can answer a direct question before the first spansule?

"Well." He shook his head, continuing to squeeze oranges, pouring the juice into clean crystal glasses. I thought of Laurie's first wife. Of unconscious limitations placed on others—they must not exceed (succeed?). A certain kindliness could keep us in our place. And keep it all light and lovely as fresh orange juice.

Father's immaculate country kitchen; my mother would strongly resent any associations made between her and that room. In our Hollywood mansion, the legend was, someone asked my mother if he could get a Coke from the kitchen and she said, "I suppose so, but you'll have to ask someone else where the kitchen is."

"I guess you'd rather not talk this morning," Father said. I was staring out of the window into the landscape. It was like looking out into the bottom of a swimming pool gone to algae, the swimming pools at the back of old Beverly Hills estates owned by movie-studio singing maestros.

"I'm thinking," I lied, "about my new book—some cuts I want to make. I think some of the satire is a little rough."

"I'd like to read it when you're ready."

"Yes. Well. It's very raw . . . I'm not sure you'd like it."

He handed me a glass of orange juice and I followed him to the dining table, where he had arranged straw place mats and white linen napkins.

"Don't cast me as a prude, Jill; I've been around a lot longer than you have. Nothing shocks me. I just find certain things unnecessary."

There are eating sounds. Why are the sounds of parents' chewing so infuriating?

"I just don't want you to hurt your mother. That's all."

He was reading my mind. I hadn't thought he could do that any more before noon.

"The book is not about me. Not about you. Not about Mother. It's an historical novel which I've happened to place in the future. To avoid similarities with the past."

He took a deep breath, dabbed at his mouth and sat forward, folding his hands, fingers interlocking. Was he going to say "Laurie was drunk last night and your mother and I are worried"? I waited: I will say he wasn't drunk and it's none of his business. At least we both knew there was no point in beginning such a conversation.

So my father pushed himself away from the table and put down his napkin with such force that it could be called a fling.

He walked away a bit, hands in pockets, then turned. "I know you think your mother and I are hard on you. And I know we are highly critical people. Highly critical. We make judgments. And perhaps we have no right to make such judgments."

He could tell I was fixing up my defenses, adjusting them like a military person, checking the gun, digging in the heels, sucking on the roach and flipping it over my shoulder. Fixing my bayonet in stoned silence.

So.

I went up to where Laurie was, to watch him sleep. And Father took Mother's coffee to her room.

When I think of the song from *Fiddler on the Roof* that the father sings about his daughter, "When did she get to be a woman?," I hear a father singing, "When did we get to be a menace? When did it start to be so bad?"

Highly critical. I can hear how they would be talking now: "Such promise she had." How (heads in hands) had they failed? No—reassuring each other in an empassioned duet: "You, you, my darling, did not fail." My mother would point out, again, the example of my hair. "Her hair," she would say, "feels like material."

"And he," they would say, "we sent him a check to buy a suit, he must have gambled it."

"He leans to the left when he walks," they would agree. "That's how one can tell he's drunk."

"I wish I had a lot of money," my father would say, "and I would try to do something."

"But what can you do?" my mother would remind him. "They would just spend it. She," my mother would remind him again, "never has enough. I love you. I wish they would go away. We were so happy."

"It is only noon, darling," I told Laurie as I woke him again, "but I feel we have to go." I almost said "home," but it occurred to me that for the first time in my life, I did not have a home.

When I was a child I dreamed once that I came home from school late in the afternoon, and where my parents' mansion had been, there was a vast amusement park, with lights and music, and all around this new place it was night. I wondered where my parents had gone, but I decided to look for them later, after I had gone on a few of those glittering rides in this nighttime place.

With assurances that we would turn in the rental car safely in Manhattan, we left my parents' house. Laurie drove me to the Chelsea Hotel. Through the sooty two-thirds of window above the lumbering air conditioner in our room, I saw another

East: a city that is the color of rust and a black/gray that did not correspond to any color I had seen in California. I moved the furniture and set up the typewriter, tacking my timelines and notes for my book to the wall while Laurie went to turn in the car.

I washed his dirty shirts in the bathtub and called *Cosmo* to see if they'd received the little articles I'd mailed in. Money would be the customary problem. He did not have the job yet—

But then, look how pessimistic I am: already I know it will take four or five hours for him to get rid of the car. I've heard it's very tough to drive a car through the middle part of Manhattan, where the skyscrapers are stacked like ice trays.

I smelled his shirt; the gamier, the better the fetish. I leaned over the bathtub, swishing the shirt in the water, rubbing the collar with the small complimentary bar of soap that said "Hilton Hotel." Two brown beetles strolled out from behind the toilet; Jungian comprehension: roaches, these are roaches. Well, what about saying they are made of tortoise-shell parchment? What about it?

I can't wash the dirt from the shirts, the roaches aren't antique mechanical jewels, and I don't think he is still just turning in the car. I left the shirts swinging on wire hangers to dry and went downstairs to a Spanish Restaurant/Bar which pretends to be the hotel dining room ("Enjoy your meals in our convenient, delightful coffee shop, adjacent to our spacious lobby." Everything about the Chelsea is a copywriter's parody.)

This is the kind of restaurant/bar that always gives the impression, no matter when you come in, that it's getting ready to call it a night. There are plastic Christmas decorations fading and a sign in sparkles over the bar, "HAPPY FOURTH ANNIVERSARY, 1953." There are Spanish posters and pictures of bullfighters on black velvet. They were selling small pitchers of a new drink called Sangría for a dollar and a quarter. I waited at the bar for Laurie (except when I was checking in the lobby to see if he had perhaps gone straight to our room). I remembered him saying once that things would be different for us in New York. "There's more energy—a sense of commitment I get in New York."

Geography may not be so transforming after all.

But it was just summer. Heat lay like a lox on this city land. I would have to be patient perhaps until autumn. My mother had told me the seasons are refreshing; everything comes alive in the New York fall.

I had two small pitchers of Sangría. Punch with a punch. And I was talking now to a German veterinarian with her leg in a cast. She said she would rather be a motorcycle mechanic for Hell's Angels. And she grinned, swigging beer.

Before she got sick and had to give up her brandy, my mother used to say a lady never drinks beer. "It's not how much one drinks, darling, it's how you do it. Properly."

Damn. I had come within beaming distance of them. Now they would not get out of my bed. I mean my head. My head, yes, my head.

One good thing about being an orphan is no parents. Laurie had it made. Oh, yes?

There is no answer.

My German friend said, "It is late where is this husband you have." She grinned, implying it's OK if I want to lie.

I wished she were more attractive. Since she had shared her dream job secret with me, I shared mine with her: I wanted to be a star of my own television talk show. There. I said it. Beaming. "Nope," she shook her head, pointing at me. "Nose is too big. Just a little bit. Why don't you have it done?"

"It's a good nose for peace marches," I said, wanting to rearrange the German's nose. Veterinarian. I could imagine: the mind cringes in horror. And I thought quickly of Jasper and Cats. I felt my arms wrap around myself to hold them to me.

I miss my animals.

I miss my children.

I miss my people. And my land.

A delicately constructed older man came over with his drink and his gray hair in a ponytail.

He told us he had taught his iguana that he keeps in a friend's rain forest on the hotel's roof to do fifty-six different string tricks while balancing on a hundred-year-old egg.

"Would you be interested in observing this feat or William Burroughs, who, he pointed out, "You can see over at that table there." Burroughs looked very much like the wiped-out computer man in his austere chalk-striped suit. I had the impression of a small collared white shirt and a thin tie. He dressed like Ralph Nader.

My new friend brought me over to Burroughs' table. We left the vet slowly sinking into the west. I was fainting with the excitement. Now, *there* was a star. And, moreover, a star who would know how to connect—a star with connections. I forgot in my passion that I was actually in the same building with a lizard: an "L." I could think of the word. Terror faded into pale menace under the Burroughs allure. (But I still felt "L" feet tapping over my head: Pounce.) My passion was more for legend than literature. All I knew was a book about, I believe, lunches with Hemingway in Paris while stoned out of their minds, and naked. Something like that, I thought. But I said I loved all his books, using the sort of mutter I adopt with seriously hip people so they will not hear that what I'm saying is probably boring and indicates I'm a closet square. I'm thinking also of asking around about speed.

He whispered now, to someone else, "The city has become very dangerous."

I thought, my God, here I am meeting Burroughs and he is speaking of law and order.

But he continued, very quietly, "I wouldn't go around with anything now. Leary's been busted. It's bad business. You have to be careful."

There was a gasp and such a hush. Someone clasped my knee. I felt as though I were sitting around the revolutionaries' table in *For Whom the Bell Tolls*. Katina Paxinou will bring the paella and the guns.

When you're near enough to William Burroughs so that theoretically you could ask him how to connect (even if the situation is so hot you can't ask)—that's Arrival.

I wanted to be cuddled by everyone in a mass family welcome. My darlings, I have come home. This felt like home. Here I wanted to leap upon the table, arms stretched out, in a triumphant musical number, sequins flashing from my Mexican smock, satin bows on my tapped-out sandals.

I am as hot as Little Richard, thinking of flashing my eyes, thrashing a hip this way and that and flinging off my clothes to be torn apart for souvenirs by the people who will dig me. Pussycat, you have arrived. Sitting at a table in Chelsea, New York, with this real William Burroughs . . .

Here's Laurie! Have I failed to miss him for a moment? Is such a thing possible?

"Hello, Laurie . . . darling!"

"Oh, hi," he said to everyone whom he seemed sort of to know. He had been hiding out on me: here, here is the cabin the groom builds, the brass bed she can see her eyes dancing in; the moon, the stars and the diamond solitaire; here is my present: the Chelsea, full of wonder. Kissing, kissing!

"Thank you for bringing me to New York," I whispered.

"Ran into Nadia," he said. "She would like to meet you. So we might get together tonight."

More wonders yet to come—a horizon full of wonders.

The others had been nonoperative prototypes. Nadia is Fame.

Her hair is black and thick and crisp with waves that are capped as she moves, with deep-blue highlights. Wonder Woman's hair. Energy and panic roamed about her, like pets, as she opened the door.

"Well," she said with enough amused implications to go around, then dashed back into the huge loft-room space searching for something. If the harassment was designed as a detour around amenities, it worked. She let me plunge right into her chaos and so I knew her all at once.

Clothing seemed no more relevant to Nadia than to the Sphinx. I had an impression of a smock the color of wet cement. A sculptor's cloth idly draped about the statute.

"Listen, you must help me, Larry, I am going out of my mind. The *Times* sent me a book to review and now I can't find it to send it back. I put it right down . . . It's the size of a table, and the pictures have as much insight."

I would not know where to begin. Huge matted black-and-white photographs were propped up on all surfaces, except where whitewashed cratelike bookshelves leaned, jammed with books, portfolios, handfuls of yellow Kodak boxes here and there, and newspapers piled up.

I thought the photographs were great ones because I had been told that she was a fine photographer. And the pictures—the eyes especially—made me look at them. She had caught something in everyone. But I would try Laurie's impressed nod: I don't want to be trapped into a specific comment that would turn out to be totally inappropriate.

And she had not spoken to me, actually. There was just that look catching me fast, to be developed later. Her eye knows: selects–rejects in an instant. Gets it just right.

"What are the pictures of?" I asked, assuming from the size she described that it was a book of photographs. Looking in a gingerly way—not to put hands on too many things. Remembering from somewhere—photographers have a horror of fingerprints.

"Who knows; who cares? It should not be known I have even heard of such a photographer, let alone to review him! But I can't find it."

I had to chew on the inside of my lip to avoid saying, "Teach me how to be you." The flash of longing had the same "This is it" impact as when I met Laurie. But it was more than Fame —it was forbidding discipline: the critic—I recognized here. The myth that challenged me to achieve and then challenged my achievement.

She tantalized me by dismissal. The pure sadism only an inventive masochist could begin to contemplate, let alone exercise.

We were now bustling about looking for the book. I noticed how coolly Laurie strolled into the partition that had her bed. I hung back a bit outside. Even the bedroom debris seemed so adult. A good hairbrush and a bottle of Cabochard were the only sexual clues. This was a professional place. Even in misplacement she maintained the impact of her powerful identity. The kinds of things I lose are beads, a sandal . . . or the phone bill. Things that anyone could lose.

Laurie found the book beside the bed, under a portfolio that Nadia was organizing, she explained, for her friend, the owner of the loft. "He was over here until five in the morning. He's completely undone, so what am I to do. I'm exhausted. Have you ever taken Valium?" she asked me.

"No, I'm sort of more into ups. But I can get some if that's what you mean." Immediately I had to be helpful. What was I thinking about? I hadn't even connected myself. But it was always easier to be urgent for a friend, to take chances; to make the convincingly desperate phone calls; to hang around in the right places that were usually the wrong places to be.

"Would you? That would be marvelous," she purred, arranging herself into a chair with her long ivory legs drawn up in front of her. Such healthy legs, the skin shining. She was not tanned, but her pallor had a richness; there was a depth to the skin tone. Under the impression of chaos she might prefer is a woman who takes care of herself.

With the side of her hand, she flicked back a ruffle of her black Chantilly-lace hair, a gesture of such luxurious quality. Then an expression of puzzlement crossed her forehead. "But I'm not sure if Valium is good for me. Do you think it really helps depression, or just makes you too drowsy to complain?"

"I don't know," I said. "Actually, I sleep under speed."

"But that's very dangerous," she said, now pleased to see me. A slight upcurve on the posh, bowed mouth.

We could test some preliminary conversation to determine if there was any basis for a possible friendship. I love lips that go like hers. Cushions. Plums. The sass in the full squareness of the lower lip.

Laurie kept the glasses filled. I thought he was amused. Watching a child with a new toy. Which, however, is the child, and which the toy? How much, I wondered, are we playing at for his amusement?

I knew she knew exactly what was going on. She knew I preferred not to know, and she was right. I hadn't a clue. I felt as perplexed, frustrated and anxious as I suppose a young boy feels—a boy trying to make the most popular girl in school.

She moved her legs from time to time and I half listened as she directed the conversation; I was longing to nuzzle at the slash of black she flashes.

How to attract her? I wondered. Hollywood stories, perhaps.

It is said that English intellectuals find our everyday experience rather odd and interesting.

She helped out. "So, I understand you were raised in Hollywood. Did you feel that was extraordinary?" Not as extraordinary, I wanted to say, as your voice. Actually, I thought she would have a cleverer answer than any I could give. Even if I thought I was being honest in my answer, she would know a purer truth.

"I did not know how I felt," I said. As usual. "I think I thought that most people in the one-story houses were poor. Places where the mother cooked. But lucky—they were definitely luckier. And I knew that to notice such disparities was impolite.

"But," I went on, "I also felt that somehow, in some way, it was my fault that some people didn't have projection rooms, and when it was explained that I had many advantages, it came out more like an accusation. A challenge to overcome."

"Which," she said to Laurie, to no one, really, "you've evidently been able to do. Even the guilt is a Hollywood fantasy. Tell me, are all of you so unconscious that when you begin to see reality you come apart? Every sensitive, rich American seems to end it all passed out in the 'Eighty-Six.' "

"I haven't passed out there yet," I said, "but I'm not rich and actually I haven't been there yet. To the 'Eighty-Six.' "

"One can't have everything," she said and then, to Laurie, "You haven't shown her one of the great attractions?" Laurie lit her cigarette; they looked in each other's eyes. And such wide eyes to look in. Karen was right: "extraordinary." But not just green. They looked golden now, gazing at me as Laurie said, "Jill doesn't pass out, She naps on the floor of the ladies' room. I try to see she's not disturbed unless there's a line."

"The 'Eighty-six' is a pit," she said. "We shall have to go there sometimes when I must deepen my depression. But I wouldn't advise you to sleep on the floor. I should not put my shoe upon that floor." I wondered if being an advantaged fuck-up makes failure any less painful and degrading. The sickness is just as cold and sour; the creditors just as persistent. "I guess," I said "the failure is what happens when it changes—when all the lovely expectations get pulled out from under you. And you only see the ones who got out. Who tried to find something to be. There are others out there who couldn't even move. They lie about and clip their parents' retrospective reviews, giving little brunches for the formerly famous."

"I imagine you're wrong," she said. "I believe the decision to fail comes first, and the clever ones devise methods to overcome any opportunities to succeed, including," she added, "turning evident advantages of birth into disasters.—I really think Hollywood is a terribly boring subject. Could we change it now?" Without waiting, she changed it herself. "Do you ever have dialogues with Larry? I don't see that you talk to each other."

Was she warning me? I was so busy defending my naïveté, I did not see what she understood: the destruction, and the encouragement I was giving to it.

We were finishing another bottle of Scotch now and I was having the customary spaces in time and communication that happened when I was drinking a lot.

I landed. For an instant. In the middle of a conversation she was having with Laurie about a jail in the Middle East she had photographed.

"They confiscated all the film. It's fortunate I wasn't killed. The prisons there are full of artists and intellectuals . . ."

I wanted to tell her, I realized, that I was much more interested in politics than Hollywood myself. I wished Laurie would mention my radio show.

"Actually," I said, "I'm writing a political satire. And I'm number seventeen on the list of the top Los Angeles subversives." Or was, I thought. What's a subversive with no audience to subvert?

"And Father's only number forty-six," I added.

"Must you call him 'Father,'" she snapped. "He's not *my* father."

"I'm sorry. I meant my father. Anyway . . ." I drifted out. Top L.A. subversives. Yes. And one of Pacoima's major revolutionaries. So. God. The squareness of me.

She only really said that because she was restless or bored— I wasn't even sure she meant to say it. But there was nothing else, at that point, that needed to be said. The tension was flying around like mad birds. And we were all drunk. There seemed to be some more spaces in time. But it was as though she plucked me, mad bird, down from the rafters of her loft where I'd been ricocheting in and out of consciousness, and holding me by the throat, she said, "Since we do get on together so well, why don't we all just go to bed?"

Oh. She does like me. She does. "Please mean it," I said, grabbing on to her hand, "please don't change your mind."

Washed and combed, Laurie and I sat on the bed like polite guests who don't start dinner until everyone's at the table.

We were waiting for Nadia, who was taking this exceedingly long bath. If I leaned back on the low bed, I could see her shoulders against the tub. White on white. Different kinds of porcelain. She was smoking. After a very long time I whispered to Laurie that Nadia probably didn't care for houseguests. It occurred to me she was probably wondering what she would do with us tomorrow morning.

I watched as she dried her body. Her body betrays her. It is all gentleness. A dappling of the flesh here and there like the shadows of small leaves. Her breasts are high enough to leave some rib line clear and give the effect of energy. But they are also full enough, soft enough to be nonthreatening (she is of my own generation). These breasts, they would give pure Devonshire cream. And, after the bath, hitting chill air, the tips gnarled up like tawny acorns to teeth upon.

She swung a towel around her neck like a tennis player as she walked out of the bathroom, snapping off the light. Then, with a shrug, she snapped it on again, leaving the door ajar.

A few wet curls of hair hung down from where she'd pinned it up to keep it out of the tub; the drops of water ran down her shoulders. Now she unpinned her hair, making the gesture seem brand-new. Standing, not looking in a mirror, she brushed her hair until it swept like glamour over one-half her face.

Someone said that beach people live in a pile: at first we made love in a pile. I was busier than my fantasies and the best part was her fragrance. We separated after this first nonspecific tumbling—sweating—and Nadia flicked back her hair, lit a cigarette and turned on the air conditioner.

"Just until we have low-grade pneumonia," she said.

She came back to bed and looked at us. Appraising.

I drifted out of focus. When I returned to present time, Laurie was up, bartending; he brought us all new drinks and then, bedtending, he pulled both of us close around him again. I drew my hands down her back. I loved the way she felt like a strong person—and a woman. It had not been my experience that these two were compatible.

And she moved naked with the ease of someone who is accustomed to being wanted. I had the feeling she has written "No Involvement" on a few cocktail napkins in her time, returning them solemnly, to many anxious lovers.

She was all the allure I used to find in rejection.

But I could not altogether separate my feelings for her from Laurie. The three seemed a complete system.

I do not like to believe it, but I suspect part of what I felt for her, too; for all of us making love together came from this urgency I had to connect on some level with every moment of his life. To understand and to have an element of each moment to examine.

I felt a similar urgency to get close to her life. Was it because she is also unique?

Who goes first now. We kept wrapping around until, whether it was choice or the sudden proximity of the right parts and places, Laurie slid into Nadia.

For an instant I felt a wistful, left-out feeling that I tried not to acknowledge. Was it partly that neither of them chose me first?

However, I found diversions.

Places along the edges to touch—to give a helping hand, as he found also a hand for me and I could touch her hair. There was enough of everything to go around and nothing to spare. Sex for only two? Such a limit on the options. He raised up above her so I could hold her heavy, lovely breasts and she reached up, eyes closed, pulling on mine. There was her wet mouth to kiss; always something to kiss when it was not being handled and there were no parts of any bodies left alone. He was not stopping, still. So, turning down now, and getting right under their thundering hips, feeling the muscles, was like being present at my own conception. The moment of fuck.

No planets or stars coolly charted her conception: I saw Nadia being conceived in a fantastic battle of wills. A flaming passionate fury of a fuck. A flying fuck started at opposite sides of a room, lovers running at each other, heads lowered, great lines from Welsh ballads, epic war poems hurled at each other . . . crediting, between each breath, the right poet. An *ibid.* thrown here and there in the midst of a cry.

As he slid off, beaming, stroking us both, I lay alongside her upside down with my face on her so she should still be warm where he had been. I want to see, to kiss where he has been. Such a comforting blend of creative juices. Could I get in there and be born again an intellectual? The expression of her private face here was just as tantalizing and assertive as her public face. Her construction seemed more polished than mine. Richer, purer lines. Modern sculpture—sort of rose burgundy finish. Three dozen coats of deep color. A long crest streaked down the center with the majesty of a medal, a bas-relief obelisk.

No wonder Cock Robin responded so cheerfully to this joy ride in this gorgeous imported machine.

With the bitter familiar flavor of being outside, I had loved to see how they went together. More than that, I loved my turn. She sat, now, cool director, with a cigarette. "Larry, go down on Jill . . ." I closed my eyes. Why, in fantasy come to life, did I close my eyes?

"Make me a fantasy," I said, laughing.

"Shh," she said, in that perfect Night Queen voice, "be still now."

I heard the cigarette hiss and go out and felt her hands on me, her hair brushing across my breasts. My trip guide. It seemed her fingers, just the tips, siphoned at my nipples. Sensation so strong I couldn't feel what she was doing. I wanted to devour her—I grabbed her thighs.

"Get over me, over me . . ."

She stayed where she was, turning me on by turning me down. I tried to get my hand inside her. Her lips were close to my face but did not touch—teasing. Teasing. Laurie's hands stroked my stomach; he wound up along my body and I held him in my hand, he was ready again . . . "Incredible," she whispered. I felt a hand of hers (she must have three or four, yes, she is Kali, goddess of good and evil) holding him as my hand moved away. Don't move so fast, Jill. Where is your sense of ownership, your pride of possession?

Property values.

I am un-American. But not enough so it did not occur to me to question how I felt about her hand moving mine, ever so gently, off his cock. Did she read me as she watched my face, returning my hand, giving me back my totem? She stroked my hand as it clasped on him.

"Come . . . come now," she said, deep and distant, and her breath came on wings, from somewhere. I had a sense of flying . . . her hair is really vast wings, tied up for everyday, now unfolding to carry me off.

"You're beautiful, beautiful," she said.

I adored her. I opened my eyes to look at her.

But she was winking at Laurie with a cool grin.

Close eyes fast. I did not see that. Such a perfect jolt for the S-M set that lives inside me: there is no joking at such a time. No mocking. She must know that. I hated her wit. She is not a lover, she is the ultimate weapon. Of course, cool queen, I'm beautiful.

I put on my middle-of-the-week-I'm-busy pretend orgasm. A light job with a twitch or two of the hips. A fast sigh. Head to left, to right, then over. Three could playact as well as two. "Well," I said brightly, "next?" I did not see, could not see, that she had given me the show she assumed I had wanted— or expected—from the way I looked to her. And the allusions I may have made about hipness. I had not indicated I wanted more than a game. And at the time, out of mind, it seemed again, to be enough, as a slow strobelike effect moved over us as we each came into focus for our own time on. As though a light glided slowly across a stage, catching, and printing in the mind, an image—a furred dark place here, turning warm against the mouth into a cool wet opening that turns into dry hard strong forearms, the linking of soft female thighs, and it was her turn. Now I could not pretend to take it less than seriously.

We loved her, changing places up and down, as she twisted and grimaced and threw a perfect arm across her forehead, another hand clutching at his hair.

Is she feeling, is she feeling, can I make her care that I care? Her eyes opened slowly, like guns coming out from doorways, and fired lead at me.

I moved off the bed in an instant. It was Laurie, of course, that she wanted. I took two Coricidin and lay back down beside them to go to sleep. There was nowhere else to go. I watched how beautiful they were together.

Then. Was it a moment; was it an hour? Laurie was kissing me, lying over me.

"Are you all right, darling?" he asked.

"Fine." I opened my eyes very narrow—am I a spoil sport? The "butterfingers" who drops the softball that would have made the last out—was our team captain enraged? "I just want to sleep for another minute," I told him. Permission is granted, I was saying, to concentrate on her.

When I awakened, Nadia seemed to be asleep on the other side of the bed. Laurie was in the middle.

"I'm exhausted," Nadia said suddenly, eyes open, staring up at the ceiling. "And we must be dying of starvation."

Laurie put his arms around us, and kissed me, which was not thoughtful. He should kiss the hostess first. He walked out into the studio area, stretched, looked around for cigarettes and disappeared into the kitchen. Nadia just stared at the ceiling.

She looked at me balefully, as if she thought, perhaps, this is a mirage. If not, then we must deal with reality. She sighed, then said to me as one who is sharing a perfect filet of sole à la bonne mère, and remarking upon the subtle fragrance of the fresh tarragon, "Larry gives fine head, doesn't he?"

I would not have been invited without him. Of course not. But I was still surprised. The egomania of the self-determined inferior.

She turned back then to lie, staring at the partition wall over which whitewashed board of some fibrous material has been stapled. Everything ugly seemed, here, industrious, therefore beautiful. She was smoking. The dark hair near her neck had a cordovan cast to it in the dim morning light. I could almost feel how she was wishing me away. So I lit a cigarette and went out, around the screen into the studio.

What's wrong with this picture? I thought as I looked at Laurie. I see: he has his clothes on. He was silhouetted against the linen cloth that hung over the half-moon window at the far end of the loft.

"Why have you got your clothes on?"

"Going out for some clams. No food here."

"Laurie, listen"—I lowered my voice—"Nadia seems depressed. Why don't you give her some head?" I did not think she had mentioned it for no reason. She never just says something.

"Well . . ." He was thinking. A decision of equally attractive alternatives—not a major decision. "I guess I'll get some protein," he said. Nodded.

I didn't ask, "Will you be back?" I tried the positive approach. "You will be back?" Then I looked at how he was smiling.

"You like both of us like this," I said. "I can see you now, purring—forever. Superstud."

"Yes," he said, "one of you going over proof sheets, the other typing out novels. I could just lie around with something cool to drink . . ."

"In a bed of satin sheets to match your eyes," I said. "Disgusting. Get some food; we have to keep up your strength." Notice how it is "we."

There was an edge of hysteria in my voice. And something well-considered about his manner. Not pride exactly. Or only partly. Poker player. Winner of games. What games are we playing?

Maybe I could be very soft and so sweet now alone with her. If she would let me, I would love her just as long and just as well. I was lying next to her again. I put my arm around her and stroked back her hair. Then I moved my body down, cradling her hips in my arms.

"No," she said, "I'm tired." But she did not seem angry.

"I'd like to be just with you, I mean," I said. It was so extraordinarily comfortable to be alone in a bed with someone who was not like me, but who was also not the other. In some ways he and I are much more alike than I am like her. But she must have had some of the same feelings I was trying to pin down.

I was lying on my side, raised on my elbow. "Nadia," I said, kissing her neck.

"What?" she asked.

It was not the subject that was hard. It would not be much easier to ask her where, for instance, she bought shoes.

"Nadia," I repeated, very softly.

"What is it?" she snapped.

"I wonder: Can you make it, I mean, come really from straight fucking?"

She lifted up on her elbow and stared at me. We were like breasted bookends. "Are you out of your mind?"

So quickly she could make me feel terrible. Perhaps I should leave. I picked up a book idly from the floor near the bed.

She said, "It's a bad book."

I put it down.

"What I meant," she said, referring to my question. "is there isn't any satisfactory answer. I knew someone who couldn't come at all—she'd acted out all her fantasies. Consider that."

Was she warning me?

Then I said things to her I didn't mean to say, but I thought if I said enough, she would find something about me she would like:

"My fantasies are all cinematic, but most of the time, when I'm really getting everything happening, I notice someone wearing a costume that's faded or anachronistic. I put cat masks on men screwing each other, and then I change my mind. I have to cut and start the action all over. It's from being on too many sets. You never get through a scene to the end . . . And I've always," I continued, my hand creeping up on her thigh, "had a terrible time getting men to understand. I told a husband once about the production problems. He said I should make up my fantasies while I was doing the dishes after dinner so I'd be ready. I smashed the dishes all against the wall one night."

"That's a good fantasy," she said. We were lying side by side. It interested me that I did not assume my behavior with her could be the same as it would have been with a man lover: I would simply go at him, as he would with me. Maybe that is the trouble with heterosexual relationships; too much is taken for granted.

Except, I thought, Nadia may be more like the lovers who feel they can't get out of it gracefully, so it is easier to make love and get it over with.

The time friends waste dieting, buying clothes, coloring each other's hair, catting, eating: why didn't we go to bed? And why weren't we taught how to seduce?

It was different now that he was not there. Because I was in charge. It was now a completely new situation.

Do you say something or just touch? It was as though I had not touched her before at all.

What did Laurie do the first time we were together? He had just blurted out, "I want you," and put his arms around me. Now I looked back and it seemed so ingenuous—that kind of expression, I thought, could come out of what I felt for Nadia.

"Show me," I whispered, putting my arms around her, "how you do it . . ." We lay there next to each other, touching ourselves like small girls on the first day of nursery school. Was it a reassurance? Perhaps for me. Certainly this was not an occasion of any significance for her. That made me sad. But it often had meant more to me than to the other one.

"The only other person who understands is Laurie," I said, "it is exciting, watching. And comfortable when you're tired. Laurie says—"

Not missing a stroke, she snapped, "His name is not Laurie, it is Larry."

"It's Lawrence, actually," I said. She managed to brush so softly, across the tips of her breasts as she worked the other hand. Perfect orchestration.

"And so 'Laurie' can also be a nickname. I'm sure that's what his mother had in mind. She was Scottish and it seems right."

"How do you know anything about his mother? You make everything up, don't you?"

"Right on the spot," I said, "so I won't bore you." I felt rejections crosshatching. And I realized that what she was doing was only an act. Suddenly I knew it. I wondered if men can tell as clearly and it took me long enough as it was. To really do it; to show me—a stranger she did not trust—her own orgasm was a privilege I had not earned.

Laurie came back with clams in cardboard bathtubs with lemon boats and a dark cider in a plastic jar. It seemed more intimate than the sex—to know what clearly must have been their private love feast.

We ate. He lay down in a hammock at one end of the loft to read the *New York Times*. I wanted to be just with myself. To clean up. To see if I had new feelings about this. And part of me understood that they, having been lovers before, would want to talk things over. Such gentlemanly consideration would not last long, but while it did I dashed back to the hotel; I pretended to be interested in working on my book. I made new dates on the timeline. That way I would not be lying when I came back and said I had been working. I wanted to show her I did not feel threatened.

But I could not concentrate. I showered, dressed and went back. Running all the way through the steaming streets. I did not know which one I was more frantic to see and touch. I must get back before they forgot me. Is she convincing him to lose me fast? Is he telling her that I read *Vogue* cover to cover? Or worst of all possibilities: have they not even mentioned me? Too occupied . . . ?

When I came back, they were sleeping back to back on the bed. One thing I shall not do is ask him, or her, what happened while I was gone. Could it be I had made a resolution designed to avoid discomfort? Even for myself. Quickly I found something to be depressed about.

I did the dishes. Even in a *ménage à trois,* I would be the one.

Now Nadia came out and sat at the long worktable watching me. "Will you have some tea?" she asked. And I found the tea and boiled the water for us. We sat there. I felt as though I were being interviewed again and that she had made up a list of optimal, acceptable answers to the questions she fired at me. In her head (accounting, perhaps, for the colored flashes coming from her eyes), there was probably a panel of lights to indicate how I scored on each question. She made me feel so stupid, so sentimental, so confused. And so longing for her.

She swallowed the hot tea rapidly. In gulps. Smoked very fast. Jabbing out cigarettes, half lit. She did not stop asking me questions about my father and my hometown. It was not only to feed her intellectual concept. It was the glossy serpent— Hollywood—as fascinating a pushme/pullme to these existential animals as the Roman Church. I did not think an intellectual would be so anxious.

What was the panic I saw there in Nadia? Would she like to believe in magic? Yes please/no thanks.

Pushme/pullme. She does not want to be alone/She cannot wait for us to go.

I remembered how my mother always says I am self-involved and I made up my mind to ask Nadia about herself. "Have you ever wanted to photograph movies—I mean, films? In Hollywood. You'd be fantastic."

"Oh, I've done film work in London, Documentaries. But what a bore to go to California and live like a fool for two years and come back to this—as broke as one started? Hasn't anyone else observed what happens?"

"Well . . ." I started to say, then shrugged I was feeling jealous. I am never asked to do anything, even if it's something I don't want.

Suddenly she put down her teacup and looked at me. "We didn't make love, again. I would not do that."

"I know," I said. Her eyes missed nothing—trapping the

smugness of my suspicion before it could take cover. "It wouldn't matter— No—there isn't any right thing to say."

"I thought you might be thinking about that," she said, then, changing the subject, "Before you leave, remind me. There's this box of things Larry left with me. I brought it over just on the chance I'd remember to ship it. It's largely rubbish—letters. I don't think he knows. You might as well have it." I had not expected she would have remembered. She is also more thoughtful than she tries to appear. When Laurie awoke, he climbed a small ladder up to a kind of storage balcony and came down with a small cardboard carton. It was fascinating—because it was heavier than if it just held papers.

Nadia announced later that the exterminators were coming the next day with a sack "to exhume this entire estate," and "I," she said, "will be moving on in fifteen minutes for Czechoslovakia, so . . ."

It was time to go.

Picture me now in the rickety old elevator with Nadia. Laurie had gone down ahead of us with five or eight huge bags full of trash to put in cans on the street.

I didn't know what to say to Nadia. Her trenchcoat was so nattily belted, her cameras and shoulder cases slung at the right defiant angles.

"Wow," I said, "I've never been with a chick before. I mean, I really dig it."

This is the kind of remark one would have heard from sixteen-year-old boys who pet in packs, and there haven't even been sixteen-year-old boys like that since probably the August 1954 expiration date.

She didn't look at me. She sighed and stared at the elevator door, willing the car to go faster, willing the doors to open now. She walked out. "Look, I'll try to call you when I come back."

She was trying to figure out how to be firmly discouraging but not unkind. I know my crushes are like anvils, my love a sack of cement heaved against the stomach.

When I say I send you my love, step aside.

"So, that's Nadia," he said, holding his small cardboard carton in his arms. I watched her walk down the street, bag over shoulder, suitcase in hand.

For an instant I felt abandoned. Then suddenly I was more aware of Laurie than ever. He had accepted all of my selves. And not just to say so, not just theoretically, the way we had talked about it at Esalen. He understood all this, and not from a distance, and he would take all possible risks. Including the risk of introducing me to someone so powerful. Perhaps this was what I was supposed to see:

Her power.

I said to him, "She is not afraid of anything."

"Only," he said, "of giving up herself. Her privacy." He was right, of course. She had revealed much less, in fact, than she had captured in a photograph of a woman standing clothed in a shadowed room. She must, then, be deeply vulnerable, to have developed such a confident camouflage. It was for this—how she manages—that Laurie had brought me to her. I saw that now.

But, I wondered only, at that moment—when would she come back, and would she call, and what kind of present would she like me to bring her?

Laurie said ominously, "That is not something to spend time thinking about; Nadia turns up. Or not."

"Okay."

Not, he thought, was how it was likely to be.

He put his arm around me. Understanding. This is a specialty kind of love: when a person's husband helps the person handle a preoccupation she is going to have with his former wife. I would not say I had fallen in love with her. I did not know then that you could love more than one person without taking something away from one of them.

"Well, listen," I said, "I have to finish the book. Or find a place to live. Something like that . . ."

Laurie had been working for a month. The company not only returned some of his seniority to him, they also regarded the job as a transfer, so they would pay our moving expenses as well as hotel bills until we found an apartment. I began to be more selective in my hostility toward the military-industrial complex.

Every morning Laurie went out in one of his two new suits. He looked accustomed to prestige and position. He looked like the picture of his grandfather as a young man I found in that box Nadia had kept. A highly respected man; he had been a senator from a southwestern state.

"I did not know," I told Laurie, "you also come from former fame."

"Well," he said, "in this case it was my father who had to deal with it."

"You have something about you I admire. Resourcefulness. Teach me."

My projects came in threes, like dogs with saucer eyes, bears and wishes.

1. Find a place to live.
2. Track down schools.
3. Finish the book.

I have accomplished these things:

1. Connection.
2. Agents.
3. Depression.

We could begin with a day in the life of the depression:

It was the kind where you can walk for miles because you are too depressed to decide you have gone too far. At home, in such a depression, I would drive to Palm Springs by accident. Here I walked one day to Central Park. It was Spanish Connecticut: armadas of people rowed boats on the pond.

I sat on a bench, full of hate, across from a woman with a fine neck and one badly blackened eye. She was drinking from a bottle wrapped in a brown paper bag. Legs were swollen, with deep red sores. Old sneakers had no laces. Her hair was greasy and the handle of her purse had been replaced by a length of Ace bandaging, attached with safety pins. She was not much over forty. I felt I was looking in a mirror as I looked at her.

I had moved on now, walking along past a glass window on Sixth Avenue, going downtown again. I tried to adjust my stride, the angle of my shoulder bag. Have I got it the way Nadia does?

Perhaps she had already come back. I doubted it. I called. She had. Quickly I remembered she was interested in Valium.

"I'm on my way back from my connection," I said. "And since I go right past where you are," I lied, "I thought I could drop in."

"I think not," she said. "I'm working. What connection?"

"Oh. Speed. You know . . . want some?" An offer of diamonds.

"That's for teen-agers! You'll wreck yourself . . . and all that energy is terribly unbecoming."

"Nadia, I'm very interested in you, and it isn't easy to say that. I want to see you."

"Well, not now. But I'll call you."

"Sure," I said. "I want to be with you. Sort of. And I don't know what to say to you . . ."

"Listen, my dear, only in pornography are problems ever solved by sex. I seriously doubt if even sexual problems can be solved with sex. And you obscure things."

"But it's not just that. The sex. I like to listen to you." (Listen to her wither me?)

"I really can't talk right now. I have put some negatives into the bath."

"Perhaps we can develop those negatives into positives," I said. Stupid.

She sighed. "Look, I'll call you soon and we'll talk. All right?"

"All right."

Not all right.

Since I was on Sixth Avenue I wandered by to see a TV agent in the same agency as my literary agent. He said, the TV agent, that I throw away some mean one-liners and when I've made a name for myself, he can get me a lot of work.

On the way down the hall from his office to my book agent, I took one of these terrific new black capsules. I felt it coming on with a low steady climb. It was a come that did not arrive. I stopped at an empty desk and called Laurie, whispering, "Hey, listen, I am getting these incredible horns. Can I pick you up and we'll go to the hotel?"

He laughed. "Just hang on. I really can't get away right now." He always speaks so softly to me that even when he is hurrying, he does not sound brisk.

We agreed to meet later at the "86."

That was not a new plan. Only an alternative to meeting at the bar near his office where he drank with a group from work.

Now I wanted to say hello to my book agent.

"How's the book?" she asked.

"Book? Book? Oh yes, sensational, he's a very good writer," I said, trying to confuse her. She might think she had sent me someone else's book, perhaps. "But I think the ending kind of falls apart."

"You know what book I mean . . ." She was not in a mood for games. I never knew how to leave. Perhaps she suspected I was desperate.

"Well, I think I'll go back home now and finish this chapter . . ."

I went to see *Fantasia* again, on Fifty-seventh Street. A woman sat in front of me with her two small blond children. I started sniffling. She looked back and hustled her children down a few rows. How soft the children's little arms were when they touched her to ask a question.

There must be no more months without my children.

I was watching the movie the third time through—this sitting. I would be late. Laurie would perhaps be slightly worried. That was appealing.

"I've decided to get a motorcycle," I told Laurie, who was waiting for me at the "86." We were an excellent match because when I said I was sorry to be late, he said, "Oh no, no . . . just a few minutes." And didn't even look at his watch. I was certain he didn't know I was over two hours late.

Actually, I only felt comfortable in New York below Fourteenth Street. And most comfortable at the "86." It had a seedy door below the street level. You had to look hard to see the tarnished numbers "86" nailed to the door. If you looked even more carefully, you'd see a dull orange glow seeping through the barred window. Inside, rows of people hung heavily like sacks dumped up against each other for storage along the bar.

I remembered the first time Laurie brought me there—groom taking bride to meet the family. "Well, goddamn, hello Larry, how the hell are you?" said the bartender and then, to a semiconscious group at the other end of the bar who indicated curiosity, by a slight opening of the eyes, the bartender announced, "This man's the best goddamn poker player in the whole world." There had been a noticeable flicker of interest, a few waves at Laurie, before they got back to the business of pointing at empty glasses for refills. I had not known I had married a legend.

The bartenders of the "86" were gentlemen alcoholics whose tabs had run up high enough to warrant a little low-pressure employment. They were fringe members of the part of the Village, Laurie had explained to me, which ran on a kind of feudal system. Five or six extremely wealthy neurotics had organized informal fiefdoms, winning fealty from impoverished tenant alcoholics who would pay them honor, tend their egos and provide divers amusements.

It seemed an exceedingly decent arrangement. For instance, Marianne had been helpful to us until his job began. Marianne was one of the richest and mistress over many gourmets and several writers. She had greeted me that first time with a large hug and introduced me to Sandy. Marianne chortled, "When I was keeping Larry, I never did expect to keep the Eel on a short chain. But, my God, he had Sandy sleeping with him on my couch for six months—that's where they lived together. On the couch. Now, that's the first time I've ever heard of the house cat having its own pet. But you put up with anything from him. I suppose it's partly the way he smiles when he sleeps."

"Yes," I said. Ordered another drink and changed the subject.

"I am writing a difficult book." It didn't matter to her if it ever was finished or published. She appreciated the process. And she savored the quality of dependency—the aura of convalescence—writers have during the writing time.

"Have you found an apartment yet?" Marianne asked.

"Impossible," I said. "And to live without a yard. In a bunch of closets just sort of thrown together . . ."

"Why don't you try the Upper West Side? They have huge places up there. Fireplaces, high ceilings . . . and the loveliest paneling in New York City. And you do get more for your money."

"Because the Upper West Side smells like pot roast. All of it."

"I don't think you're really trying, now, Jill."

"I am. You can hear roaches running hunt breakfasts through the layers of newspaper real estate ads in our room. But apartments," I grumbled, "do not have space for possessions and people."

"Well, darling," said Marianne, "you don't worry about the possessions, anyway. What you're not wearing will be stolen."

A person down a few stools lifted her head, with much effort, off the bar at this point and said why hadn't I asked her, since she was the broker around here?

Ollie the Broker lumbered us off to an area near the Chelsea Hotel and laid before me possibilities in renovated brownstone houses, each one of which had a tree in the back of a species known as "plain." Just plain tree. Colored in that green of theirs. Children could live there. We signed up for this garden duplex at an amount of rent that turned out to be half of Laurie's monthly salary.

But with his poker games and the magazine assignments that I would have when people read my book which was almost finished . . . and the radio show I would certainly get . . .

"Don't worry," Laurie said, holding me tight. We sneaked into our new house without the key the way Ollie had showed us, and looked at the light from the windows of the Chelsea Hotel shining down just like moonlight on the nice dark oak floors, across the charming used brick fireplace wall. We noticed our tree cast a shadow like a giant hand. And we imagined the garden I would make in the brick yard. The pots of geraniums.

"This really is our first home!" I said to Laurie. "I know it's expensive, but you know, you have to aim high."

"Oh, it's not too bad," Laurie said. "Now, you just finish your book, and we'll have everything all ready when the children come."

So that was the house. Now school:

First I tried to locate children who could tell me what district they were in. And, incidentally, to give some advance information on how to be a child there. I ran after everyone who seemed to be or have a child. Imagine my delight when one day, out of the shimmer of the steaming heat, came a person of Emily's size. Oh, dear. I tried not to let my face fall. He was a dwarf, meticulously dressed in a well-cut pale linen suit.

"Excuse me, could you give me a quarter?" He was so gracious. "I'm a well-educated man," he continued, "but I'm a dwarf and can't get a job."

I saw a mother one day with a pale-faced girl walking primly by her side. I ran up to her, panting, "Excuse me, is that a child living in this area?"

The mother huddled the child to her side; they walked away on straight little legs, like llamas running.

Two boys were playing: riding around on each other's shoulders. Were they Wright's size?

"Are you boys, any of you, about ten?"

"You wanta fuck, lady . . . eh?"

School . . . I thought I would have to try another approach. Later.

I would go up to my room and lengthen the book. A less difficult process than finishing. Easier. No choices, on decisions. Write it all on out.

When our furniture arrived, it looked terrible. It would never distract the childern from the fact that there was no beach down the street and that Emily's room, it occurred to me slowly, had no window.

Jasper, who had arrived already, with his cats, was not deceived. This was not home. There was, for instance, that business of the leash.

Because I had been able to attract her attention in emergencies, I called my mother. (They—parents—had returned from Connecticut to their city apartment.) "I'm going to kill myself—there is no furniture! Only one untorn sheet for a family of four."

"Jill wants something," my mother said to my father.

"It's a disaster," she said on a survey of the house to see what I needed. "I'll have to tell your father. You used to be such a neat child."

"I don't want a lot." What I meant was "Just do everything for me."

"We are just people." What she meant was "I don't know where to begin with you any more."

"Mother . . ." When will I let her be who she is?

But I would never really know who she is, who he is. For I was seeing with these angry daughter's eyes.

My mother and I went to Bloomingdale's. I glared at myself in a mirror as she signed charge slips. A fantasy came through the mirror to me: I set up huge crosses on my parents' green, green landscape. I tie my parents up on them. My mother reminds me, "After we are gone, remember, no one is permitted to use your father's cross."

"I remember, Mother."

I am dancing about their crosses in my beaded moccasin snakes, slithering below with my fangs bared. The ungrateful child.

As she gave my address to send the things for the house, my mother said anxiously, "I hope your father likes this lamp."

I say, "It is for me, not for him." But you don't beat people over the head when they are trying to say "I love you."

Wright and Emily arrived with ten tiny field mice in a cage. One had died on the trip. Our first act in the city was to bury the mouse in the landscaping outside the JFK Airport.

The children loved their rooms. What my parents had not given us I bought with a real credit card. (East Coast credit bureaus didn't seem to check with the West. Then.) I shopped in the flush of the speed optimism. I knew we couldn't pay. And I knew in a couple of months they would take the card away.

Emily said, when she saw her room, "Mommy, it's just like a

child's room from *Vogue!*" And Wright liked his wood-burning fireplace.

But then they stood in the yard, so golden and healthy in that bleak, rust-colored space, eyes scaling the walls of the Chelsea Hotel looming behind our houses. "Oh, look, Mommy," said Emily, pointing to the ground. "A tiny balloon." Her eyes flashed at Wright, who giggled, but said, "Don't touch it."

"Ick to that!" Emily said, flicking the hideous little white thing over the fence. Chelsea confetti: condoms, roaches, dead ammies. We were awakened the next morning by shouts and barking. Jasper had learned to shoulder through the doors opening onto the yard, and he was out there with a boy and the boy's T-shirt between his jaws. Wright said "Hi." Emily scolded Jasper, who retreated under the glass table.

The boy, Herm, explained in pieced English (terrified at Jasper, who was using a low growl I'd never heard before) that he had come over to see the children. Jasper thought he was lying.

I did not think it was so terrific that he could just climb over the fence like that. By afternoon three women, one of them Herm's mother, presented themselves on the doorstep to tell me why legal action should be taken concerning my dog. I said the dog had really been in his own place and that the boy had climbed over our back fence. "But you know how kids are," I grinned. "Why don't you come in and have some coffee?" They sat very straight and sipped the coffee with discomfort.

I asked about the schools. "Oh," they said, they sent their children to private schools—they would not put their very own children in New York City public schools.

The main trouble we had with school was getting there on time. Wright was in intermediate, Emily in grammar school, and they were in kind of opposite driections.

At first I dropped the children off in cabs, making a wide circle from one school to the other, until it occurred to me that this would eventually cost more than private schools. California people don't take naturally to walking places.

y outrageous—people like that aren't allowed to be customers
ck home!"

We were whisked right to the security department. "Re-
pts?"

"Well, they were in the bags of course." I did happen to have
ouple of receipts to show. There were apologies, excuses that
sort of thing does happen in New York, but that they would
ertain to apprehend them . . . hopefully.

Of course, I insist you adjust my bill immediately . . ."

Of course, they couldn't do that. "Those items had been
hased, madam."

Do you mean to say that anyone can just walk in here and
off with customer's purchases—and I'm to pay for your
rity negligence?"

he children, sensing a tirade coming on, pleaded hunger
exhaustion.

we approached the Seventh Avenue downtown train I
o the kids, nourished with jelly doughnuts, hot dogs, orange
and crullers, "well, those are the risks you take. Nothing,
all, is for free."

we started getting on the train, a man in a uniform of
sort said, "Hey, lady, didn't you hear the announcement?
the uptown train . . . you'll have to wait. We're running
now, and we're running the uptown train here." Uptown
n downtown track. Yes, I could see how things were going

pping at night was also good because the later we got
the more likely it was that Laurie would be there. He
t eleven that night to say he was playing bridge in the
. At two in the morning he called to say he would be
the morning and not to worry. At six he called to say
ked up a razor and would go straight to work.

ven-thirty I knew we were embarked again upon a trib-
Outside now there was a slush storm and it was as cold
I could remember ever feeling in my life, when Wright

Laurie helped us get accustomed to moving on feet. He taught
us about buses and subways. We were slow learners. But he
would come home from his all-night bridge and poker sessions
in time to take at least one of the children to school. It was indeed fortunate that Laurie had these games—this source of
extra income—because the first time the rent check bounced he
was able to cover it quickly.

As for me, I could not visit the uptown because I was afraid
to pass by the offices of the magazines to which I owed articles.
One of which was called "Why I Send My Very Own Children
to New York City Public Schools."

There was, I had realized, no way to explain it in less than
three hundred pages.

It seemed there had been a day and a half of their big deal,
"Autumn in New York," and winter was on the second time the
rent check bounced. Eve, who owned the brownstone we lived
in, was a born New Yorker and accustomed therefore to catas-
trophe. She laughed nervously, more embarrassed than I was,
hating the role of landlady. Laurie's secretary said he was still
out at lunch at three-thirty when I called to scream at him.

Gone. I thought. He's gone.

I was just paranoid. He called me back at four as the children
and I were deciding which store to raid that evening to complete their winter wardrobes.

"Listen," Laurie said on the phone, "tell her to run it through again. A check I got from my game last week hadn't cleared; I'm certain that's what happened."

"Laurie"—there was veiled threat in my tone of voice—"I hear that bad theme music in my head. Like an Eduard Franz science-fiction movie. The thing is not dead."

"Richard Carlson movie," he said. "Now, don't worry . . ."

Gimbels, we decided finally, was ripe for a little hit. There wasn't much difference between Macy's or Gimbels, except Gimbels was a little more depressing, but they were both open late—we all liked to stay out. Me because it was harder to wait and wait for Laurie at home, the kids because I would get frantic waiting and waiting. And we could take the subway we understood: the Seventh Avenue IRT. There weren't many tricks to it, as long as you stayed on the local.

As we started out this afternoon after school, a huge black man with a face of anguish strode back and forth through the Penn Station/Macy's stop, crying, "Let me out!" Repeating, "Let me out!" There are many ways the New York desperation hits. Some people become charged up for success. Others use the big sense of urgency to fail faster.

The first shoplift had happened quite by accident. The salesperson had just packed the other things we had been looking at in the box. The second time I'd said, "I wonder what the store's going to give us this time," as I slithered my eyes quickly from side to side and whipped the inflatable basketball into my bag.

Never have three people gone so fast down escalators or been so hot with terror as we clutched each other in the subway car, sighing as it lurched us off. But Wright had a ball now, a lure for the street kids who played in the parking lot on Sunday.

As I said, we never discussed lifting; it was simply a matter of "What is the store giving us today?" To talk about it in advance would have been too frightening. Part of my informal lifting technique was to create confusion in each department; to make ourselves highly visible.

At Gimbels then, this evening of the second bouncing rent,

we bought some socks and a sweater on the cha
we tried on several things at once, right over
and sent salespeople looking for lots of things. "
from California," I said. "They need entire n
complained about the merchandise on one hand
how it was so marvelous that I'll-need-six-of-
other.

Emily and I were arguing about a purple
gold gypsy braiding—was it ideal for wint
school in Manhattan?—and Wright was tryi
because none of them were real Levi's. W
far was already stuffed into two large sho
corner. Legit stuff on top. Our other stuff
into the bottom. One of us, I've forgotten w
be keeping an eye on it.

When we'd finished fighting over these l
down the escalator. "Something's wrong," I
at each other and Emily clutched Wright'
Wright said, managing to dash up the dowr

He met us at the candy counter, whe
lounging, looking suave, popping chocolat
"They weren't there."

"What do you mean 'not there'?"

"I guess," Wright said, doubling over
been stolen. There must be shoplifters he

Emily started to laugh.

"Well, that's outrageous!" I was fur
store police!"

Emily said, "Mom, you can't."

Wright said, "Mom . . ." I was of
chortling behind me.

The floor manager did remember
coming back. "Oh, Mrs. Robinson,
maced. "Did you forget something?"

"We," I said, "were robbed. I shou

took Jasper to the door for his morning walk, Jasper looked at him as if he were insane. "He's not going out there, Mom."

"I don't blame him. Put some newspapers in the downstairs bathroom and we'll keep our fingers crossed."

The children and I argued about who would go around the corner and get the milk and cat food.

When I got back from getting the milk and cat food, I said, "We're not going out in that."

"What about school?" they asked merrily.

"It's too cold out there to think." No. I am where I am because no one ever made me go to school.

By eight-thirty I called his office. He was not there. Suspicions confirmed.

If the children don't go to school, I thought, I won't be left all alone to wonder if Laurie has run away again. I shouldn't have told him about the rent check on the phone yesterday. I should have waited—mentioned it next week. In bed, so he wouldn't notice.

What do they learn in school, anyway? About how things are.

But see. I can be more pessimistic than required. At eleven he called. We were all in bed. Me and kids. And animals.

"Laurie, darling—thank God. Listen, don't worry about the rent." It's better to be evicted than to give him guilt.

"Why don't you try to get some sleep?" he said. "You sound exhausted."

"I wasn't up all night playing bridge!"

"You were probably up all night worrying, and that's worse. More tiring."

"Well, the kids are home. It's too cold to go out." By noon they were bored and there was nothing to do. We had to get out.

So we went to see the new *Ape* movie.

Truancy and shoplifting. A model parent.

When we came home I made a fire in the fireplace and put the little hibachi in it, with marshmallows on bent-out wire hangers. I wrapped the children in afghans and went downstairs to get their warm flannels. But this is not, I thought, a terrible mother.

There was a half-written letter on Wright's desk. A letter to Berenger in California and Berenger's Pat.

Dear everyone, I miss you a lot and I wish I was back in California. It's cold and eicchy here. Jasper running around, Larry sleeping and mom nervice. My school's nice but I've been late a lot and my teachers are getting mad. I'll probably fail typing that's why I'm writing. A few days ago I went to a slot car place with my friend. He's not very good at sports, but that doesn't really matter out here . . .

You can tell a real Californian when New York is "out here." Like the man in the subway, we're all yelling "Let me out!" And although we can hear each other, we don't stop to help because we can't handle the distraction. We have to get where we are going. In New York the getting is the thing. I must explain that to Wright. "Darling, if we stop, we might realize we don't know where we're going." And grownups have to act as if they know. That's how they show they love you, by knowing more stuff; it makes you feel secure.

The children fell asleep in our bed. I attempted to write at or on my novel for about a half-hour. Or three hours; then I lay down on the bed next to the children and stared out the black window. What lives have we invented for these children? This city is not life. It is as cold and dead as this blind window that looks out only at another rectangular black eye.

I did not know I had fallen asleep until I woke up screaming. "Hello, darling." Laurie was sitting beside me. I was shivering from a nightmare. And I had amphetamine eyes: prismatic images flashing around the edges.

"What's the matter—a bad dream?" he asked.

"Where are the children?" I patted about the bed, looking for them.

"I put them downstairs in their rooms—I didn't want to wake you, sweetheart."

"You never do." He was always trying to get me to rest, to sleep. I walked to the window. The street was empty, silent in a dull dawn.

I sat silent, covering my wrists to keep from ripping out the veins with my teeth.

"It helps sometimes," he said. "To tell."

Because he knew enough about speed to suspect I was beginning to hallucinate, I did not tell him of the mirrored shards breaking in my eyes. But I told him the dream:

"I am married, but it is years ago and I have gone to visit a friend. She is telling me marriage is nothing but dishes to douches to diapers.

"And diaphragms, which we all wore then. And marriage was all that then, and I feel, with that closing-in sense of a nightmare coming on, that I must remove my diaphragm. I excuse myself, and pulling it out, I see it is full of the L's."

"The what, darling?"

I started crying again. "My children will be smashed like they were." I put my arms around his neck, and made him see the scene that had glided through my conscience almost all my life:

It is 1942. I am six. I am wearing corduroy overalls and my grandmother's flowered, veiled hat. My father's gardener has brought a load of grass cuttings through my play yard, to the service yard beyond.

I am running, chattering, after the gardener who resembles Gilbert Roland, a movie star who comes over to play tennis with my father on Sundays. I notice a garbage-can cover that has fallen into the wet gravel and I pick it up.

A silvery mass of lizards nestles in the center of the circle created by the garbage can lid. Frightened/curious. I pull back slowly; tiptoes, come closer to see if there are any babies. There are a lot of lizards, seven, nine, eight. Tangling together, squirming and gray with pearl-white bellies, some lolling on their backs with tiny, reaching claws. Something about the big ones slithering makes me scream. And I am thrilled by the sound of the scream. The gardener pays attention to me.

"Watch it, now!" he shouts and hoists a huge shovel into the air. My hands reach for his arms and freeze. Too late; I cannot stop him. Now my mouth is empty of sound. He slugs that shovel down, mashing them all to bits. Skin like silk slit to shreds. Orange and vermilion insides bursting out. Little eyes going blank dead. Little teeth in the pointed open jaws.

In a gesture of dismay, my stubbed fingertips bounce frantically against each other. Birds trying to get away. To get somewhere.

It was so hard to tell him. I had never even been able to say the word before. "I used to think," I told him, "that I was scared of L's—I mean lizards—because they were like snakes . . . the Freudian things. But it's the vulnerability I find so terrifying. I've only seen them in jeopardy: run over, eaten by cats, pounded to death. And the violence that comes to you when you are so vulnerable." I used to think I was terribly vulnerable. I was beginning to see that I was not always my own best victim. That was terrifying. I cried and held on to Laurie. My hands clenched like traps into his arms.

"Darling, I think you're a bit strung out," he said. "I think you ought to cut down a bit, darling."

"Laurie, no. You said you'd never try and rule me. Don't take away my speed. You will see you have married no one. Please . . ."

"No darling. I won't take it away, but you just be careful, a little cooler about it. I don't want to lose you."

Now he was holding me too tight.

"Don't put pressure on me, Laurie. I can handle it. And when the book is finished . . ."

"It will be an epic, darling, ten years in the writing, not to mention the rewrites." He said so softly, "Don't pull away from me; come, let me hold you."

"Oh, Jesus, Laurie." I pushed him back from me. "Fuck it, you're drunk." I cried harder.

"No, darling, I'm not."

"When you call me 'darling' every sentence, you're drunk." My mood switched like a devil's tail. "You pick on my scene so I won't notice yours. You spend your good awake hours everywhere else, and come to us when you're out of it. Checks bounce. Nothing's changed. Except where we live. And that's worse! I want to get my children out of here . . ."

He sat on the bed, removing his crumpled clothes, his shoes with the white salt marks from the frost-covered streets.

"Don't go to sleep now!" I yelled. "You'll drink coffee and you'll take a Dexedrine, but you'll hear me."

"I don't need any speed," he says. "Some coffee would be great. With a little brandy."

"You're destroying us by drinking and now you ask me right here for brandy. Am I crazy?" Shrew hands were on my hips.

"Okay," he said, "I won't bug you about the speed."

"That's different, anyway. It makes me function more—which one of us ought to do!" I made him his coffee, with brandy. And finished the bottle off by pouring the rest into my Coke.

When I handed him his coffee, he put it down and held my wrists. "Don't touch my wrists!" I screamed, pulling them back; he was looking at my hands.

"Listen to me"—I was shouting—"our things are stolen, the

streets are full of pain and filth and shit, the kids are scared—
and you don't do a fucking thing. You live as though we don't
exist. Jesus, Laurie, we hardly get a chance to make it any more.
I don't feel in love. I don't feel anything except terror. They
throw rocks at Jasper, and the kids are isolated. You don't know
how it is for them . . . you don't understand."

"I do," he sighed. "I really do. Darling, let's try to rest. Let
me make love to you. We'll talk about what to do in the morning. Later. Please." He kissed my forehead. "That head is sore
—do you want some Excedrin?" He looked puzzled.

"No. We'll talk now," I said.

He reached for me, I pulled away. When he is drunk he is
awkward. He hurts me. Everything hurts me. "It's no use," I
said. "All you understand is booze."

"Hey, come on," he said.

"I try to handle things. You just smile with your pretty face.
It isn't enough to look at you."

I ran downstairs and got Wright's letter.

"What are you doing, Mom?" he said, half asleep.

"Nothing. Fighting," I snapped.

"Yeah. I can hear. Don't yell at Laurie, Mom."

"I won't. Go to sleep."

I showed Laurie the letter. He handed it back to me. He sat in
the rocking chair, his elbows on his knees, his hands under his
jaw, his eyes looking nowhere.

I paced the floor in front of him like a prosecutor, whipping
around, my voice low and mean.

"You left your own kid," I said cruelly. "You never wanted
to be a father. You haven't a clue what's involved."

"I've tried," he said. He looked miserable. "I never want to
make our kids sad." And he started to cry. "I love these kids.
I'm sorry I don't have money. I do try." He was sobbing.

He tried to pull away when I went to hold him. "Laurie,
don't cry. It will work out." How could I do this? He is my
thoughtful, vulnerable child. The man-child. The man-child

I could keep forever. He probably doesn't even know how people live when they're good.

"Don't worry, Laurie, I'll try and get some bread so we can put Wright in an after-school sports program."

"I don't know," he said. "I don't know."

He looked so beat. I kneeled between his legs and put my head on his thigh. He stroked my hair with both hands. I must not lose control. He cannot handle trouble.

He nodded. "Yes, I'll take Wright to a game this weekend."

"Laurie, forgive me. It is going to be all right." (Does he hear there is a question to that?)

"Yes, it's going to—you may be just saying that, but this is my fourth try. I'm not going to let you go."

"I'm not going," I said. "Besides, where would I go?" I was too scared to go anywhere new, and everywhere I'd been they wouldn't take me back. We sort of laughed and held each other desperately tight. We were skidding out together.

It was now mid-December. One morning there was snow. For an hour Manhattan was looking good. Sun came slanting sideways into our yard and everything glittered. Like an old drunk, the city looked cleaned up; sores cooled, covered in soft fresh bandages.

Some days, it was true, I got the kids up so late that it seemed easier if we just skipped the effort it took to get to school. But the kids had not been too late for school today, and they had gone. I sat at my desk anxiously counting out pills. I did not have enough to get through the weekend. My connection said there was a new shipment coming in. ("Sorry, the electrician's out of town, ma'am, you can reach him this evening" was the message.) I'd learned to expect different approaches. ("No, we're not casting now; don't call us, we'll call you.") That meant they were hot; I'd get a message at some point with a new phone number.

Just knowing I was running out was bad enough to make me feel as though I was already crashing.

I had an hourly speed schedule, an intricate chart with drawings of tiny cars in the colors of the pill I had to take. There wouldn't be enough. My mouth was dry with panic. I mixed a screwdriver to calm down so I could sit at the typewriter and work.

There were twelve new well-filled pages lying on the floor when I heard a small sound downstairs. Not just Jasper, who spent most of his days under Wright's bed, from which vantage point he could watch the cat who, for her part, stayed guard over Emily's bathroom, where her collection of twenty-three field mice was living. On New York rents, you don't have mice on purpose. Mice with rooms of their own.

I think I'll just drop it.

The something downstairs was not alarming to Jasper, who greeted me at the foot of the stairs with a yawn and a stretch, and there was Wright snoring like a pony on his large bed.

"Hey, Wright, what are you doing home?" I shook him gently, ruffling his thick blond hair. "Wright, are you sick?" Stoned? Drugs? Those maniacs have got him hooked. Jesus god.

He opened his eyes. "Oh, hi, Mom. I'm not at school, I guess." He shrugged, blue eyes waiting to see if I thought that was funny.

"What have they put you on?" I looked at him anxiously. "I'll help you, it's not good for you—Jesus, you know I understand."

I didn't discuss my drug thing with the kids. But I felt subliminally—they knew.

"Mom, what are you talking about? I'd never go near drugs. Don't get so wound up! I just didn't go to school."

"But you did. You left."

"I came back. I left my window open and climbed over the wall. I hate it there, Mom. I'm not learning anything."

"Okay. I know. I saw that letter. I read it because if you didn't want me to, somehow you would have mailed it or hidden it, you know what I mean?"

"Yeah, I guess so."

"Can we talk to the principal?" I didn't know what to do. I shouldn't let him know that. "What do you want me to do?"

"Nothing, I guess. But at home I felt like someone. And we did more things. We had better friends. Hell, we had friends, period, Mom."

"Wright, darling. People are not someone because of what people think or how many people know them."

"But, Mom—you know—it was fun when you were on the PTA board and drawing pictures of me on the newsletter. Come on—you know what I mean."

"I know. You learned this from me, I'm afraid. And I don't know how to help you unlearn it. We can't go back." I just wanted to keep talking to try, at least, when the chips were down, to seem like a real mother. He was listening. But he wasn't any happier.

"Am I telling you things that feel right to you?"

"Not really," he said with half a grin.

"Well, maybe I'm too involved in the book." (Or not involved enough to finish it . . .)

"I know. When you finish that book, everything will be better. You're always finishing a book and you never do. It's like 'maybe' or 'pretty soon.' It means 'never.'"

"Okay, so I won't say I'm really doing it. I won't promise any more. But I will promise to see what we can work out at school.

Come, let's go get some pizza, and we'll take a taxi down to pick up Emily."

I will call his school Monday. If I can connect well enough, I can finish the book by then. It is so close now. While Wright waited for Emily, sweltering in his storm jacket in the over-heated hallway of the school, I called my connection on a public phone. Tonight. Nine-twenty. Precisely. Buoyant, I was really buoyant.

Then late-afternoon slump hit me and a feeling of stark panic. The kids were squabbling in my room. I sat at the type-writer in the living room.

"What do we have for dinner, Mom?" Wright called.

"I don't know. I'm working."

"Mom," Emily shouted, "could we have spaghetti?"

"We had it twice this week already, Emily. Listen, I'm work-ing."

"I'm so sorry," she says sarcastically.

"Emily, don't be such a pig," Wright said. "You interrupted her to begin with . . ."

A cat jumped up beside the typewriter. The other one sounded in heat. This one howled. I threw him down. The other jumped on it. My hands grabbed the typewriter to pick it up and smash it down on the cats. I gasped and grabbed them to hold them. Forgive my compulsion, Cats. Stay away from me. They defended with arms at attention, claws alerted. I flung them down. I must get out. These hands were flexing and un-flexing almost automatically with tension. I got up and wrapped my face in my muffler, putting on all the dreary winter clothes, slung my bag over my shoulder, slamming the door open. "I'm going to the market!" I shouted.

"Mom, did you walk Jasper?" Wright called.

"No," I screamed.

"You walk him," Emily ordered Wright.

"What about you, fatface?" suggested Wright.

I closed the door hard behind me and spent an hour and a half walking around the supermarket in a cold sweat. Staring.

No blink rate at all. Ideal shopper. I got all the messages. I almost belted a couple of shoppers who bumped me with their carts, and a checker who ground and cracked a wad of green gum and tapped a burgundy-polished nail against the counter. I came home with a *TV Guide* and ten packs of Doublemint. Laurie brought in cheeseburgers again. The kids continued their war through dinner. Emily switched her plate from the table to my desk and sat there alone, one perfect tear coming down her face. Her eyes army-green with fury.

I couldn't take it. To try to keep from screaming, I grated my fists behind my chair against the chic unfinished brick wall. I scraped the knuckles back and forth until the pain was soothing. "Listen, I've got to go out," I said in a low voice. "So cool it." If I took some more Ritalin I might calm down, but it would make my head feel funny. I could feel, when I took a couple, my brain sort of crawl away, as if prodded with a hot wire. And my supply was going faster than I had planned. I looked at my knuckles as they all got up—and sucked on the blood.

"Laurie, they're driving me crazy." I got up from the table.

Wright followed me. "Well, sometimes you drive us crazy . . ." They were always following me. We were now poised like animals, the kids and me, in the hall. Emily was looking at my hands.

"Everyone drives me crazy. All of you," I shouted. Laurie was to the right in the kitchen. He was getting out ice cubes. "Even you," I screamed at him, "with your goddamn drinks all the time. You don't say a thing. You just rattle ice cubes to show you're alive."

"Well, what about your goddamn pills?" Wright yelled.

"Don't scream at Mom," Emily shouted.

"You shut up," he said. She went for him.

Jasper started barking. The kids were yelling. I looked at the clock. I'd never get the pills on time. What if I couldn't leave? "I'm all trapped. Let me out of everywhere." I picked up a captain's chair and threw it down the length of the hall. It ricocheted against a wall and the frame split. I ran to get it,

to pick it up and tear it to pieces, to beat myself into unconscious-
ness. To get out of my life.

Jab this jagged post into my belly. Tear myself to shreds.
Split the skin like lizard skin, so the blood that runs as thick
as shit comes out.

Laurie moved so fast that I didn't see him, and now he
grabbed both my arms in his hands with a toughness I'd never
felt. Such fast, hard motion—was this Laurie gripping me? I
looked up. I was seeing a new expression. His eyes were angry.
I thought he was going to hit me. I loved the terror I had stirred
in him. This anger—so frightening because it came from him.
And so satisfying. I have such power, I see.

"Now," he said, pushing me into a chair hard. He held me
down. "Now, you just cut it out. You just stop it. That's
enough. And you"—he turned to the kids who stood frozen with
amazement—"get to bed now. I'll take care of your mother. You
just get ready and I'll be down to tuck you in, in a moment."

As he turned his head to watch the kids, I slipped out of the
chair.

"Where are you going?" he asked.

I sat back down.

"I have to finish my book this weekend."

"You told me you were going to cut down."

"I have."

He had wrapped ice cubes in a towel which he put on my
hands. Then he picked up the chair pieces and put them in a
corner. "It sure doesn't look like it."

"It's not that. Wright's playing hooky, and I'm scared. And
I'm crashing because I'm running out, so the dose is out of
sync. How would you feel if it was Saturday night, liquor
stores closed Sunday and you'd just finished the last booze in
the house? Think about it. I'm going."

I was halfway to the corner when I stopped pretending I
didn't know he had followed me, running, his coat half on, his

breath coming in puffs. "Jasper will watch the kids for a while. You're not going alone." He hailed a cab. "Where do I tell him to go?" he asked.

I gave him the address. Way uptown. Any other man would have hit me. Pulled me back into the house. Yelled. Or said, "The hell with this crap." It wasn't as if it was the first time. The trick, I think with the people who seem crazy or difficult at times, is not to react. Especially not on their terms. When people love each other, pride—battle points—must not count.

"Listen, Laurie. I didn't mean I'm hysterical because it's the last speed. Really, I meant when I get close to finishing a book, I get hysterical. That's all." The knitted gloves made my hands sting. I took them off.

"You don't have to get hysterical. That's all, too."

"Well, the kids, they just drive me bats when they fight. Why do they do that?" I was sucking on my hands.

"They're literally jumping out of their skins . . . they're both getting into pre-puberty, I suppose. And I suppose what they feel could be the beginnings of sexual tension. So they fight. But it's wrong for you to get in the middle. Or try to stop it. They have to work it out."

"I know." I was trying to work out how much the speed would cost this time. Connections don't take checks. Or credit cards. And Laurie must be running low on cash. He drank beer, not Scotch, with his cheeseburger. But I think: I don't like Laurie coming here. It is not his kind of crazy. "86" people have a sort of seedy cachet. Like old colonials. They like their peace and quiet. And no matter how drunk anyone is, if you misuse or mispronounce a word, you will be corrected at length. But I didn't really want to walk alone there at night. So I was glad he was with me. I held on tightly to his arm.

It looked worse at night. Half the windows on the buildings in the block had sheets of steel over them. "They remind me," Laurie said, "of the coins placed on the eyes of the dead."

As we walked up the four flights I rumpled his hair. "You

look like such a nark sometimes. Loosen your tie maybe . . ."
When we went to visit my parents, however, I straightened his
tie. And told him to comb his hair.

Rock music was playing, live and taped. The ceiling of the
old apartment was covered with flashing lights and a vast fake
rock garden slid along the floor and up one wall. A king-size
spring-and-mattress was occupied by a young kid who kept
scratching in his sleep. His hipbones stuck out like shelves. A
couple of others were fooling with a tape deck. On one wall
there was a large chart on which my connection, Dana, and
his friend, Mary, were working out a new system of numerology.
It claimed to predict success potential by adding together the
number of letters of your grandparents' names and dividing
by three.

"It's called heredity," Laurie said quietly. "You can do it
without numbers."

"I thought you'd be interested because it did have to do with
numbers and math and stuff," I said.

He just looked at me sort of over his shoulder. He gave
me the impression he thought he was slumming.

He didn't even take the red wine that was offered.

I went into conference with Dana. He was looking around
through his stuff. "Won't be any black beauties for a while now,"
he said. "Can you imagine, a guy got picked up with ten thousand of them the other day. Confiscated."

"There goes dinner," I said, snapping my fingers.

Black birds. Black bombers. One of the few truly great pills.
Sleeks Biphetamine 30's. Pure black capsules. Long and low.
"I need twelve a day to work, Dana. You know that. Jesus, I'll
be in real trouble."

Mary was saying to Laurie, "We've just gotten in some very
good methedrine, and if she'd only learn to shoot—it's distributed
more uniformly, also you can mix it with vitamins. That way
you can take a hundred and fifty milligrams of meth morning
and night and vitamin B12, lots of good things. You're not
popping pills all the time. It's easier on the body."

Dana was still looking for my spansules. I was getting anxious. I hoped he had not lied to me. Perhaps it was because I was late.

I looked at Mary. She had been a model, but as she was saying to Laurie, "I was sweating it for nothing. I was paranoid that the photographer would yell at me. You can shove work."

I wished she would keep her arms crossed. They looked as though they would break and the marrows would spill out clear as methedrine. I had a terrible feeling of pressure in my own blood vessels, in my own arms, and they didn't look like hers. I was staring, she saw, at her bruises. "If you bruise easy, I can teach you to find veins in other places. You practice on an orange."

"Jill doesn't go for needles," Laurie said, standing up.

"Suit yourself," she said.

He put his arm around my shoulder. "Ready?"

"Well," said Dana, "I've only got ten little ones. Red and tan's."

"Maroon and peach." I am precise about color. "That's not what you said."

"I told you what happened. I can let you have a couple of meth tabs." He handed me little white tablets. "Powder them up and mix a quarter in with one of the first morning spansules. That should pick you up." He added, to Laurie, "I've never known anyone with such a heavy habit to stay on pills." He shook his head. I was trying to decide if that was a compliment.

Like dieters and convalescents and other addicts, speed freaks spend a lot of time talking about new methods and systems, exchanging hints on crashing and coming down, and tips on getting the best highs.

"How much?" I asked.

"Oh . . ." Dana was scratching out some figures which we all knew was a put-on. He had figured out a price the minute he saw I was desperate.

"With the meth thrown in, I'll have to get fifty."

"Fifty! Dollars? I can't do that." I looked at Laurie.

"I've got thirty cash," he said. "That's all."

"No," I said, "this is my thing. You don't use your money. I have twenty. That's enough."

"Thirty-five," said Dana. "That's it. I'll let you know," he said to me, "when we've got something new."

"Right," said Laurie, handing him neatly folded bills. Putting my hand with my money back in my purse. "Happy Mother's Day, or something," he said, handing me the little envelope of pills.

"I can't get by on this." I was afraid I would cry.

Dana shrugged. "Best I can do right now."

"Really," Mary said as we were leaving, "you'd do a lot better shooting." I clutched my arms. I could almost hear the clicking of a slide machine in my head as the images flashed through: shot; doctor; pain; needles; lizards. I closed my eyes.

He was silent as we walked through the dark side street to a cross street. The wind was freezing. It hurt to breathe. I had to stop. I couldn't walk fast in the cold.

I clasped my arms tightly. "I've got to stop being so scared of shots. It's just self-destructive . . . absolutely irrational."

Laurie had his hands shoved into the pockets of the old reversible raincoat my father gave him; he feels like my father in this coat: mad at me. But also safe, on this black, deserted street where the shadows were guaranteed to be full of horror. I sneaked one of the meths out of the envelope carefully. Hard to do with sore hands. Carefully, carefully, I rubbed my front tooth across the edge, rubbing off just a tiny bit to drop on down to my tongue. Then I licked it back down my throat.

He made me tea when we got home. "I think I'll have some coffee, too . . . later," I said, peeling off the nail-hardening polish I hoped would strengthen my nails so I would stop finding edges on them to bite off. The one knuckle that really was bleeding was doing it again.

"No," he said, "tea has plenty of caffeine. That's enough." He gave me the towel I had left on the floor. With more ice.

He walked about a bit, sat down and lit a cigarette. I wanted him to go to bed so I could prowl around, doing this and that, on my own, getting into my working rhythm.

"What do you think about the shot idea?" I asked when he sat on the couch again.

"Not a hell of a lot," he said. "But it doesn't matter because you're not going back there."

"What are you telling me?"

"You've had enough speed now. You're going off. I'll help you get that book together this weekend. I'll keep the kids out of your hair, but after Monday there will be no more speed."

"That's very hard, Laurie." I was chilled and started to cry. I could feel it. "I told you I'll cool it a bit, but I can't just stop. You know that. I'll get fat and dull. Gail Sheehy said I was when she interviewed me after my first book. Fat. Right on the front page of the old *Tribune*. I'll lose all my sex interest . . . everything. You didn't know me when I was off it once. I was terrible. I skipped around in dirndls. I had no wit. Laurie, I'll wheeze. You won't be able to get to sleep from the wheezing." I was pacing around the room, clutching my arms. He was just sitting there, hand in front of his jaw. "You're programming my reconstruction. But what are you going to do when I won't get up? My last withdrawal I was in bed with a coma for a month."

"Three days. You told me," he said.

"Four days. It seemed like a year." I looked at the broken chair. A cat cowering near Jasper in the corner. My hands.

"And how can I work if I have that hanging over my head?"

"You've had it hanging over your head for months and you know it; you've been just putting it off and now we've all had enough. I don't like that place or those people; I don't like this violence." He looked at my hands. And the chair. (I'm glad he did not see me throw the cat. He is very into cats.) "And it's no good now for the kids. Listen, Jill," he said and opened his arms, wanting me to come sit next to him, so I did. I couldn't go anywhere. "You wanted me to go with you. Somehow you set it up to happen like this. The chair. Then running out—but you were waiting there—you knew I'd follow. You just need confirmation. So here it is."

"Yeah. I guess it's time." I sat down. I felt as though my body were already drained away.

"It's such a goddamn great drug. And I love it so much. I need it so much. I'm so frightened."

He held my head tightly against him; I tried to pull away a bit. I felt smothered and I felt caught. "We love you. We don't want to lose you."

"I'm not dying." Why was he so frightened? "You're lucky," I said bitterly. "At least your thing is legal. You don't have to overdo it out of the sheer terror they're going to ban it or un-invent it tomorrow."

I finished the book. I executed the heroine and cried as I wrote "The End" at six thirty-eight that morning. Then "The End" looked pretentious. I X-ed it out. Wrote "30," then added scrolls. I was putting glitter on the scrolls when Laurie came in with tea and some scrambled eggs.

"Don't touch . . . don't touch." I edged the last forty-two pages over to him. "My perimeters all hurt," I said. "Oh, Laurie."

He had taken the kids on excursions, and play equipment had stealthily been brought up and down the steps from their rooms. He'd brought me cheeseburgers and milk shakes, leaving them on the desk, kissing the top of my head and splitting. The speed had been singing through. Hardly a lavish amount, it felt like luxury because it was the last speed in my world.

It wasn't bad to finish that damn book. I asked Laurie to type over the last page and leave off everything, just putting a couple of asterisks or something.

"Well," I said to him, "since everyone's got to have something, now, I guess, you'll have to teach me to drink like the big kids."

"Foiled again," I said, when the therapist at St. Vincent's clinic said the antidepressant he would give me to help cover the withdrawal would not work with booze. I had gone there because I remembered when I was looking under "P" in the phone book for "Public Schools," I had seen "Psychiatric Clinic." I'd had an idea I should keep it in mind.

"It will only make things worse," this kid doctor was saying. "It's a bad idea to drink on Milleril."

"I did the first time when I went off under Tofranil and Milleril and stuff."

"Well, you shouldn't have."

"How long will I be on?"

"I don't know. After two weeks we'll switch to Stelazine; then, after a few months, we'll see how we're doing."

"Months! Nothing. No beer. That's crazy."

"That's how it is."

"Sort of two for the price of one. Withdrawals."

"Maybe." He had a sly and evil grin, this young doctor. I think he had talked to Laurie. I didn't care. I felt, finally, drained and almost relieved.

"You'll see . . ." It was half-hearted, the argument. But I can't simply cooperate. "You'll all see. I will be so fucking boring. So depressed. So terrible, you will go running together arm and arm to my connection—far be it from me to tell you where it is—but you'll know I'm right. No more radio star, no more

TV person, no more writer. End of story. Maybe there's a little basket-weaving department you have here, you could work me in. I studied that the last time. Actually they thought I should knit. But I screwed up this piece of wool so badly . . ."

I started weeping quietly. Then hysterically. He just sat there in his white coat taking notes.

"How are you feeling?"

"What do you mean, how am I feeling? I'm hysterical. But you have to have me tell you so you can write down that her perceptions still are relatively accurate. Have you noticed how I'm tearing at my nails? Shall I hold out my hands for you to see the shaking? Would that be good? Well, let's see . . . where did I put them?"

My hands.

I will not go into a hospital to withdraw this time. What happens—after the Milleril begins to take effect—appears to be primarily a lot of heavy sleeping, clear improvement over my recent behavior. Under the sleeping is the panic, but it doesn't show to onlookers, except at the beginning.

That first night Laurie sat up with me, waiting for the sleep to begin. I am made of fear. Afraid to bite my nail for I might rip it from its plate of flesh. I paced about, tramping back and forth like a mad animal, throwing myself here and there, falling onto our bed, tearing at my hair, beating my hands against the brick wall behind the bed. Laurie sat on the edge. I grabbed at him, trying to find handles to hang on to.

"Hold me!" I cried, and he covered me then with his whole body, clasping me hard and tight.

Then: "Get away," I screamed, "I want to get out of here. You're smothering me."

I am a rubber chicken from a joke store, empty thing—to take by the neck, to pound and pound against the wall until it is dead.

"Kill me." I grabbed his back, biting like an animal at his neck. Sucking at it desperately. "Don't leave me, don't leave me alone."

The nonspecific feeling of terror ricocheted from one fear to another. My insides were coiled to pounce out.

"Shhh . . . shhh," he said.

"Jordan is dying," I sobbed.

Jordan breathed speed. "Jordan died the last time, too." Then I was quiet.

He brought me a cup of soup. Suddenly I pitched it onto the floor.

"You hate that part of me," I shouted. "You said you accept everything, but you don't—you're just like everyone else. You want me to be good and sweet and soft. Oh, fuck softness, man —I want to be someone! You don't think I really mean it, do you?" I yelled at him, "You think I'm just being a bad something, a no one."

I meant "child," but could not think of the word. I saw images of small people. I cannot connect them with the word.

"You don't think it's funny. You hate me. When I go down dead on that bed you will go away." The crying wouldn't stop.

"Jill." He cleaned up the soup. For an instant I thought how patient he was, then that thought was ripped away. He would be a good chambermaid to beat. I saw red welts across his haunches. I watched him. How busy he was being to keep from feeling helpless.

I was falling away from him. God, how fantastic it had been when I went back on that first time: the first quarter bite of the speed gum hit, and I said to myself, "Well, hello, there you are again!"

If they can go to the moon, why can't these fucking doctors make a speed that stays—just a thing to get around good on?

"Why did it have to go bad?" I cried. "I fail even addiction. I fail even breathing. I'm falling away from myself. Oh, Jordan," I cried. As if for a dead lover.

One of the first movies I remember was *Green Dolphin Street*. In it the sweet-faced star, Donna Reed, is trying to escape from a sudden tidal flood that's engulfed the beach she's been walking on. She climbs up through a rocky tunnel. Her hands are bloody—they claw and stretch up over the rocks as she fights up to a small space of light. I feel the waves lapping up at me, the foam hissing at my ankles, my knees. I can't scream: I must put all my strength into staying with the fight. Into the climb-out. There were gentle nuns waiting for Donna Reed. There are no gentle nuns waiting for me. I watched my struggle. Like when I had asthma—before speed—when it was bad, I'm trying to scream in the snow, but my lungs and chest and throat are packed up tight.

I was clutching to stay above. Someone was helping me, rocking me on a boat. Safely drifting out, I came back up out of the sleep pit and he was rocking me with his body, covering me light as a summer comforter, and he was holding on strong with each of his hands clasped onto each of mine, his legs around my legs. "There, baby—there, now . . ." he was crooning to me softly. A Gestalt game—he had learned from Esalen. Recognition did not lessen the impact.

Mother-man-baby-man. How can he be all such things? "Hold me, Laurie, hold me."

"Yes, my baby, I won't ever let go. I'll hold you all our lives."

He blew softly on my face now, so cool. And held me so warm against the chills.

The book was accepted. I stayed awake through my editor's phone call, until he mentioned there were, however, four chapters he was sending back for a rewrite. I kept nodding off. He had to repeat himself.

"Jill—those four chapters just don't work."

"Four chapters? I'll look for them—oh, you're sending them back for a rewrite. What's the subject of the book again?" On speed I felt as you do when you're feeling well. Off speed I felt the way people say they feel when they are "coming down with something—a cold." My eyes did not see, it seemed, as sharply. My head felt full of lint. My limbs felt heavy and dull.

"Sure," I said to my editor, "I've got the time. I'll call you right back and let you know." To dial the Time Signal was a challenge for my ingenuity. I had to avoid telling him I can't write without speed. I couldn't even think. And I directed my limited attention span to the children, who were going to California for Christmas, to visit Berenger and wife. I conducted all preparations from the armchair. The soul of docility.

Would we all enjoy pizza again for dinner, Emily wondered, with a quick lick of the chops. "Not again," said Wright, knowing pizza it would be, although it could be take-home bought cheeseburgers. I had burned them once, trying to heat them up. I peeled carrots in bed. And frozen vegetables had made their appearance in the house.

"I am under a spell," I said to one of Emily's friends who

looked at me sideways to see how I would look when I was not lying down. The morning before the children left, Emily woke me to tell me a dream. I took her with me into the depths of the red armchair. She held on to my neck; she feels so full of shape in her flannel nightgown; heaven would be sleeping through the years with Emily curved in warm beside me, my arms around her, her head tucked up under my chin. "I dreamed," she said, "there were two little Fiats parked outside Grandfather's house and they were painted gold. One of them gets stolen by a man. And while I'm watching," she continued, "I'm holding a box with two kittens which have coats just like the little shelty dogs you like and then I look down and one of the kittens is gone, too."

"What do you think about that?" I asked her. I wondered if the man was her father or her grandfather. Was she afraid somehow of going to California? Fiat. Had she heard the word used in a legal connection? We were divorced when she was so young—it must be hard for her to disassociate her father from lawyers. Maybe that was it. She and Wright were legal tender. But it would be so good for the children to have a little sun. They were looking almost like New York children now. So pale from the cold.

"It's probably about growing up," I suggested when she said she really didn't know what the dream was about, "that kittens have to grow up, too." Perhaps, I thought, it was about Wright switching generations, suddenly, going into adolescence while Emily remained in childhood. I didn't know whether to tell her that. Sometimes you feel it's better to say nothing rather than the wrong thing. I felt especially fragile with the children right now. I wanted to tell them to observe closely how I was and not ever to be like that.

We took the children to the airport. They were wearing stolen coats, and shoes that were not paid for. I stood there crying, of course.

"I shouldn't—send you off for a holiday like this. With tears. I always say that to you and I always cry."

Wright said, "Then, Mom, just stop crying, okay?"
I never change. How I hate everything, every bit of my self.

When Laurie went to work and I was home alone, I remembered I needed distractions. I tried to focus for a moment on what it was my editor had said. All communications had seemed like vague dreams. Yes: he said extensive revisions were still required on four chapters which he was returning to me. That had been a few days or weeks ago.

I stayed all through the holidays in the red chair when I was not reading very slowly, very carefully. Absorbing little. I pondered whether to call my editor. But he would be busy now. Everyone out there had friends and parties to go to. Such an excellent season for self-pity.

Four chapters to rewrite—mailmen have invitations and gifts to deliver to other people. No time for chapters.

Christmas. I slept through it. But I had a new bag Laurie gave me. Handmade. I crawled back into the red chair, squinting at the bag, trying to remember what my clothes looked like and how this bag would go with them. Once every morning Jasper and I went down into the children's rooms and fixed up or neatened just one thing. Then we napped.

On two afternoons I called my editor's secretary to say, "Isn't it funny I haven't gotten those chapters back yet? When did you mail them?" She remembered who I was each time, which is such a kind thing to do for someone like me. "Yes," she told me again, "the chapters have been sent. We're rather afraid they may be lost."

I had mentioned to my editor that I didn't have a copy.

To be sure, if the chapters had been sent by registered mail, they wouldn't be lost. I would like to mention to him that I am not a writer any more now, so it will be a big problem if those chapters are lost. Perhaps we can just have blank pages, since it is a political satire. And stamp CENSORED on them. I will have to think over whether that is a funny idea. I don't want him to know I am not crazy, just dull.

I could handle calls to the children's schools concerning

post-holiday opening schedules. There seemed to be some half-days involved. And some hangups with the hot lunches. It was amazing how much reorientation these eastern educational people needed after their holidays. One would think they spent their Christmases speeding.

I had to study up on the children's routines quickly. We were to meet their plane in two days now.

The phone rang. That would be my editor's secretary calling back to say she had traced the chapters through the post office.

"Everything is fine," she would say. "In fact, they won't even need rewriting now; they mellowed, we feel, rather well during the postal experience." In signing off she would add, "Sorry to hear you can't write—it's a terrible loss, you know . . ."

Even though I was under the impression I had already picked it up, the phone was still ringing. It was not my editor's secretary.

"Hello, Jill," said Pat, Berenger's wife calling from California. "Hi." She was bright-eyed and bushy-tailed today—even I could tell. "Happy Christmas?" she asked.

"Fine, fine," I said, borrowing responses heavily from Laurie until I learned some of my own. Was, I wondered, one of my children ill? A change of reservations?

"Hey," she said. "Listen, we've decided it's better for the kids to live out here with us, okay? Just wanted to let you know they won't be on that plane."

She was saving us a trip to the airport.

"I'll have to call you back on that," I said, using the tone of someone who has to check out availability of house seats or a particular car a Hertz customer has in mind.

"Oh, sure, no hurry." She sounded relieved. She would probably say to Berenger, "She took it very well. I was quite surprised."

I hung up the phone, and then came such a scream that Jasper galloped to my side. Such a rush of adrenalin from what I felt must have been a reserve pocket of speed beads somewhere that suddenly burst into action as blood poured through and my heart pumped and I called Laurie.

"Mr. Robinson is aways from his desk at the moment," she said, "Can I—"

I hung up and called my father. "You have to buy me a plane ticket to L.A. They're trying to take away the kids. Help me."

I went to my father's apartment to pick up the check for the ticket.

"Oh, I love your green suit," my mother said wistfully, looking at my father.

I was wearing a navy-blue jeans suit.

"You should have worn something trim," my father sighed. "Correct. To show them."

"Your father hates women in pants," said my mother.

That's why I had taken off the green suit with the skirt and put on the jeans before I left my house.

"Well, I thought I'd just get there," I said. Defensive: "I'm not applying for their approval."

"How dare they!" said my mother. "Who do they think you are!" Berenger, unhappily, knew only too well who I was.

"I talked to Wright on the phone," my father said. "He does want to stay in California, but you talk to him—see what you think. How much he's been influenced . . . He's very determined, you know—very determined."

"There's nothing to think," my mother said. "They're your children. They belong with you. They'll grow up idiots out there. Your whole trouble was being raised out there."

"Thanks," I said. I was numb again with Stelazine, So I couldn't overreact, as usual, to every word they said.

Before the plane left, I called Laurie. He was in his office. "Actually they wanted me, I think, to be wearing black and pearls—does that mean this is a situation to be avoided?"

"No," he said. "And the children don't expect black and pearls. It's only important to keep in mind who you are going to see—what they need."

"Well," I said, snuffling, trying not to start crying, "I hate flying, too. Are we ever going to fly somewhere together—ever when it's not a disaster? But that doesn't count, Laurie. I think they really may need different things. I think he may need Berenger's kind of order—Wright just may be more comfortable with that kind of discipline."

I didn't want to say "security." I didn't want to say "his real father." But Laurie said it.

"I think . . . he's coming into adolescence—he may need his own father."

I stopped myself from saying, "What about *your* son?"

"But I think it's a terrible thing to separate the children."

"Traditionally—" Laurie said, "but I think they'd love it. It wouldn't be bad for either of them. The individual sense of identity is hard to have, I think. It's always 'the kids.' I think they hate that."

I put a nickel in the phone to fend off the operator. I saw passengers assembling at the flight gate. Nuns. I saw nuns, for good fortune. Nuns, Linda Goodman had told me, will cancel out the prevalence of dark clothing, which is never a terrific omen on a flight.

"It's not ideal to separate them, but mainly because it's not traditional," Laurie said. He had said it now three times. He'd had too many drinks for lunch. Hell.

"Well, Laurie, just don't do anything—I mean, be where I can find you, please. You don't know—they may not even let me have Emily."

"I think they'll have to. Now, don't fret. And call me tonight. Darling, I know . . ."

"I know you know . . ."

What else was there to say?

On the plane I thought that I had been thinking traditionally. On certain subjects it was still difficult to separate my opinions from my parents' opinions. Even though their opinions came from a different place. A different world.

I am the traditional bad mother. The traditional punishment is to take her children away.

No: the children, by being removed from one who uses them at once as target and weapon (however unconsciously) are being protected and saved.

Yes, Berenger was rescuing his children and was to be commended. Disarm this woman.

I would have been grateful, perhaps, if it weren't for visions of Pat in triumph, visions of my parents' horror. The last twist of the ungrateful child's knife in their honorable, estimable bellies.

But I only saw the children running on the beach with animals. (Jasper—yes, this was no place for him, either. They would get custody of Jasper as well. And perhaps he would, in return for the sunshine, just once, give a little puncture wound with his teeth into Pat's ankles . . .)

And I saw the children in spacious, sunny classrooms, surrounded by lawns.

I saw them . . . there.

I remembered what Laurie had told me once about his own child. I thought it was a cop-out. And I hadn't really heard what he was saying.

How understanding changes. You take the same pieces—
like bits of glass in a kaleidoscope, and with a small turn, there
is a different picture:

It is shortly after Laurie came to live with me. We are talking
on the patio. He shows me a picture of a small child.

"She was very young—nineteen, twenty. I married her after
my first marriage fell apart without thinking very clearly. She
wanted a different life than I could give her. Dancing. Uphol-
stered furniture. Order. We tried for two years. I am not, you
know, good at confrontations. So I left her.

"Her family had a lot of lawyers. They employed lawyers the
way Californians buy cars. They traded them in the moment
they suspected they were not getting enough mileage for their
money. Anyway, they kept finding me. Having me arrested. She
would explain it was for my own good. She really did believe
she loved me."

I understand that girl already. But I do not say so.

"One night, after we filed for divorce, she found me—I kept
living in new places, but she found me—and she said she
wanted me. She was always so attractive to me—it was late . . .
I was, of course, drunk.

"The only thing I really didn't like was when she said that
even if I was married or in love with someone else, she would
always come and sleep with me any time I wanted her to."

I don't ask why he did not like what she said because I was
busy thinking how I would have done the same thing she did
and made the same offer to him. I hate all his women because
they did not make him happy. And I adore them because they
let him go, so I can have him. And because from what I have
seen and heard of them, they are all something like me. (Except
Nadia of course. And every comparison can always correctly in-
clude the words "Except Nadia.")

"Then six weeks later she found me to tell me, 'It worked. I'm
pregnant. Now you'll have to come back to give your child a

father.' So I even tried that. But I had not intended to be a father and to continue this marriage would be a lie a child could see and hate.

"I left her. Oh, they found me, a lot of lawyers, her father, her brothers and cops, the night the baby was born. They broke down my door and my two cats almost got out. I was just standing there, naked, holding on to my cats. And thinking I was the only sane one in the room because I knew that the best thing for my child would be for them to forget they knew me."

I feel sad—the way he said "My child." But I say, "Laurie, I'm glad you didn't go back because I wouldn't have you, but I think you're precisely a wonderful father because you don't try to be Authority, to play the role, and because you are wise enough to ask those questions."

"But," he says, "when I say the same thing to you, you disagree. Maybe it's okay here, now, because the kids see an agreement between us that is secure and comforting in itself. But with her—there wouldn't have been that. And it was easier for the baby to get used to someone she could get along with—without being torn. I did not see that I could give a child much of a life. That was when I went to London. It had seemed, at first, far enough.

So, on the plane, now flying back to where I had started from, I thought that the best thing I could give my children was a clean new life, a life of less complexity. Berenger—even that woman he married—were well programmed as parents. They would definitely get a license, if there were such things.

The transcontinental jet flight is a condensed metaphor of the escapist's Geographical Change. One starts out with the gorgeous hope that the self one abhors can be left behind. Three thousands miles is a powerful distance; such speed, such height should get you away before that self can catch up.

I could hear Nadia gagging at the tatty little melodrama I suspected was flickering around in my head somewhere, carrying a miserable string shopping bag. But I would like her to believe I have made my first intellectual decision, although, as she had pointed out once, no self-respecting intellectual would ever apply the description to herself. Or her activities.

But this was a decision based upon reason, after all. Not emotion. We could give up the brownstone. Save money. Or go all the way to hell without taking two remarkable young people with us.

Love (today—in this time zone at least): When you love enough to know the best thing for them is not only not you but may well be someone you detest—and when you not only know it, but make that concession, and really let them go.

But then. The plane landed. And I was three thousands miles away from the Land of Intellect.

I wanted my kids. That was all.

I tore through the mess of people in tourist, elbowing the businessmen in first class.

"This is an emergency—they're taking away my kids," I said.

My friend the lawyer was waiting there as I got off. She ran after me, trying to catch up as I dashed through the airport parking lot until she grabbed me, reminding me that since it was her car and she had parked it, I didn't even know where I was going.

"Now, there are many different courses of action to consider," she said soothingly.

"One." I stamped my foot and pounded the dashboard of her car. "Just one. Getting my children right now. Nothing to consider. Drive!"

Lawyers are trained to have patience. That's why they speak and listen in the precise manner of people who open presents slowly. Lawyer said Berenger had called her. He had not reached his own attorney yet— however.

"However, what?"

"Okay," she said, "they feel it would only upset the children if you see them this evening; they want you to wait until the custody papers have been drawn and signed."

"Blackmail. No papers. I'm coming with police."

"Just be patient now. We have to take these things step by step."

"I will see my children tonight. Or—no. There is no 'or.' "

I felt for an instant that she was going to argue, and then she shrugged and drove me to Berenger's house.

Feelings: There was an interview in the *New York Times* with a rancher about his cows. He told the reporter how the small calves are raised in terms of expenses and how much you have to get for their bodies in order to make a living for yourself. "But," he says, "you can almost get sentimental about these little fellers. Did you know," the rancher tells the reporter, "the mothers can tell their own calves in a herd of a thousand or more, and did'ja know," the rancher continues, "that when we separate them calves into the shipping corrals, the mothers stand outside there, standing by that fence shrieking and bellowing in sounds you ain't ever heard no cow make. As if they know what's happening. And sometimes they'll stay there for a week or more without eating, nothing. Some of them, their throats get raw from that bellowing. Time comes you have to drive those mother cows away from there or they'll likely starve themselves to death."

Berenger and Pat knew I was coming. Lawyer had stopped to phone them and tell them. Come I may, but I would not see the children.

So they said.

I heard the sound of the baseball/football TV game that is Berenger's theme song before I went into the house. "Hello," Pat said. "Would you like some coffee, dear?"

I looked around, cool, making a frost with my eyes, hands dangerously hidden in pockets, a gangster. I was Richard Widmark. "Just don't call me 'dear' any more, okay? Where are my children?"

Oh! Teeth, point: Go into her neck!

I could barely resist tempting Berenger to rage so I could go for him, kick in his TV ball game, shatter the glass and set his hair on fire.

The tension—this patronizing good behavior: "Of course," Pat said, "you may see the children."

"*My* children. What the hell do you mean 'may'?"

"But we wanted to clear up a few things, and you know how they are—well, we've got them cleaning up a bit. They get so messy out here, with the beach sand, surfing and the mud in the garden and all the animals, you know, and they were out riding the neighbor's horses . . ."

Yes, I knew how nice it was here. And I might be a bankrupt person from a chill and barren city, but these are my children.

"I'll just go to them now," I said, eying the door that would lead to the children's bedroom wing if this house followed most suburban home plans.

She said, stepping quickly in front of me, "I think we have to settle this first."

I will not become hysterical. I will not give her that.

"Give me my children," I said again in a new voice I had borrowed from one of the cow mothers. Inside I am cheering: Hey, notice how you have instincts! These are instincts. This is not that formal, mournful child: tradition. Instinct is a lusty born child—

Now came what seemed to be a row of mmmmm's trammeling up from my gut, rumbling along like letters drummed out on an electric typewriter, like the x's just stamped out in a murderous row crossing out everything in their path. I leaped around her, as behind me I heard Berenger say in a voice a mouse could not hear, "Children, your mother is here," and I was through the door and they were running into my arms. Emily was crying and clinging, and Wright hugged me. But it was a partway hug. I felt it. They had gotten to him. They had laid on the guilt, the conflict, choices—that's where it was: choices. But then he came back to me and hugged me real as I held my arms out for him, and I bundled both of them close, on my knees, crying with whooping sounds, and I felt how he, Berenger, looked at me. I didn't need to see with eyes the contempt of his expression: Dirty bird I am to him. Smarmy.

"Listen," I said to him, the father, "you just planted them. I grew these babies. I fed them in my body, with my body. They are my people and you don't do this to people's mothers."

I was allowed then to sit and speak with the children in the room they had and Emily said she wanted to come back with me. Wright, however, refused to go back.

He was so sad. I hated how he had had to make this kind of choice so young. I hated what drove him to it. "Mom, it was kind of my idea, I didn't mean to make things bad for you, though. I just want to be with my dad." I wanted to reach my son, to get him to feel I could and did understand—that he must split because he had to. To save himself. I thought he had become an adult in a way I never had: he had learned what he needed to do for his own self.

Now I must let him go without the guilt wagon.

I thought of Emily's dream: Golden cars. Gilt wagons. Are these what we build our children into?

"Wright," I said to him, holding both his hands, "I hate it—but I think it is a wise choice you have made." His hands had a new roughness now. There was a young-manhood texture in his skin. I touched his shoulder. It was more sculpted. Sinews were coming here. Unfamiliar territory. Forbidden. But his cheeks were round. And soft as a duckling's wing. For how long, I wondered? I could not think that question. Would those boy cheeks have changed to man jaws when I saw him next?

I had spoken to Laurie once during the two-day trip. All I did was cry collect. I tried to call him again, but the voice said our number was temporarily out of service. The bill had not been paid.

I did not call his office in case he would not be there, which would have been too much to think about. He had been under a lot of pressure lately. Enough to drive anyone to drink. And the time I talked to him he had sounded as through he was already there . . .

Although Berenger tried, he could not prevent me from leaving with Emily. Legally, because I had custody—or, I supposed (grudgingly), for the same reasons I would not force Wright to come with me.

But when I flew off with Emily, I clutched her so tightly to me she could not breathe. I did not take my eyes off her. I would not fail this child as I had failed Wright. I had forgotten completely that without speed I could not stay awake for more than an hour at a time.

"Ambition is destruction, only competence matters," I told Emily as we dragged the typewriter out of the camp trunk where I had put it when we came home. I had been determined to concentrate on Emily. Not fame. But waiting for me was a message from my editor. The four chapters had been lost in the mail, after all.

With the rage that provides mock speed, I knocked out—from memory—four chapters to replace the lost ones. Then we rearranged rooms so that Laurie and I slept in Wright's room downstairs, near Emily.

Laurie said, "And you can always write upstairs in our old room."

"I don't do that any more. You forget . . ."

"You wrote those chapters."

"Don't reason with me."

I put the typewriter back into the camp trunk and locked it. Then I put the trunk key in the spaghetti pot.

"You know," I said to Laurie one night, "Emily must have felt a terrible ambivalence . . . wanting to come with me but feeling rejected because Berenger did not fight as hard for her. She must feel very confused."

"I think you can talk that over with her," he said, "and I also think Emily will work it out better than we have because we don't pretend to know too many answers."

Actually it was Emily who often had answers:

Emily and I had decided to make a garden and so we were in the back lifting bricks out of sand.

"Emily," I said, "I feel so isolated. I don't know where to begin."

We had pulled up seventy-hundred bricks and we now have a gray sandpile and a dustier dog than usual.

Maybe Nadia was in town. She would have an idea—I went inside and called. She was in London, her friend said. She would be coming to New York, perhaps, in a week. More or less. "One never knows," he said. I have heard that before.

"I think you need friends your own age. You always had friends in California," Emily said. Now she was walking around, helping me arrange the bricks into a little wall, indicating where we might put pansies—a border of dwarf marigolds "like we had at home." We always say "at home."

"I know, but there aren't any here. I can't seem to find them." Friends at the "86" were not what I meant. I must have been talking about contacts.

"When I said exactly that same thing about not having anyone, you made me have a party."

"But you had people to invite—kids you go to school with. Darling, don't pay any attention. Everything will work out, really. In spring we'll be able to go to the park . . ." We'll be living in the park. I thought it was not just contacts. I needed a job. Laurie couldn't manage alone. And I couldn't write.

"You do know people to start out with," Emily insisted. "You just get them to bring friends." That's what you made me do, and I'll help you."

I did have a friend: a practicing writer who knew everyone.

"Listen," I said to her on the phone, "I'll have this party if you'll bring the friends."

We were in the middle of the party: Emily and I had been cooking all night. Laurie was bartending. Nadia had returned and was here. (Although with some reluctance.) My friend had come with a set of guests that moved like the crowd scenes in early U.P.A. animated films: as a unit.

In one thrust they conquered a couch and a corner like a street gang and, indeed, they slouched, looking warily at the outsiders as they talked nervously, clearly distracted and on guard. Laurie's friends from work hung out in another corner— after a couple of attempts to talk to the gang had been put down.

As for the host, he was smashed. My friend who had brought The Writers said to me, "My God, he's really cute—like the boys we used to want to go to dances with and they would never ask us—but, Jill, people like us don't marry people like Larry Robinson."

I thought it was a compliment, but I decided to think about it more in a year or two when I would be off Stelazine.

Nadia, who was her own gang, had been observing from yet another corner. She put things in a way I comprehended immediately. "This," she said, coming up to the open counter of the kitchen, "is the first time I've ever seen Larry drunk. Do you give him vitamins? He's never looked drunk before."

"No. What kind of vitamins?" I felt accused, as though she had given me something in perfectly good condition and I'd wrecked it. I wiped my face with a lettuce leaf instead of a dishtowel.

"Look, I'm hardly a registered pharmacist. How would I know?"

"Well, I just thought— Actually, he's really tired. He's been working very hard." (And playing cards even harder.)

And his back has been badly broken out for some time. Vitamins. I will get some tomorrow. All that I can find. Or perhaps I will ask my young therapist. That is a better approach. Look how I am considering better approaches.

Emily returned to the kitchen with a report that we should throw dressing on the other bale of salad. And put another vat of water on for the sixth batch of noodles. Oh yes. "And what," she asked, "was the key to my camp trunk doing in the spaghetti pot?"

"Flavoring," I said. "A Russian Jewish trick."

Nadia: My eyes turned on her like a searchlight all night, searching for her to like me. She was watching a group of women writers: wolf eying lambs. Novelists, journalists, a poet —they were, I thought, not quite allied with the couch gang. I didn't know when they had arrived. It was exciting to be in my house.

I was thinking of pointing out that I had written a couple of books . . . saying, the way I tried to at birthday parties, that I knew how to play games. But you don't say you know how to play—you just go up and get in it. Announcements give rise to suspicions. I would have to go tell Laurie my envy was operative again.

I heard, as Emily pressed more garlic and I mixed more butter in the noodles, talk of such things as grants and awards, agents, galleys and paperback deals.

"I miss something," I said to no one.

Emily patted me. "Tsk," she said.

The women writers reminded me of women I knew in my twenties.

Then we stood about in our various nurturing phases: anxiety of the early nursing of someone into the housebreaking stage. An occasional sibling rivalry to be discussed. (Oh, you're getting a full-page ad—really?) How you want that baby (book) to be born and how your body mourns when it leaves. The sound like a dove in your heart when it goes off to nursrey school, and the letting-go must begin. And. What do you feel? Oh, the urge to be pregnant again. I stood there like a dummy, with my wooden spoon in my hand, watching the real writers, and I thought of how it was to have a book in the belly.

Would the longing creep up on me in the dark, would I turn to my lover, Electra (for Electra is the name of my typewriter): "Fuck me." Or, actually, I would become the lover and make my typewriter pregnant. (It's easier than trying to make her come. Sex without speed is simply a pause for affection.)

I ran to Laurie and held him. "I'm having an analogy. Or something," I whispered. He held me around the waist and kissed me. I wanted to call it a robust, winy kiss. But it was a drunk's kiss. Nadia was right. It was different now. His smell was different. His eyes seemed to whirl around in spirals. You expected to see red, white and blue sparks come out like from those old sparkler toys.

This was no time to think of another book/baby.

So I looked at the women, eating, talking books, such accredited women, hearing the heartbeat of the book in the night, waking them for pages—a kick of a phrase to be scratched down on a pad next to the bed. "But you have your book coming out darling, and it's a nice book," Laurie said.

I looked at him. "Stillborn." I shook my head. I ran now to help Emily gather up the plates, to ask Nadia if I could get her some more of anything—run down to the corner for a dish of Beluga caviar, if she'd like, or truffles to eat like grapes . . .

I offered coffee to a writer who was great with book. "Another chapter sold last week to *The New Yorker*," she was saying.

"You're still working on that one?" A gargantuan labor. A young writer said, "I've only been working on this one three months." She is nauseated, queasy . . . afraid to talk or walk too much or go too far away from her notes, for fear of miscarriage.

Someone sneaked up behind me and whispered in the voice one uses when one expects sad news, "Weren't you writing a book?" They had already heard the book is stillborn (although, horror beyond cruelty, I must carry it full term). My agent, the midwife, had reported, at a cocktail party, that (sotto voce) it's a Monster. "No, I had an abortion. It's gone. How do you take your coffee?"

We thought, anyway, that it was a nice party for three hundred dollars. "What!" cried the denizens of the "86" who expected not to be invited to certain parties, like poor relatives who always want to hear about them, anyway, because it makes their feeling of deprivation more justifiable.

"Three hundred dollars . . . what did you have? Potato chips?"

When I woke up the morning after the party, I found this poem taped to the bathroom mirror.

ESCARGOT D'AMERICA

Last night, walking in the moonlight
In the yard behind my house,
I came upon my neighbor's son
Lying naked beneath a bush.
He glowed from the tracks that snails leave,
Dashed lines, like a chart in a butcher shop.
I gently bore him through the gap in the hedge,
Hoping they had snails in the garden next door, too.

—Robinson

It is pretending to be a political poem. But it is a poem about guilt.

The letters my boys leave around.

I held Laurie and told him how sad and beautiful his poem was.

I looked at him. How sad he was. Not so cute right now.

Someone must be in charge. This time the someone is me.

Everyone has a subliminal nickname for a lover. That is Laurie's for me. It just slipped out one night.

I learned to like chirpy little old Fuckbucket. A sort of used-up wench who, nevertheless, gets on with it when it needs to be gotten on with.

So, I remembered what Lennie Godfather had said about putting on my black and pearls and going to Saks. Some writers make a living from writing. And some writers don't. Especially when they write what a person can't read and only do it on alternate Thursdays.

So I saw in the paper that Gimbels was selling midi-skirts for $13.99. In black. And I found the pearls my godfather gave me when I got into college. "Someone," he had said, "should go to college in your family."

And I bought the midi-skirt. "Don't wrap it," I said, "I'll wear it here . . ." I put on the pearls, with my black sweater. I went to Saks and got myself a job.

In the sales training school, my sample sales slips were very neat, although it was suggested I work on my speed. "Yes, that is something of a problem here, I'll work on it."

Laurie was so proud of me that he took Emily and me out for dinner after my first day "on the floor," as they call it when you're out there pushing rags. Dinner cost a day's salary, but I couldn't cook, anyway, because my feet hurt. I was reminded of "The Little Mermaid." How the witch described the pain of growing legs instead of a tail. Legs to stand on.

I was on the fifth floor in Designer Dresses. It could have been Hosiery, mind you. And I was, after all, the only Commie-hippie I knew who could have a sex flush over the set of a Norell collar.

Primarily, there was an order to our lives. Emily went to school on time. At first Laurie, too, seemed to respond to my routine. Plunging down the steps, hand in hand, in what we called the Mole's Charge, we took the same subway, and he was early for work every morning.

It was appalling that by having a schedule imposed upon me, I could influence everyone else. But any alarming sensations of power it gave me were obliterated the moment I walked into the employees' locker room and prepared to go on the floor.

Possibly even more than your first lover, you remember your first customer. Mine: She pulled a leopard-printed raincoat off a mannequin and whipped it around her, executing a terrific variety of lunges, leaps and other exercises at her mirror image. She slapped at her stomach, did flipping things around her collar and wound up in a sort of neck-wrap position with her arms, where, for a minute, I thought she was strangling herself. After this little demonstration of how the coat moved, or how she could play D'Artagnan, she turned to me and demanded, "Well, is it me?"

I was standing in the approved posture for younger sales personnel, hands held modestly behind the back, hair pulled into a tiny bow, feet together. I nodded meekly. "Oh yes, madam, it's very cute. Very."

"Cute!" she bellowed to an escort consisting of a sort of daughter-in-law type, a friend, and a possible niece or sister. "Did you hear that? What the hell kind of word is that—'cute' —for a Donald Brooks raincoat?"

I lowered my head, eyes on the floor. "Forgive me, madam, I'm new. I meant to say the coat is very striking."

"I'll take it!" she said, triumphant.

She stood there. "Well?" she demanded, hands on hips.

"Is this a charge, madam, and will you be taking it?"

"Yes, it's a charge," she said, "but I won't be taking it. I'm sending it to my sister's house, where I am staying."

"Charge to one; send to another. Oh." The most complex sales slip to write. I had to recheck all my carbons to see that each was in its right place so all the receipts for all the separate tallies and reports would come out properly. I asked, "Well— may I have your card?"

"I don't have a card," she sniffed, looking to her associate shoppers for verification that this was indeed the stupidest salesperson ever encountered in any allegedly high-class store.

"Well, oh—I think I'll have to ask the service manager what we do, then . . ."

"I'm from Cleveland, you know," she said, assuming that was either impressive or self-explanatory.

"Well," I said, "I'm just from here." I grabbed hold of Fitzgerald-the-Fearless, fastest dress pusher on the floor, who followed through absorbing an enormous amount of static about "that dumb kid."

I hobbled into the women employees' rest room to take off my shoes, to have a cigarette and to feel very sorry for myself.

Presently Fitzgerald came in. "You've got to learn to hustle a little, that's all. Chin up."

"No. I like just watching, really."

"Listen, kid—we'll get the same lunch hour next week, and we'll practice, okay? you've got to think of your record. You can do it. I've been keeping my eye on you; you've got a good head on those little shoulders."

Fitzgerald was a parody: I watched how she went after customers. She'd wink over her shoulder at me, and hunch herself together like a tackle going in hard, then screech to a halt at a customer's side. "Listen," she'd say into Customer's ear, "I just got in a new de la Renta. Not everyone can carry it, but I saw you coming and said to myself, 'You gotta hang on to that dress because it's got that woman's name on it.' Come on." By then Customer would be whipping out her charge plate . . .

No one seemed to take what I was doing seriously except Wright.

When I told him on the phone, he said, "Gee, Mom, you're not a salesgirl." He knew how sad it was. Symbol of failure. Such sacrifice.

My mother, for instance, laughed.

Emily and I usually made dinner together. Such unrelieved times she had. Came home, with keys around her neck, walked Jasper, sort of did her homework. All alone. I destroyed her options by presuming my own as an adult could be as limitless as they had been when I was a child.

Maybe when you have children you have to fall in love selectively. By God, I would teach Emily priorities, not birdsong and stardust. I believed that until my feet stopped hurting at night, when I got into bed.

Birdsong-and-Stardust had not taken a shower in God knows how long.

Lying next to him was like lying in a bunch of towels left over from someone else's alcohol rub. He felt clammy, and when he tried to make love he was so out of it he pulled hairs; his nails were jagged. He scratched me.

"Stop it! Stop it! I can't stand you like this!"

"What, darling?"

"You're so fucking drunk!"

"No, darling, I'm not . . . It's just that you don't drink now, so you notice it."

"Damn it, Laurie—don't they notice at work? Doesn't anyone else tell you?"

He slumped back against the wall. His pillow fell down to the floor. I wished we had a headboard. No. Those things don't matter. I have lost my sense of perspective in the store.

"No," he said, "I don't drink at work. I just had some drinks this evening because one of the guys, Dick, you know, we wanted to talk over a project . . ." He was like a kid explaining.

"Laurie, don't. Don't let me grill you." And I kept on doing it. "Are you taking your vitamins—do you eat protein for lunch?"

"Don't worry." He put his head on my shoulder. He is more hangdog, these days; it's not that romantic sadness. When he came to Saks, I tidied him up. Like shaping up a mannequin. Who am I trying to impress, for why?

"Laurie"—I clutched at him—"no matter what happens, just don't leave me alone. Just don't leave me alone."

My sales tally was bad. And I talked more customers out of dresses than into.

Fitzgerald cornered me. She told me, "You think this is how anyone started? I had a damn happy marriage. My husband died and I have four sons to put through college . . . Two are almost through. Kid, you want to make it—well, the way you do, I figure, is whatever you got to do, today, you do it the best you can. You look at every day as just a practice for the big time, and if you don't make it, at least you can look back and say you did a good job."

That, I learned, was Fitzgerald's word about how love goes. You do what you have to—and not as a martyr, for then everyone is miserable, including the people you say you're doing it for because you love them.

I asked one of the ladies where she got these shoes I can't stand. She swears by them for people whose feet hurt. So I got the shoes. And sold dresses.

Being good makes my teeth hurt.

After a few months I was called one day to Center Desk.

"We certainly hope this is not a personal call, Miss Robinson."

"Oh, no . . . I don't have any persons—"

"Hello, is this Jill Robinson?"

"Yes," I whispered.

"Hi—my God, have I been trying to find you!"

"What . . . madam, if there's been a mistake, an alteration can be—"

"No"—the voice laughed—"I'm a friend of Nickies' over at *Cosmo*. I have a small ad agency—she told you, I'm sure. She showed me some of your tear sheets and said you wanted a job."

Yes. Months ago. I had never expected to hear from them, but I had not, of course, forgotten. Every rejection is engraved—

"Well, I've been trying to find you, for two weeks! What the hell are you doing at Saks Fifth Avenue? Have you ever written fashion copy? Never mind; of course you can. I've got a job for you."

"Now?"

"Any time you can start."

"I'll get my coat and say goodbye to a friend."

Fitzgerald said, "Well, kid, what did I tell you?" There were tears in her eyes. "And you aren't going to stop here. I'm going to watch for you and, you believe it, I'm going to be seeing you on television one of these days. Now, don't you let anything, or anyone, get in your way. You're one who's going to make it."

FUCKBUCKET HITS THE BIG TIME

Madison Avenue. Terrazzo floors. My very own office. Triple the salary.

And I had been writing copy as cool as you please, turning

it out for a few weeks now, when I had a call from a Mr. Erwin.

"Whoops," I said to Sally Receptionist, "that could be something uncool, a creditor." I was cleaning up bills—when I could find them. Many, it turned out, had been garnisheeing Laurie's salary. He didn't tell me. Bloomie's did, when I called to make a payment. A dollar and a half I was ready to give them.

"Let me see," Sally Receptionist said, "what I can find out." She buzzed again, laughing. "He says he's not dunning you, that he's a friend of your husband's and that he's cool, but that it is kind of an emergency." She switched over the call.

"Hi," I said.

"Hi. You met me, Richard Erwin, remember?"

"Oh, of course—right." I had met him. He looked like Ravi Shankar, and he spoke great wisdoms, which he attributed to his grandmother in Tennessee.

"My grandmother tells me we should get together."

I had left Laurie at home with a cold this morning. "What's going on, Richard?"

Then I froze. What else could it be: "He's drinking too much —not showing up. Right?"

I'd known Laurie had been coming in late. I was taking a different subway now, and half the time Laurie wasn't even up when I left. But I had this tentative feeling about my work, about myself, that I was, in some way, on probation. If I let down for a moment, if I allowed myself fifteen minutes leeway, I'd go all the way down. So I wasn't able now to chivvy Laurie along in the mornings.

"Listen, can we have lunch?" There was urgency in Richard's voice.

"Now. Right now," I said. And I sped out, noting nevertheless, it sure beat Saks, where you were put on report to your manager for leaving five minutes early.

Goals change: To take off my shoes in the john just for five minutes had been a kind of goal. It only seemed maudlin now.

But I remembered that then it had seemed very real indeed, although its importance had surprised me even at the time.

I loved this job. I loved being asked to meetings. I loved it for me and for Emily whom I could send to private school. I loved this job with a kind of ferocity. I would not let him or worrying about him fuck this up.

Richard looked very unhappy. And it was not just the meditative look I remembered.

"Jill, we all do a bit of drinking; he's not among teetotalers, but he's got a problem, and they've noticed. Which doesn't mean anything except he's going to have to get some help . . . he probably should get dried out and get into therapy. The company pays for all that. I've heard it's an excellent program. Of course, we have to figure out a way to get him to want to. None of that works unless he's motivated."

"But why would they do all that? For him."

"Because he's damn good. And even if he wasn't brilliant, it happens to be part of their policy. They fix. They don't fire."

"He won't go. I know. We tried that." And I told Richard as much of Laurie's history as I could.

"Well, darlin', they're going to put it to him, that it's either/or. I think he knows that, and that's why he hasn't showed up."

"But he's home. He's got a bad cold. I mean, it's real today."

"That may be. But then he ought to call in. He's been starting late, leaving early, and with long lunches—you know. It just doesn't look good. And then," Richard said, "not to come in for two days without calling . . ."

"But he's only been home today. Oh God! Two other days?"

He had probably been just sitting at the "86."

My jaw felt like the Tin Man's in Oz. The hinge would squeak if I talked.

"You just stay here," Richard said. "I'll try him at home again."

"He was asleep when I left," I said. "He won't answer because he doesn't hear the phone when he's sleeping. Damn him."

I called my office and explained my husband was ill and I had to get him to a doctor. Then I went home. Laurie was lying in our bed. It had rained hard in the morning—a summer thunderburst—and as usual, the water had collected on the floor of our room. It was like going through a lagoon; the small fake Persian rugs from Lamston's floating like barges.

His breathing sounded heavy.

I leaped over the water onto the bed, landing on my knees beside him. He stirred, and automatically, he reached out his arms and put them around me. He wasn't really unshaven because he had faked going to work and coming home the two days before by dressing and shaving. So he did not seem completely seedy.

I thought of the young-looking drunk on Seventh Avenue who reminded me of Laurie: he had a new scar, a new bruise every day. And there were times when he was gone for weeks— to return with new bandages. His old pants hung down and showed a sore, white backside. His toes were black and purple.

You don't notice such drunks unless there is an alcoholic in your family, and then their faces come at you like punchy previews of coming attractions.

"Don't feel too well . . . How are you, love?" he mumbled.

"I'm okay. I know you don't feel well," I said. "Listen, Richard Erwin is very worried about you. Why did you fake going in yesterday and the day before—Laurie? Let me help you. If you don't feel well enough to work, then at least, darling, see a doctor."

Richard and I had decided it would be good for Laurie to feel we were concerned only that he was ill; we should not try to approach him on the whole drinking issue at this point. First, the point was to get him to a doctor. From the restaurant I'd made an appointment for him with an internist Richard recommended.

I had told the doctor, "I think he is an alcoholic, so please give him those tests, but don't scare him. I think it's primarily that he has a bad cold, but he ought to have some tests."

"Laurie," I told him now, wiping the 100-proof sweat off his face with a corner of the sheet, "I've made an appointment with a doctor. So you'll go."

"I don't like doctors. I've just got a bad cold; it's going away."

"I know." I looked at his back; the sores were worse. The antibiotic ointment had not helped. The new vitamins I bought from a health-food store didn't seem to be helping either. Megadoses of B vitamins and niacinamide. Calcium magnesium for nerves. Why aren't they helping? He sat on the edge of the bed smoking, feet wading in the watery floor. My dear boy. I put my arms around him.

"Laurie, I love you so much. I want you to feel better."

"I know, darling. Can I have some coffee?"

We weren't saying much: "I love you" wasn't much just to say. Once we had both talked to the doctor, we would know Laurie had to give up drinking.

But Laurie would not listen.

Laurie was too much of a maverick. I had to think of something.

I dropped Laurie in a cab at the doctor's office. I had to get back to work. Saks' mentality still operative to the extent that I expected to be yelled at.

"Call me as soon as you're done," I told him. "Please . . . I wish I could go in with you." I did, and I would have, except for worrying about my job. And there was the beaten look he had these days. It seemed a very precious thing to give him pride and dignity wherever possible. To take himself, for instance, to the doctor.

When he didn't return home that first night, I called Richard to see if he had been to his office. Then I kept calling Richard at home. He and his wife, Joanne came over and we went out for dinner with Emily. Richard said, "Don't you worry—we'll find him."

"Not if he doesn't want to be found. And I think this is it. Somehow."

We placed an emergency call to the doctor that night. Laurie had been there. Yes, he seemed to be in bad shape. Tests had been taken.

"What did you tell him?" I asked. "Was he scared?"

"No, I didn't want to scare him, but look, Mrs. Robinson, he's feeling pretty sick—he's bound to know he's in trouble."

We would have the test results in a couple of days.

"Well, you let us worry . . . now." I knew Richard was telling me that I had to consider my priorities. This time I would. I had Emily to consider and this job. And I had learned now that maintaining a routine is the best way to hold on. I wondered how much of my cool was from that, and how much from the Stelazine. If worst came to worst, I could go on to a higher dosage. I'd already called my own doctor and checked. Knowing I could made it easier not to.

Emily would go to day camp as soon as school ended; then to a real camp by the sea. I was glad I had already paid for that. I could not have afforded to if I'd thought I might be trying to live on my salary. I could not now be sure what would happen.

That first night I didn't allow such thoughts to go places. Emily and the animals crawled into the big bed with me. She said, "Don't worry." And we held each other tight. The house seemed twice as big and empty without Laurie—a kind of absence that was immediately different than when he was simply out.

I went to work. Emily went to school. We went through the morning like mechanical dolls.

I had called the doctor's office right away. It was his day at the hospital, the nurse said. He would get back to me later. No, she did not have the test results yet.

I had to do something new that afternoon—go to a client with

Ann, one of the agency's owners. She was slick, cool and polished, tall, with silver streaked, dark hair pulled back into a long braid, always perfectly coiled into a chignon. She ate up sidewalks without even seeming to walk. I had to go into a fast trot to keep up.

She talked the fast New York jargon, too. No sentiment. No time-wasting. She made the day brisk. There would be no time for me to cry, to fall apart. I felt that the more I worked, the more I had to do the easier it would get. If each day could go by—the next one would go a little faster.

"Things going well?" she asked.

"Fabulous, I love it."

"Dynamite," she said.

That night Laurie's doctor called. "The liver is very bad, Mrs. Robinson, dear, and . . ."

I listened, folding into myself like a night flower.

I called Richard. "He's dying, Richard . . ."

Richard and Joanne came right over. I explained that according to the doctor, Laurie was not, for one thing, able to absorb any vitamins. That explained the cracks in his mouth, the look of his eyes, and the sores on his back. If he did not stop drinking, he would die. It was that simple and this soon: a month or two, at the most.

"Well," Richard said, "we're going to find him, and when we do, there won't be any choice. You'll commit him. And that will be that."

"Yes," I said. "To hell with his dignity. I want him alive. Please find him. Will the company get detectives . . . should we do that?"

"I don't think we do that yet. My feeling is that he'll come back. He can't have much money. He didn't pick up his check this week . . . I looked into that."

"Oh, money's no problem with him. That's why his cronies call him The Eel. He plays cards. His checks bounce. He borrows. If he stayed with another chick, I don't think I would even be jealous, because he'd just do it for convenience."

"You've checked with all his friends in the Village?"

"Oh, yes. He knows where I'd go first . . ."

The "86" was on alert. And I had even called Nadia, more, I think, for sympathy of any kind than out of conviction that he would be there, of course. She knew that, too.

"Maybe we ought to case a few places, anyway. You know, they tend to stick together."

So, Joanne, a medical school instructor, stayed with Emily, explaining to her various new techniques that might apply to animals, and happily inspecting the pet mice for flaws Emily might have missed. Richard and I combed the Village.

"I give up," I said.

"I think we have to wait a day or two," Richard said, "and then we'll put out an alert."

I began to feel I might be running down. I sat in my office the next day trying to work and thinking of him lying somewhere. I could not keep out the image of him—sick, perhaps unconscious, perhaps he had fallen or passed out and been mugged, and perhaps . . . Stop it.

"Laurie"—I concentrated all my will, all my thoughts, all my force onto, into his head—"Laurie, please let us help. Laurie, come home, come home."

I couldn't handle it. I put my head on my desk and just shook with crying and the fear and the grimmest sense of hopelessness.

Ann walked in saying, "Listen, would you come up with some names for— What's the matter? My God . . ."

"It's no use," I said. "I didn't want to involve personal problems in my work. I know that's not right. But it's just so bad."

She sat down and leaned forward, her elbows on my desk. "What's so bad? Hey, listen, we're all people. We all have problems. Tell me; I may be able to help."

"My husband is dying. He's an alcoholic. And I can't find him to put him in a hospital . . ."

"Now, wait. First, it's not your problem to find him. You can't help him unless he's ready to help himself. I know something about this. My aunt was A.A. She lived with me until she died last year in an accident. I went through everything you have—the bills, the blackouts, the disappearances, the sickness. Now, do you know about Alanon?"

Ann did not look as though she would have permitted chaos in her life. Or even knew about such things. Her life seemed too chic for public problem-solving places such as Alanon. One thought of Fifth Avenue doctors. Hospitals perhaps somewhere in the Southwest that looked like dude ranches.

"Yes, I've heard of it—for the relatives of alcoholics."

"There's a meeting tonight. I'm not going, but I have a close friend—you'll meet her there. If you want to, that is."

"Yes, of course. Thank you." I knew that this exchange—my need, her competent help—put me in a different light somehow. There would be less leverage, less professional regard; even people who have had trouble—or, perhaps, *especially*—don't quite trust the reformed and recycled.

"Don't thank me, sweetie. It's not easy to keep your life in order. Now I need forty-three names for a new pantyhose, all of which will be rejected because they will use the one the sales manager comes up with which will sound like every other brand on the market—but it's something to do, anyway. Now, you'll go tonight like a good girl."

Giving advice is very much like loaning money, and borrowing. Before you give it or take it, consider: Is the relationship worth more than this exchange? Because whether or not the advice is taken, or proven sound, or the debt repaid, the relationship will be gone.

The meeting was to be held in a church. Religious, like A.A. And uptown, besides.

I called my friend-landlady, Eve, who was always willing to do anything for us that did not involve Jasper. She would check on Emily.

Then I called Emily. She was having a friend sleep over. (With school almost over for the year, there were more relaxed rules.) Her friend would also be going to the new Village private school next year. I had been so proud to get Emily in, but now I wondered. If Laurie—my God, how could I think about that kind of thing, about how to get along financially without him? I could not believe my coldness; when he was dying, I was thinking about money.

According to the people at the Alanon meeting, the majority of whom were women, that was precisely how I should be thinking.

They were gathered around a large table in a bare stone room in the cellar of a Park Avenue church. One woman, who looked as though she'd been blown in through the door and hadn't quite settled her feathers yet, was explaining that she hadn't been able to get her husband to A.A. "Maybe he would listen to someone else—but who? All his friends are worser drunks than him."

A Spanish woman discussed her husband. She referred to him as "Mr. O'Connor." He did not bring home his money and she was worried about the children, and no, it didn't seem proper for her to get a job. A man, she felt, should support his family. He was vulgar, and she would not be used if he came home drunk again.

Ann's friend, Eleanor, seemed to be the leader. She was very forceful, very cheerful and brisk. There was another woman like her, but more tentative; an old, sad-looking man, with a very red face; and a young woman whose stepfather was an alcoholic. Everyone seemed to speak in turn, and the way Eleanor directed her questions and those of the others, the idea seemed to be sort of gentle group encounter. The point was: What are we doing about our lives and how have they been affected? The point was not: What are we doing for Them?

The stepdaughter, for instance, was advised to let the problem become her mother's—that she was perhaps permitting what was not really her personal conflict to get in the way of what she should be doing with her own life. It occurred to me that I must help Emily not to be over-involved in us. Was it, perhaps, the only way she thought she could capture our attention?

I listened quietly, but these careful, unemotional appraisals started moving in on me; sensible considerations; pragmatic suggestions.

"My husband is dying and I can't find him! You've got to help me," I suddenly shouted. Tears burned like an infection.

There was an attempt made to discover what I was talking about, in the same orderly way.

"You're so dispassionate . . . Don't you see that I have to find him, get him into a hospital?" I said his treatment would be part of a company program.

"First," Eleanor suggested, "you must find out if the company's program is A.A. I also think you should ask the doctor if he's had A.A. experience."

"But he hates group things—religion, all of that . . ." My emphasis, again, was wrong. It was as though I were in a game without knowing the rules. I was glad when the meeting ended

—with a joining of hands and a kind of prayer about having the power to change what we can change, and dealing with what we can't.

Then Eleanor said to me, "Now, come, let's go to my place and have a talk—I know this is a hard time."

"The power," Eleanor said as I sat with her in her elegant apartment, all cool chrome and sunglass-lens-colored glass, "is what you think of as 'the religious part' of A.A. And the power can be religion, but it need not be any kind of religion you've ever heard of—it's whatever you can respect and use as a source of strength. Remember it's the alcohol you're fighting, not the alcoholic. He is also a victim." Laurie is now The Alcoholic. "You'll read about that in 'The Twelve Steps.' " I have a pack of leaflets about "Alcoholism," "The Alcoholic Husband" . . . and "The Alcoholic Woman." In case.

I didn't want a drink. But the frequency with which the words "drink" or "drinking" had come up in the meeting made me want to swallow. I wondered if people who got involved were not just as alcoholic in some way. "That is the point . . . or *a* point," Eleanor said. "And that is why the first point is to put your own life in order."

"No, I can't think of that. I only want to get him to stop drinking."

"Jill, you can't get him to stop drinking, but you can tell him he can't come back unless he does, and you must follow through. You must give him a chance to hit bottom. Generally that happens when he loses either his family or his job. Sometimes it doesn't happen until he hits skid row. From what you tell me, I suspect that if you turn him out, that would be it—if he believes he has lost you."

"Well, that's impossible. I can't do that when he's dying. If alcoholism is a disease, then why should we treat someone as if he's bad? I don't like that. No." I shook my head.

"The moment will come when you understand what must be done."

I shook my head. She did not understand this kind of feeling I had for him, and my need. "He knows, also, that I can't manage without him in any way. Emotionally, financially . . ." I explained, not without panic, precisely what I would have to manage. Facts and figures tumbled out.

"Of course, you can't manage a brownstone duplex you have no business living in, even on both your salaries."

"I know, but what can we do? We have to have—"

"What?" she said, and I resented her. Such an authority, here in all this elegance she lived in.

"My husband thought he couldn't live without his yacht. When he slipped—started drinking again—I leased out the boat. I told him, 'I can't afford your drinking.' He stopped drinking again, and he's working now. He may make enough to afford his private yacht, but he's not getting it from me."

Listening to Eleanor was like looking in a curious kind of amusement-park mirror: half of it gives back the true image, half a distortion, and never in any consistent way. So you tend to think the whole mirror is screwed up and dismiss the total image.

"The first thing you ought to do is move."

"But I can't until I've found him. And you have to have cash to move."

What am I doing here? I should be combing every bar in the city.

"Ask your father," she said. Suddenly.

Instinctively I had felt she was taking an unusual amount of time with me. Ann had told her. My father was what made me special, interesting. I could say he wouldn't help, but that wouldn't be true. He would if I demanded help. If he had the money.

I said, "No, I won't do that."

"Pride is just stupidity."

"It's not exactly that. I can't." I think she believed for whatever reason that was an impossibility. She was still hellbent on finding answers.

"You'll borrow money for moving from the company you work for."

"I could never pay it back."

"You're playing a game with me. You have to go on the assumption, now, that you will."

"But where could I move? The animals . . ."

"If you have to get rid of some of the animals, then you'll do it."

"But Emily will feel I keep dropping everything out of my life. She may think she'll come next."

"Listen, you have put her into camp and into private school—she can't feel disowned. She'll accept more than you think for an atmosphere you can afford."

Why was she being this patient—now? I cannot wear down her patience. Do I want to win? Or do I want help—do I want to learn how to change?

"But if he comes back, he won't know how to find me if I'm gone." I dismissed the fleeting thought that if he hadn't been found by the time I was moving, he would probably be dead, anyway.

I could hear him saying to me now, "You're playing 'Why don't you?/Yes, but.' "

"I'll move. I'll find a two-bedroom apartment . . ."

"You can't afford two bedrooms."

"Emily can't sleep with us."

"You'll get a convertible couch, and you'll put it in the living room." I looked around the study we were talking in. Through the doors I could see a vast gallery leading to a spacious dining room.

Envy. Shove it, I tell myself.

"Look, this is only depressing me. You see, I really love him. It's different." True love never lives on Park Avenue.

"You'll have to say to him, 'This is all I can afford. I can't rely on you.' "

She punched out every sentence with the thud of a judge's mallet. She was a harder woman than I could be.

I heard the sound of a key in the lock. "My husband's home from his A.A. meeting," she said. "That's another thing: he should go every night at first if he has to. No less than three nights a week. The alcoholic is accustomed to meeting his cronies in bars. The meeting must replace that."

I saw her husband, ruddy-faced, stocky, hustle lightly across the floor, almost on tiptoes.

Such choices for my person, my Laurie?

Shades of my Careers game: she has money. She doesn't get love. I won't allow myself to see that.

"You must understand," she said before I left, "love should not be confused with indulgence."

Jasper looked at me when I came home with "Just us?" in his eyes, and he knows that is not quite sufficient.

I heard the little mice partying in Emily's bathroom. And then I walked out into the yard. We had planted some flowers, finally, in the sand, after lifting up the slabs of slate lying right under the layer of soil. New York is all rock. Hard-core city. Could we grow in New York? Jasper sat next to me as I perched on the little brick wall we'd made. I regarded the sweet william, the daisies, and the three or four little zinnias that seemed to be coming up. They could grow. We could grow.

Emily and me, I mean. A terrible black void came into my consciousness as suddenly as the black monolith arrived in the book 2001. It was a void that was, because of its arresting emptiness, a total presence. It was the space Laurie had filled. A space I would have to learn to live with. Like a permanent injury.

Saturday, the next day, I went with Emily to a fair at the school she would attend next year. She knew many of the children from public school, and some from seeing them in the Village, where most of her public-school friends lived.

Jasper had come along for the walk. Emily saw a group of girls she knew. They ran off in a flock together to exchange notes on the flaws of certain teachers, and the really awful boys in everyone's class next year.

I saw people I knew from the party we had before. The Writers. One had just had a book quite favorably reviewed; she was talking with an artist about their small children. I noticed, looking around, that so many of the women seemed to be my age but had much younger children than mine.

I probably started too early. If I had been older, I might have given them more of myself, I might have been a more conscious mother. But they got out of my body while the getting was good. Before it all went to hell.

I stood gingerly with Jasper, who also seemed to be standing on less than the customary number of feet. The women were discussing plants. Hanging plants and how you water them and what kinds and: "When you come for supper Sunday, I'll show you. And, oh yes, I've also invited . . . It makes a mob, but—oh, hi, Jill."

"I loved your review," I said, "and I have to talk to you."

One says to the other, continuing their conversation, "I've just got to look at those geraniums . . ." And they wander off.

Perceptive women, they had sensed I was going to be very depressing. Probably the navy-blue shirt, not tucked in, the huge navy-blue canvas hat with the vast brim, covering my face, and the jeans, dragging their edges on the ground. It looked as though I had no feet, as though I slithered along on slippery stalks like an especially damaging mushroom. Dark and very poisonous to the system.

"Jasper," I said, noticing a husband who was a writer speaking with another. (Just as, at home, I had only seen movie stars, in New York I only saw writers. Perhaps it was the same: writers—stars of the East.) "We seem to be taking the wrong approach; let us try something new, let us be more concerned with something else. Let us behave like writers."

I went up to the two writers. They had been at my party. I did not fold back the brim of the hat or remind them that they knew me. It was a test. How hard were they going to work to know me?

"Hi . . . listen," I said, insecure and unidentifiable—someone you need to have around on a Saturday afternoon. "You're real writers; do you have trouble with deadlines? I have a piece due . . . and I wonder if you write along every day, or really only respond to deadlines."

"Well," said artist's husband, "I don't put a word on paper until an hour before the piece is due, and then I call up when I've got that word down, and say I am just finishing up and will probably turn it in a day or two late. Isn't it that way for you, Cal?"

"Sure. Any editor who's been around is relieved when the writer calls to say the piece will be late, because he knows at least the bastard's finally stopped screwing around and started writing, which reminds me of a great story I heard once about Tom . . ." And he put his arm kind of casually around the other fellow's shoulders and they too walked off.

Emily came up then with her quick kiss meaning, "Please, is it okay," to ask me if she could spend the night at Allie's house.

"Of course." A good place to be.

So that was Emily settled.

"Jasper, marry me," I said. And I walked through the Village streets heading south and east in the late-June heat that warned of summer coming.

"Well," I said to Jasper, "look where we are."

We seemed to be in Soho and I was standing in front of the building where Nadia lived.

No.

I walked off with Jasper trotting smartly along. We walked two blocks. We turned. We walked around the two blocks coming up short right at her building again.

I buzzed. She would not be in town. So it was safe.

"Who is it?" She did not ask. She demanded.

"Me."

"Who?"

"Laurie's wife." The way this day was, I didn't assume she would remember my name.

"I'm working."

"Okay. 'Bye."

"But I will see you for a minute."

I pulled my bangs out from under the hat as we rode up the elevator.

She opened the door, standing there in a translucent Indian shift, a periwinkle shade.

"You look beautiful," I said.

"I look like hell. What are you talking about?" Why have I come here for this? I think I wanted her to tell me how to handle being by myself. Or at least to tell me, as she would, what I really was thinking about. I could steel myself for that.

"I'm going out of my mind with the prints they made for my new book. They refuse to use the dual process. It's a technical problem you wouldn't understand. What has become of your book?"

"Oh, I guess it will be out in the winter. But there aren't going to be ads, I don't think. It's sort of dead. Those things happen, so I've got a marvelous new job. I mean, it's really so fantastic. Huge salary . . . and then I've planned to do some more magazine pieces on the side, and—"

"Your industry is really so boring, you know . . . and that dog!"

Jasper, picking up that she was not into animals, had made himself quite obscure, curling up under my chair into a shape half his normal size.

"That's a very boring dog," she said.

"Listen—shoot, if you must, this old orange head, but don't burn down the dog, or however that goes . . . and we'll just go, I suppose."

"I'm so exhausted," she said, which I took as a signal to stay. But not for too long. Maybe it was something about the way she sat down at her table, legs stretched in front of her, or something, that showed me she was taking a break from her work.

"Why do you need all these projects, all this busyness? It's tiring just to hear about."

"I like it, and Laurie—Larry—feels that I try to do a lot to keep from falling asleep—that since I gave up speed I have to keep moving or the momentum will stop, or something . . ."

"That doesn't sound like him. That sounds like you. I've noticed you have no conviction of your own opinions. You're always giving them out as quotes from men: from Larry or your father."

"Laurie's gone, Nadia. I'm very depressed, actually."

"That was what I meant once when I told you that you made up a fantasy of who he was. Larry never has made a commitment. He just tries to find women who will make the commitment for him."

"I know, he looks for mothers. I don't think it's so terrible to need what you need, if you can find it."

"What if someone wants to die?"

"I don't think you let him. I don't think you do." I suddenly forgot I was intimidated, forgot to be on guard about my Hollywood background. "Listen, I watched a lot of people dying out there. I heard Montgomery Clift calling up my father and crying for someone to talk to at six in the morning. 'Help me, please, get him to talk to me . . .' He was dying."

I told her all this: "I do know something about people, about not letting people die. There was Robert Walker, and Judy Garland, and even Marilyn Monroe . . . and, my God, how many more that hang on half dead? I think they died their various deaths not because of the fantasy, since that was part of who they were, but because people kept trying to bring them down from their fantasies. You don't give certain people reality hard in the face. They could have kept up with their screen images if someone, just someone had been around to help them support that image. It didn't, after all, come out of some director's head full blown. There are magic people who are like gifts and you don't go around tearing off their veils. There are some people who—well, you just put up with their impossibility."

I took a deep breath. She put some water on for tea. I decided to keep on because I might never see her again. I would say to her the things which I never say and wish I had said.

"I always wanted to be like you. You know how I feel. You are impossible to me. But I don't think it is crazy of me entirely to put up with that, because it is part of how your magic goes. I feel a lot about you. You don't make it easy to say that . . ."

She went to pick up her cigarettes from the worktable. I waited until she got back.

"And, listen, what the hell was it that happened that weekend? Was it just because he was there—was it a game? Do you know how much that meant to me? How hard it is to keep calling you? Just because you had a full consciousness when you were two does not mean I am necessarily stupid. And don't call my feeling for you masochism. It's fascination."

She seemed to be thinking about all the things I had said. She said, watching me, "As for the weekend—it was the situation, just the situation. And hysteria." How deftly she shelved the subject, putting it back. Hoping it would stay there. "I think you're wrong; Hollywood is enough to drive anyone intelligent to drink and suicide, or madness."

"Listen, I didn't mean to get into this. I just came because I needed someone to talk to. And I've wanted to be close to you."

She poured herself a cup of tea. "Will you have some tea?" she asked.

"No."

She wanted to be alone. I would drink strychnine. To stay with her and just to be held and to hold her.

She knows that. But she is still wiser. She recognizes destruction better. And she mistrusts me because I do not even understand my own motives. One cannot trust the uninformed.

"I don't think," I said to Jasper, "we go too well anywhere."

I bought an orange and some cheese, and started to walk Jasper around to look in galleries. He saw a cab, however, sitting at a stop sign with its light on; he yanked away from me, leaping through the open window of the cab, and sat up straight in the back seat.

"Hey, lady," yelled the driver, "where does this dog want to go?"

"Home, I suppose." But I can't think why.

I got into bed wearing Laurie's shirt and holding Laurie's box of old things. When I said to myself, "There is too much here to just end like this," I am afraid I was hoping for magic.

No.

I must not let go of how I feel for him. I must go deeper, hang on harder. I am the Moon: I pull his blood like a tide. I am Earth: come, my orbiting spaceship, plunge into my ocean. Each cell scans the night. Like eyes of feeling, eight million radar screens swivel slowly like electric fans.

I see Ethel Kennedy's face in my mind. I'm having that feeling: the outrage that is love's mirror image. I can feel it on my face.

Laurie: be found. Laurie: let me in to you.

I held my hands out straight, spreading the fingers—were they shaking? How was the tension? Was I hanging on?

I was hanging on.

I got out of bed. Went upstairs and ate some cheese, the heart of a romaine lettuce, and a pint of peach ice cream. And fed Jasper and the cats, and then I carried them downstairs to be with me.

I got back into bed. With a piece of buttered toast.

I went through the cardboard box again. There was the solid-gold medal Laurie's father won when he was a kid, for running a race. And a silver plaque of his grandfather's, and the letters his father wrote to his parents when he was fighting in World War I. A letter he wrote to his grandmother.

And each time, it seems, I see something I haven't seen before. Slipping down the side of the box, behind a picture of Sybil in a driveway, holding Laurie, is a small card. It's from Matt, Laurie's father, to his own mother; the envelope is postmarked 1932.

"Good Wishes to Mother" it says, and it shows a picture of a messenger in a cerise bellboy suit running through a storybook town. The card was made by the Buzza people. Inside the card is an illustration of a lady with a large bonnet and gleaming black bangs. Matt has written about his new apartment . . . he tells of his sister's visit, and as in other letters I have read from Laurie's father, he seems wistful for the excitement of his own home. Then . . . something about her: *"Sybil can't stand much and gets tired so easily. That liver extract is temporarily off the market, but we're having some obtained if possible. I hope it will do her some good . . ."*

I wondered if Laurie had ever read this letter. I wondered if he realized Sybil was sick long before he was even conceived. It did not begin with childbirth. I didn't like the irony of finding this out if I was never to see him to tell him. Good irony makes lousy living.

Sybil. So where are we going and what else can you tell me?

I draw up in my dream in front of an antique shop in California. I'm already delighted, for in all the best dreams I shop: I go in softly seeing outlines and shapes and new qualities of darkness and oldness. A young man emerges from the gloom. Is he Mercury? Gore Vidal? I can't quite see.

His eyes are navy-blue diamonds. "Let me show you something marvelous; it just came in."

And he excuses himself for a moment from the shapes of customers who seem to be wearing much Persian lamb. He pulls out from the shadows, sliding it out beside him on a track, an old amusement park tram car—the kind that would whisk you through doors into a "House of Horror"—an earlier version of the ones you go in on a Disneyland ride.

"Isn't it superb?" he says.

"I have to have it," I say.

I sit in the rusty tram car and think how it might do with a new fringed awning, blue-and-white. It slowly moves forward. Well.

Something this fine should have crimson velvet. And tassels of purest tinsel.

Then I am plummeting through calendars of swatches, textures of time; fine veils whisk across my face; all muted in the shadows of the shop which reveals, as the cart traverses it, a vastness.

A darkness so dark it has no dimension.

As the tram car carries me on, in the increasing intricacy of the speeding swoops and dips, it is evident that we have a destination beyond all discussed and described perimeters.

A gorgeous terror builds inside me. I must have this splendid relic, as Sinbad's sultan would have his flying horse. The chasm of dark disintegrates. We are soaring as no ride has ever soared over magical lands no amusement park doors ever clattered you into, over spinning fantasy realms so fantastic you do not need to see them.

And then there is the amazing feeling of that instant of free fall, when, as before coming, one cannot distinguish between the sensation of flying and falling.

And I am gliding close to the coastline now, over dark-green trees set sparsely into gold-beige hillsides and villages . . . white stucco with red tile roofs, and here and there, bunches of frame bungalows, already Kansas-colored.

I'm holding on to the rusted iron safety bar across the front of the car with both hands. My hair is flying in the wind. Below me in my flying car I see suspended over the landscape, in the chromium-yellow well beloved of the designers of film titles, the words:

SANTA BARBARA, CALIFORNIA
MAY, 1936

Now I am standing in front of a small bungalow. Sybil opens the screen door. I know the sound of that door. Know it was one of the first things Laurie had heard and learned to listen for.

"I thought," Sybil says as we clasp each other's arms, "this might help you understand . . . for us to meet."

She's taller than I am, of course, and her hands are long and slender. The skin has that fine, poreless texture I know, and her hair dips naturally down at one side in a wave like his— like the one I've cultivated in my own hair lately. Her hair is a darker golden-red. I've traced that smile, his smile, with my eyes and lips.

"Do you want to just watch me for a moment to get the feel of how it was here?"

I am checking out the house. She's following, occasionally. She pauses before a mirror to check her golf swing. "I've got very good form. But not much power lately . . ."

"I'd expect you to have that kind of grace," I said. I didn't want to ask how she was feeling. I wanted to put that off.

"Look," she says, reading me, "we don't have to talk about the illness—that's not the important part. And when the transference comes, you'll know. I'm afraid it comes soon. They say that when you come back like this, it's easier to visualize who you were, to discuss things if it's near the time."

"It must be, then," I say, "because I see you very well."

As I peer into the bedroom she laughs. "You're looking for the peach satin; the chenille bedspread with one swan in mint green . . . Why would I have that any more than you would have those curious trumpet-shaped Bakelite chairs or a minister's table?"

"A parson's table," I laugh. "It's named after a design school." It's funny; she knew some things, not others.

"But you're not immune to kitsch," I say to her. "An oilcloth table cover. With a lattice work of ivy. I mean—there it is!"

"And you have one tin-foil pillow in that renovated brownstone. That's staging. Actually, with the second marriage it seems you're just too tired to exchange anything. Too worn out to be smart and different."

So she had married twice too. She looks tired.

"People," I say, "don't even expect much for the second marriage. Never give you things. I guess it's not a good investment. You just make do as the failure gets worse."

"Yes," she says. "The failure. Glum, isn't it?"

She sits down at the table, neatly moving a small pile of mail and magazines from the center to one side; a clearly defined gesture of making space, not of avoidance or busy work. Just briefly she looks at one magazine. She says, "I'd hoped to hear from this magazine by now. As to failure—of marriages, for one thing. Well, the trouble is people slink away eventually from friends who seem congenitally incapable of happy endings. And that plays hell with the possibilities of having them."

She pauses. "I sent a story to the *Atlantic.*"

"Did it have a happy ending?" I ask. She smiles a rueful smile; the kind you must cup between your hands and kiss.

"That all depends on whether the story is accepted. I see you're surprised that I write. You should have assumed I'd write, that we have a lot in common—besides loving him. You've forgotten we were writing stories in Palo Alto years ago . . . you and I. Or you. Or I. Whichever you prefer. It is, of course, the same. We were in college that year. You know, nothing is by accident."

So.

I had forgotten those dreams or fantasies. So long ago. Fantasies of having a woman friend: An invisible Pan-Woman— pan-and-transexual; she would come and be with me in the Muir Woods. Encourage me to write my stories. And . . . other things. A muse in sensible shoes. So. That was her.

"Is this a karma thing?" I wonder.

"Well," she says, "call it that if you want to give it the taint of Southern California. It's really a matter of style—what you call it—whether what it is requires a label."

(That sounds like him.)

"I may"—she smiles wickedly—"be a fantasy." She stares at me, twirling a pearl button on her sea-green cardigan.

"So, that was you." I feel so complete. I remember how I saw her, how she looked in the forests; casting a longer shadow than mine on cool, mauve beaches.

"If you'd like to remember, if you need to remember—to give things some hope of continuity, of permanence—then you could cast me as the muse who came with you," she says, "on the long, fast rides on the freeway. You could even say that my foot was on the brake when you were skidding downhill on eighty milligrams an hour. Oh, I suppose there was a reason that we had to do all that," she says, using the "we" now, as the time goes by, to draw us closer.

"We had," she continues, "to experience danger and chaos. It served a purpose so we could begin to get close to Laurie's experience in order to deal with it—to understand. To stay with him." Then she looks at me slowly, rising from the chair. "I mean, of course, for you to deal with it."

"Listen," I say, "it's the same thing, whether it would have been you or me having the most of him. I'm not sure if you can understand how much I love you, or care for you, in the warmest sense of that— I don't make a distinction between our exis-tences."

She looks at me thoughtfully, and she looks so much like him. How can she be so him and so much, at once, so much myself? "I know," she says, "that you don't make these distinc-tions, or insist on what they call 'appropriate roles.' That's why you're here."

"I think there are other reasons," I say. "I think it's somehow like a Möbius strip and we are other sides of the same thing, but I can't figure it out. It's just something I feel. Or we are like a ribbon, smooth on one side, matte on the other. But woven the same together. What is that about?"

"It's about," she says, sitting down at her table, and having me sit on the other side, "that fame problem. The problem of the impressive parent. I was married to a you. Laurie's father, you see, was in his time, in his city, the son of a most important man. He would have understood how it was for you.

"It's rather," she says, "a kind of improbable difficulty, from the outside. Part of the trouble is, you don't grow up. You can't, if growing up involves breaking with, questioning and even opposing a parent everyone else seems to consider perfection it-self."

"Yes—but, Sybil," I say, "even if the parent is not what we call famous, the child never hears anything but the praise. Everyone's parent is only a fantasy finally, neither as magical as, forgive me, you are, nor as prosaic. It is the image one has created in the head that one is fighting. Not the real parent at all. You bring out my Adult. Look how I can even disagree without fear of rejection? But you talk. I don't want to take your time . . . please."

"Yes . . ." She looks out the window to tell the time. She does not require a watch. "However, I lived with a man who longed for the excitement of his home, which, of course, as you say—and you are right—was only an illusion of what he wanted to remember . . . birthdays transformed into galactic festivals. You had some of that, I know. These grand events that are only grand ten years after—in memory experienced—in a bitter present time. Such grand memories that make what we can do, in a real life, rather drab . . . Oh, these parties Matt's father gave—to hear of them, they were dances the planets do around the sun. And he, the father, was the sun—and you take away the sun, as I did when I urged Matt south to Santa Barbara, to find work on his own . . . to find his own soul-identity, as you say."

She seems flushed now, wanting to tell me everything she has learned while I've been sleeping. There is such a short time. "My husband plummeted. And he longed for what you've tried to forget. Those expectations. And by the time I had to go, he was lost."

"But," I say, almost to myself now, "are these sun figures then so great if we, their satellites, are never taught to function?"

"The point is only that you believe they are powerful." She pauses and looks at the light of the sky again—the tone of time. "When the magic is threatened with exposure, when you learn how the trick is done and you see it isn't such a trick, he's not so magic. Where's the power you need to come from? Drink? Those curious drugs? At least the illusion of the mythic size of the parent is maintained by your failure. Religion is a glad alternative for some, I suppose."

She touches my hand and smiles at me, staring with her golden-flecked green-blue eyes. Her Scottish cat eyes . . . like his, like his.

"You see," she says, "you know what it feels like to need to be someone. . . You can make him feel like that. You know how to admire. We've learned to see from the other side, and I liked a lot of that—your childhood. A warning here for you, though . . ." She looks in a couple of books, among the papers on the table.

"Yes." She looks in a small brown notebook, squinting—light or eyes fading. Then she laughs a quick short laugh. "Yes, don't reach too high for your own identity. Don't bring—I think it says here, I wrote it in such a rush—the fame down on your own head. I mean, my God," she says, "who knows where we'll have to go next?"

"Stage mothers . . . or mother, perhaps," I said. "I know it isn't likely that we will do this again. People don't often see so clearly how it ties together, I suppose."

"No, and people wouldn't. The grandson of a Senator of a Southwestern state: Presbyterian and a Mason besides, and a Hollywood producer's daughter: Jewish. It's not obvious . . . now."

"Come"—she beckons—"it's almost time." Her hands are his hands. I want to kiss her hands.

"But"—I reach out for her—"I've got so much more to ask. Where were your people from, for instance? What could he say when you—well, left? Was he talking by then, or still too small?" And I hear how he would say the word. I now race on, sensing time fleeing, the color becoming pale with every moment, more slightly sepia. The color of Kansas before Oz. Glinda's bubble-gum chariot drifting off.

"Do you," I babble, "have trouble writing in the morning? I mean, are you a night writer?"

"Well, you write when it's writing time, of course," she says, with a puzzled expression.

"But I wanted to talk about you and him. I wanted to thank you, to tell you how I feel about you."

"You don't really need to; I've told you what you really need. The rest is all there for you to find when you're ready . . . as you grow. It always has been there, you know. Now, I must get things in order. The time has come for what my husband persists in referring to as 'female repairs,' a wholly untenable description. I think the expression is more repugnant than the operation. Come, see Laurie. I'm glad he's napping; it's given us time to talk. He's been terrorizing the cat all day."

"Lawrence and cats . . . always cats."

"Yes," she says, "a lot of cats have run through his life, I understand."

A lot of cats.

"He always smiles when he sleeps," she says, leaning over; she is having some mild pain.

"I've heard that from some other sources," I say.

"I expect you have," she says. "It doesn't take a lot of observation. Hello—silky."

She reaches over and strokes his sunny hair, burying her soft sienna hair in the curve of the baby's neck. His arms reach up and clasp her tightly; she gently pulls them apart, and in his sleep he clenches a fist tightly about the tail of a large black cat who blinks at him sternly with round yellow eyes.

Sooty. I wonder if this is the cat in his letter to his grandmother.

"I'll be back soon," she whispers to her baby, "as soon as I can, so you be all right now."

She looks at me steadily. I ask her if she had just slipped away . . . like that.

"I think so. At the time," she explains, "I felt it was not a good idea to make it seem special. Or different. I didn't know."

We leave, with a quick look around—and then I am lying down. I can see the black cone come down over my face and feel my interior world going really all wrong. I screamed so loud the spirit shot out of me in terror and dared not die, dared not leave that boy. It tore up and down the coastal landscape in a sweeping desperation, needing a way back.

So it had seemed like a Santa Ana wind that night. I must ask my father if he remembers such a wind blowing on the night I was born, ranging like a raw-boned vixen down the coast until it seized upon a moment of conception . . . a way back in. A way to somehow see he was loved well enough. Someone for Sybil to look through and love him through, to warm him and keep him and hold him.

It was shortly after dinner Sunday night when Emily said to me, "Mommy, I don't think he is really hiding. I think he must feel frightened and embarrassed; you know how you say people are scared to ask out loud for help—like when Wright left that letter out so you could find it."

"Emily, of course! He will be at the most accessible place, not a place he'd normally go to hide." Emily had given me such a good hook for what I considered only a desperate kind of manic plea. No grounding in reality.

I called Richard. "Damn," he said. "There's a hotel near the office where visiting executives stay. They wouldn't even hassle him for money—Emily's brilliant, tell her that for me."

"I'll meet you there in twenty minutes."

I didn't want to call, to panic or alert him. Landlady said

she'd listen in case Emily needed her and I was off. Somehow I didn't stop to question why I was so sure.

Asked to hurry, every cabdriver becomes a missionary for safe driving, lingers over each light change. It is true, you cannot kill cabdrivers through the partitions.

Laurie was registered under his own name. Emily had been right; he wanted me to find him. I felt I had known it myself all the time.

The hotel manager would not, however, let us have a key. I called Laurie's room. No answer.

"He's maybe unconscious in there—he's sick!" I yelled.

The manager said, "Ma'am, we get a lot of wives looking for their husbands. Now, you'll have to get an officer and a warrant."

"He may be dying. It will be too late. I will have every newspaper and TV station in town here if you don't let me in that room!"

Richard quietly showed the man his company card. "We do a lot of business with you people."

We got the key.

He had been there: a half bottle of vodka. A jug of red wine almost empty. A stain of wine on a sheet of one barely rumpled bed. His attaché case sat pristinely on the dresser. A legal pad with hieroglyphics neatly penciled on.

"Where is he, where is he?"

I touched everything he had touched: willed his pencil to tell me something. I rubbed my hand on the pillowcase, stroked the handle of his attaché case.

"He'll be back," Richard said. "Probably eating something. We'll wait. And, listen, I don't think we should tell him just how sick he is, you know. Might have the opposite effect—he might think the hell with it."

We must frighten him just enough, but no more. Would I know what "just enough" would be?

Laurie walked in about an hour later.

"Hello, hello," he said, so cool, so cool. Pale, worn, thin. Hands were shaking. He greeted us as if we had been waiting for someone who is about ten minutes late for lunch.

"You crazy bastard," said Richard. After a few minutes of what-has-been-happening sort of anxious small talk, he explained the company's plan of action—I think for those first few moments we both feared Laurie might bolt out on us.

"You'll have to go to this hospital. A guy in my department went there. He'll talk to you; apparently it's a beautiful setup. Then you'll have a psychiatrist and A.A., and you'll be on full salary for as long as it takes to get yourself straight. Now, let's get out of here . . ."

Laurie sat on the bed not going anywhere.

"That's the first interesting proposal I've had in years." He nodded. "I'll certainly think it over."

His cool destroyed me; he hadn't touched me. He hadn't even really looked at me. I must remember he is sick. It's the disease turning him away. I have Sybil with me, I thought. I will play it surreal, supernatural, any way I have to—I will not leave. I will not be thrown.

Richard said again, "Come on, get your stuff together."

"Sure, sure, but I've got to have a little time to think about it, man. I don't want to rush into anything." He had a sort of mocking expression. "It's a big risk—to stop drinking, going straight. Who knows? What you've got in mind could be very boring."

"Oh, shit, Laurie—stop playing Nadia."

"I'm not playing. You're asking me to give up . . . my whole world."

He gestured around the room with a rakish, elegant grin.

After an hour and a half more of Laurie's deft, elusive charm, Richard quit. "I'm not going to force you. No one says it's easy —I've said all I know, so I'm leaving."

. . .

I felt that this was the only real fight I've ever had. The only thing I'd ever wanted and must win. I talked at him from one-thirty until six in the morning. He didn't say a word. He didn't show he was even listening. I felt a desperate fever not to let him go. I talked about what he is and what he means to me:

"The first time I ever saw you cry, and you sobbed—you sobbed—was when I asked you to bite my neck when we were making love, so how can you be such a sadist: what killing cruelty it is to get me well enough to perceive how much I can love.

"You're throwing me against a wall of razors, and you're throwing Emily too. Not that she can't live without you, but I can't, Laurie, I can't . . ."

I kept running on. He poured himself some vodka and removed his tie. Oh—alcoholic stereotype: dressing, shaving just so—grooming giving the lie to decay! "You'll be taking away her mother, is that what you have to do to get even for having your mother taken away? Do you resent Emily so much for having me a little, too? How many kids do you have to punish for what happened to you? And how dare you feel you have the exclusive on what's hard or tough, how dare you any more than I do . . . any of us. It's all hard and tough—everyone has a story!"

Silently he continued to undress. I felt as I had with men who gave me money for a cab because they were too beat to take me back home . . .

"Don't make me feel the way I do, Laurie. Don't!" I must fight this. Powerless over alcohol, perhaps. But I shall not be powerless over his will to destruct. "You signed on. Remember marriage is so we have to talk about it. And I'm talking about it. You've been whimpering in this hotel here, and so I know goddamn well you haven't pulled out."

My voice was angry. A new voice. Now he got into his bed—with his shorts on! I wanted to say, "Don't worry, I won't use sex to try to keep you." However, I must give him some privacy of motive. Some fears to keep to himself.

But he had put up a new sign, "Do Not Trespass." He had never slept with shorts on before.

He lay right in the middle of the bed. Flat on his stomach. Creating the fortress of an armadillo.

Affection. What about a little affection? I didn't even ask. I tried to lie down beside him. There was room to lie only on my side. I stroked his back and I felt the muscles tighten. The sores were huge. Infections had poured out and dried. "Your back looks worse. You know you need attention . . . you know your body can't take this beating."

"Take it easy woman. Just enough and no more."

"Listen, if you're so damned smart, Laurie, how can you think this makes any sense—what you're doing?"

He shrugged his snotty, rotting shoulders.

I got up. It was like lying next to a knife edge. I might not be able to resist running my body upon it. To open myself like an iron maiden. Only—inside he would find hot wet red meat. I would snap back into one piece. A flesh cozy to keep him warm. Or a casserole to cook him in.

How finely he is honed, I thought, this side edge of him. To slice me. But he's only pretending he is dangerous.

Play his game.

"You are—okay, you are George and Berenger and all the rest all together and much worse. But they never pretended to be anything other than what they were. I just wanted to see them different . . . so badly. I wanted a You and you're trying to make me think you've turned into a They."

I don't cry. I won't cry. My voice will not crack.

I sat on the edge of the other bed. I told him what I felt about why we had come together. "You've never thought much about your past except to be angry. There is so much more there for you to be."

Suddenly I remembered what Eleanor had said: "He has to hit bottom. You have to tell him . . ." I cannot tell him I will leave him. I will not leave. After all, I am here.

No.

"I won't let you go." I roared now like a goddamn lioness. "Cool does not impress me now. You do not convince me: I know you, Laurie. Lawrence. Larry. I know all of you. And I know you're scared and, okay, that's why you pretend to be so cool . . ."

Not working. He was pretending to be asleep. I could tell by the way he was breathing that he was not sleeping. And that he was also not too well.

"Laurie, I adore you. We're going to move. To get a smaller place. I'm going to handle the money . . ."

I am not supposed to plead or promise things, to bribe. I don't care. "I've given you too much to worry about. Listen, I'm a lot stronger than anyone thinks. You know that. Look how much I've been able to do that we never dreamed I could—well, I can really handle everything."

I lay down on the other bed. I was exhausted. "Do you mind if I rest here?"

"Suit yourself." He spoke. But it was no different than his silence.

"Oh. Strong and silent." My voice was growling, vicious. "Such laconic rage. Such a hip tantrum. You're just mortified." Yes, Eleanor had told me, "Behind anger there is usually, if not always, fear. Remember that when you deal with The Alcoholic."

"So, you're afraid you'll get yelled at. You're afraid you've lost dignity. Fear is not a dignified thing. Yes. Fear and sickness are quite messy. They don't tell you that in the 'Eighty-Six.' Alcohol hurts. And so does your head. Oh, Laurie, I don't want to scare you." I was saying too much. "Laurie, you're not going to die, but if you don't come back, I will. I love you so much."

No. Whining. That's out.

"You know, we promised Emily we'd take her out to that horse show on Staten Island tomorrow. We planned to have a real picnic. I don't see actually how you can do this to her." No. I must not give him more guilt.

I could give him less—my God, that was the point of Sybil. "Laurie, listen to me. You're killing yourself for guilts you shouldn't have. Laurie, listen; Sybil was sick long before you were even conceived. Laurie, you never even look at the proof of your own life." I told him about the card. "Laurie, we children have such enormous egos. We assume our parents do everything to us and we don't give them an independent ego, any more than they let us have one." He just lay there. Did he hear me?

"Laurie, your father was so busy being angry at his father— he was not angry at you . . . wait. So be angry back. Fight him, don't give in. He ignored you; he died like an adolescent. Oh, Laurie—don't. Laurie, let me help."

As I lay there, leaning on my arm, talking now more softly, I couldn't believe that he hated me so much, resented me so much that he didn't want to hold me. "You said, you know, Laurie, that we shouldn't try to change each other once. That we don't have ownership. I've thought about that, and you're wrong—you really are."

He hadn't even touched my arm, not even one of my hands.

He can't. I thought—without knowing it exactly—because he would give in so hard. And, somehow, he felt he needed to hold out. To pull back.

"Laurie," I continued, "I do think we have a certain right with each other. You showed that with me. You would not allow me to self-destruct. So how is this different? You are your brother's keeper. And we are brothers. And all the others are wrong."

I lay there for a while, finally dozing off, but the image of him just lying there on the other twin bed stayed in my head —behind the dreams like a double exposure.

At dawn my voice was gone. And Emily was waiting at home.

There was simply no more to say or do.

He was still rigid, unmoving, silent and frozen.

"All right," I said, "you've won. A little time. There's nothing more. Just don't come back to die. I'm not going to watch. I'm on my way up now. Emily needs a person with her, and I'm going to be there for her, and for Wright, someday . . . I cannot live with you dying slowly through the streets. I'll come and kill you off quick. I won't let you be blue and cold and pitted with these rotting, bleeding sores. I won't have that moving on my mind, getting in my way.

"So, think of this, Laurie. It's now six thirty-two A.M. Now, you be home and ready to get well by twelve-thirty this afternoon, in time to get Emily to her horse show on Staten Island —or never try to see us again. Stay away, my love, my dearest, because I'll find you in the dark and drive the knife through your back. And I won't even look to see if you're beautiful dead. So twelve-thirty or— Oh, fuck it, Lawrence Robinson. Even I have had it."

I threw the damn room keys at his head lying there like granite—fallen idol. I walked out. And I slammed the door behind me. Hard.

And so, although I had told Eleanor it was impossible, it had come to that. I had walked out.

I got into the cab. Closed the door . . . no, my God, I must go back. I must get his clothes so he can't leave.

No.

That's not the point. He has to want to come. He has to want to get well.

In that dull morning light, riding down a dead Broadway, I believed that my life with him was over. That was how I had to think and to plan. He might go somewhere else for a while, he might even try to get well. But he no longer responded to me. There was absolutely no sign that he did. Part of my responsibility now was to accept that.

I will move with Emily. Somewhere in the Village. Somewhere secure we can afford. We will make it.

And I will write about Laurie. No! I will not do that sentimental bullshit to myself.

And I will not dare to start to cry.

. . .

Emily was up. She opened the door. And silently shook her head: "Not coming home?"

"He has to think about it, darling. Maybe when he gets well. Some people, you know, are just loners." Nadia was right about my making him up out of whole cloth. It's fine to support a person's fantasy when it is his *own* fantasy about himself, but you can't impose your fantasy. He'll shrug it off and split like a cat you try to dress up.

I tried to explain to Emily all of these things I had been hearing and thinking about. Mostly to give her positive ideas about how we would have new, exciting things to do. "And we'll go to the horse show . . . so let's start making that picnic."

I had to live, and let live or die. But at least I had tried. At twelve-fifteen I started sounding the gentle alarm. I can't be so cool for much longer, I thought. But I can't let go. I will not do that any more to Emily.

I called Eleanor. "I guess I'm going to have to learn to deal with things without him."

She was having people over that evening, she said; she'd be delighted if I came, "and, of course, bring Emily, it's very informal."

I called Richard. "Listen," I said. "We lose. So if you and Joanne would like to go to the horse show, or come over . . ."

"Sure," he said, "I'll put on my jodhpurs. Now, we'll be right over." He couldn't go on with jokes. "That miserable, crazy Laurie. To hate himself so much he can't stand the idea he could be loved," he said.

At twelve twenty-two I called my father because he would have to know.

No. Because I had to say, "I need you to talk to me a little."

There are times when you just have to say you can't be brave any more and you want to crawl into a ball and be a child, whatever child you were, with whatever parent.

"You did what you could," my father said, "it would have been very wrong to take his clothes . . . I agree with you. Jill," he went on, "your mother and I want to tell you we respect what you are doing. We love you very much and when you want us to or need us, we will give you all the help we can."

Such a powerful draw parents have. Power. Could I use them as a kind of power now? Power: I thought of my father's curious little round about power from one of his movies.

"Remember 'You-remind-me-of-a-man'?" I asked my father after I told him about the "power" concept Eleanor had explained.

He laughed. It was a routine from a movie he had made.

"Wasn't it Cary Grant?" I asked.

"Yes. 'You remind me of a man,' " my father began. I was surprised I remembered exactly how it went. And more surprised that I was not throwing things around the house, screaming and slashing at my hair in frustration.

"What man?" I gave him the straight line and I saw out of a corner of awareness that was sore and present as a bruise that it was twelve-thirty.

"The man with the power."

"What power?" I will not give in. I took a deep breath. But I thought, Oh, God. I really did love him by all the definitions you could find, and so what . . .

"Power of hoodoo," said my father. He was, behind this game, sad for me.

"Hoodoo?" I said.

"You do." There was almost a question in my father's voice. I thought he really did believe Laurie would come back.

"Do what?"

(12:32)

"Remind me of a man."

"What man?"

"The man with— The door!" I screeched. "I'll call back."

"Give or take a minute," Laurie said as he walked in, calm and neat as you please. He nodded his nod, of course, looking so correct, so himself. Under the pale skin, that is, the cracked mouth and the red eyes.

He hugged me, picking me up, holding my head somehow tightly against his. Our brains must embrace each other.

"How are you, my darling, darling, man . . ." I needed a supplementary ego. A special order, we called it, at Saks. A good serious size 14, with broad shoulders to lean on. I've got to follow through now. Got to help him every step.

Emily came rushing in and they hugged each other, tears like a little woman's in her eyes. "Now, do you hate deviled eggs?" she asked. "And . . . Mom, would you get some more grapes or something? I've got to get ready now." She flashed him a quick smile. He reached out his hands, touching hers before she dashed away.

That night I did not go to Eleanor's. We called Laurie's friends from work and had what Laurie called his bachelor party. Everyone drank as if each glass were his own last drink.

Richard had already connected with all the right people, and arrangements had been made for Laurie to go to the hospital the next day. It was out in the country and I would get him there. Emily would go to her grandparents for the afternoon.

However, during the party Laurie said, swaying a bit, "I think I'll go into the office for a few minutes in the morning. There's some mail I ought to clean up . . . you know I'll be away a few weeks."

I had been told it would be more like three to six months, but I didn't tell him that.

"Fine," I said. Frantic. I did not want to let him out of my sight.

I asked Richard later if he had to go to his office. Richard said, "Hell, no."

Okay. I had waited for him to make his own decision. But he didn't have to have to make it twice. I couldn't stand that. So when everyone had straggled off, I kept him up until light came through the window. A sense of hope was coming through. As though it were the first time and the last time, I made love to him. Then I had him and made him and devoured him enough to knock him into oblivion.

And in the morning he did not remember about going to the office. Or if he did, he did not have the energy.

Getting used to trusting is not something that comes back, like swimming.

I borrowed my father's car for the long drive to the hospital. I wished it was not his car, but the independence factor is an indulgence because, after all, I did accept the car.

The real problem of the car, I began to see, as we drove along, was the Ending Syndrome. Anything associated with my parents had always reminded me there are no happy endings. The candidate you care for is shot or too wise to fight another day. A cause worth pursuing is always qualified by "Lost," and the work you love to do goes wrong.

Come too close to triumph. Enjoy it? For sure, it shall eat you all up.

There are beautiful stories, but no happy endings.

You cry at happy endings because you know the Way Things Are. The dear, unsuspecting people rushing into each other's arms are going to be clobbered in the continuum beyond the end of the reel.

I know you never get Everything. I know that. I looked at Laurie sitting so still, beside me, seeming to see nothing.

Laurie. Be all right.

What I heard myself saying was, "Listen, if you die, I'll kill you . . ."

On this July day, the thruway seemed left over from *Weekend*, the French film I hadn't wanted to see which Laurie had dropped me at one evening so long ago in California. He then had gone to teach his math class. He wanted me to experience the movie, and I had experienced it twice because teaching makes you thirsty.

The highway was full of death; there was the dead cat first, like a flat, torn, tossed-away fur collar, split to reveal, in the sun, vermilion coils. Then a dying bird, thrashing. Tiny lifts and slaps as it fell back, wing to wing, an eerie gray seesaw.

It seems now like a fairy-tale trip from one of the hard-core old storybooks with the tough tales of moralistic journeys punctuated by sequences of ever more intricate, ever more challenging obstacles.

Finally—and indeed, like all magic symbols, they did come in threes—the Black Dog. The Labrador, lying against the center divider; its head grotesquely propped against the wire fence, twisted, the neck broken, so that the head stared back over its shoulders at us with wide, terrified eyes. Accusing and forgiving; fighting and conceding defeat. All at once. And all the while quite dead.

I found myself thinking in fairy-tale jargon: ". . . and then the plucky little party turned down a narrow country road . . . the trees formed an arch overhead, and suddenly they came to a stone wall flanking a drive turning, twisting ominously up a long hill to the hospital swathed in mists and trees."

The driveway was bordered in a quite different foliage than I had seen in an Eastern summer. Bushes. Short, spiny, clawing trees, really. In a deep, brilliant plum red. Laurie said, "That's a serious red."

The cruel hedges grasped as the plucky little party made its way to the Castle of the Wicked Witch of the West—to the Palace of Night, the Palace for the Night People?

As I turned into the driveway, flights of blackbirds swept from the crimson bushes and sarcastically applauded our arrival.

The company did not do things halfway. The cottage Laurie would be living in was a guesthouse on this huge old estate which had been converted into a luxurious hospital.

I left him in the cool white room. A gentle-looking male nurse was unpacking his suitcase. The gardens were full of flowers. It was not an ominous place to leave him. I placed my hands on his sore, sad shoulders and kissed the parched, chapped raw corners of his mouth. I kissed his eyes and held his hands to my lips. And I held his forearms tightly.

"Now, *you* be all right," he said to me. "And if you need anything, you call Richard."

"You . . ." I said, not knowing, not feeling any words strong enough. "You feel my arms around you all the time. I won't let go."

It could not be good for him at first. And I would not be permitted to see him for a week.

The first night, I lay awake and tried to project myself

through space to him, to cover him with my body as he ha~
covered me. To hold him. To hold him close.

Laurie's psychiatrist divided his time between the hospital
and his office in the city. I met Dr. Jason the next week in his
in-town office which was very much like that of a schoolmaster.
He was a reserved person. Laurie will like the slight austerity,
the formal demeanor.

"He is very wise," the doctor said, "a very wise young man . . .
extremely intelligent." He paused, steepling his hands before
his very sober face. "That is the problem. He is also deeply depressed. In fact, I believe the problem of the depression is what
we must deal with. It is more serious in this case than the
alcoholism."

"Well, then . . . there's hope."

"No," he said, "the depression is a more serious condition . . .
you must understand that. And he has been depressed, I believe,
all of his life. We can begin work with the depression when he's
physically stronger. But that is if he does not resist, if he does
not drink."

"But he can't—there aren't drinks there!" Were there? What
was Dr. Jason telling me?

"You don't understand me," he continued calmly. "I'm concerned that he won't stay. There is a village nearby. I'm just
telling you things I feel you must be prepared to deal with.
The will can be very strong in such depressions."

"What chance do you think there is?"

"Fifty-fifty. No more."

"And then—will he stay . . . how long?"

"Oh, not less than six months in this case. But the company
is very good. Very understanding. That will be no problem. It's
the depression . . ."

Dr. Jason stopped. He seemed to be looking at an inner
image. Perhaps at his meeting with Laurie. Reflecting on the
memory as one would examine a notebook. He continued, "If,
after he's released, he doesn't drink for a year—I'd say there will
be no regressions. We will have succeeded."

So. It would be a wait. With milestones. Again, very much like a fairy tale.

I visited Laurie after the first week.

His color was returning, but he walked slowly, and he was shaky. I was wearing a new hat. A leghorn, with huge flowers; with streamers. Something to amuse him. He smiled as if it were a hard thing to do while he looked at me with such wan eyes. He was completely becalmed. A silence that was different. More like the aftermath of a storm. We sat in the garden and I just held on to his hands. We were very still.

After twenty minutes I knew he was too tired. So I went back to the city.

The second time I visited I had an act to perform for him— an imitation of a funny number from a musical Emily and I had seen. He laughed. And he laughed. He laughed.

Oh, if there is one thing I can do, that I care about, it is to see that I can please him.

After he laughed, we were both more relaxed. We stopped searching each other's faces silently—he to see if I was managing as well as I said I was; me to see if, as he grew sober, he still wanted me. The corners of his mouth were healing. But his hands were dry from the medications. I thought: I must remember to bring him some hand lotion.

Then he called me at work one day to ask me to bring some things to him the next time. And I called Dr. Jason: "It's better . . . isn't it?"

"He appears to be doing well. How are you?" The doctor sounded guarded. But when he asked about me, I realized that how I was would affect how his patient was.

"I'm fine. Except . . ."

"Yes?"

"Does he still love me, do you think—tell me, does he like me now that he is getting better?"

"He is very fond of you. He likes you very much, I believe." I examined the words, every possible nuance. What I never learn is that when you believe something, you don't even ask, and when you don't quite believe, you can hear the answer ten thousand times and not be convinced. I believed he still loved me when I thought about the fact that he did come home. But when I talked to him or saw the remoteness that was his illness, the deadness in his eyes, I was reminded of the night I found him in that hotel. And I thought: When he gets out he'll ditch me, especially if he's well.

And yet every time the phone rang—especially on weekends, when I was not distracted by work—I wondered: Has he run away? I could see Dr. Jason shaking his head, and hear the words: the fifty-fifty chance.

It's a fifty-fifty identity he has for me now, too—Alanon's compulsive, driven Alcoholic; Dr. Jason's wise, weary Depressive. Was the gentle man with the tweed jacket who loved me another fantasy after all?

You never get all of it, remember . . . not all your points: The Fame points, the Happiness points and the Money points.

"Maybe," I said one night (who am I talking to?), "I'll make a deal, a trade: Listen, God, if you're a little of Sybil, a little of some sort of Power, if you're my father's friend, Whoever"—I put in the capital, just in case—"you give him what he needs, anything he needs to stay well and to want to come home to me. To just want me again, and you can have all the gold stars. I mean it. All the Fame points. I don't want one. I'm switching to straight Happiness points from now on. Okay? Please!"

They said it could be anything, this power.

The fourth time I visited, I brought the lease for our new apartment. Laurie signed it with a firm hand that did not tremble, and that held my hand when we walked through the hospital gardens, instead of mine holding his. I thought, however, that the reason I was getting through all this so well was that it was the first time we were apart when I knew where he was. After one of his disappearances, I remember, he had said, in triplicate, because he was drunk, "But, darling, if you know where I am, how can I feel I'm away?"

I told him how the agency had loaned me enough money to move. And how Emily and I had already packed almost all of our things. We would be moved in two days, saving more than two hundred dollars a month in rent. And we had two bedrooms —that extra bedroom being the only concession to my refusal to admit that I had followed Eleanor's advice.

The first time we went out for dinner together to one of the country restaurants near the hospital and the waiter said, "Will you have cocktails?" I held my breath.

Laurie said, with evident effort, "No, we had to give that up."

Laurie had been at the hospital for two months when we were told that we could not only go out for dinner together but also see a movie.

"Zeffirelli's *Romeo and Juliet* is playing. Let's go see that," Laurie suggested.

"I don't think I really want to."

"I hear it's not bad."

"Depressing . . . I mean"—I hated to find myself using the word of his sickness—"the sad ending. I hate sad endings."

He was smiling easily now; his mouth was so much better, his shoulders looked broader and stronger, not pinched and sharp as a Rhodesian ridgeback's. "It's not a bad movie for us to see," he said. "Actually, Shakespeare was talking about not fooling around with liquid potions; he must have known about that too. You might say, '*Midsummer Night's Dream* was also a warning.'"

"I might also say, I still don't feel like seeing it. I just want to sit and be close with you. I want you. I mean . . ." I touched his knee lightly. I knew the drugs had turned him off. But I still had to test would he want me if he could, so to speak.

"Soon, very soon. I'll probably be out in a month."

"But . . . I thought it would be much longer."

"I know. I want you. I think that makes me rush to get well."

"Oh—Laurie!" It was as if he had been reading my mind. He said the thing I had been longing for him to say. But it made me oddly shy when he said it. "I feel," I said, "as though it will be all new. And a little unveiled. Without all our stuff—you know what I mean?"

Our captain at the restaurant seated us near the bar, where Laurie faced an army of bottles. "Are you uncomfortable?" I whispered.

"No, no," he said, and when the waiter asked, "And will you be having cocktails?" he answered simply, "No, I don't think so." He was accepting, but it would be a year. A year before you know a part of a pattern is set, will not fall into chaos; out of shape, losing all identity again. You lift yourself up once. They say the second time is harder. I could not think of that.

"You mustn't worry about us," he said, knowing, I suppose, by the way I looked that I was.

One can't just say okay, that's that, right here. In a movie they probably would have ended our story when he went to the hospital, but it was after that that I found out there was only a chance he would not run away, only that fifty-fifty chance that he would stay well.

"I'm sorry," I told him as we sat in the restaurant and he noticed my anxiety, "I just love you so. I just worry, you know."

I would sometimes turn my head to see who was standing behind me—the fear was such a vivid, heavy presence. That night we did not go to *Romeo and Juliet*. We talked, instead, of endings.

"We can make our own endings; in fact, Dr. Jason talks about what we do in terms you'll like: we've written scripts, and I don't think they were very much different. All the things you mentioned, in the dream you had about my mother, may have had something to do with these scripts. The point is, for whatever reason, we get mad at our parents when we're very small, and somehow we turn around whatever they want us to do, to become. Failure is an especially strong punishment for achievement-oriented parents, and you can really get back at them by using one of their own hangups to destroy yourself."

"I think I see . . . I like that. I like your doctor. I've decided—"

"Yes, he's interesting. Sometimes we just sit calmly together."

"I would have imagined that—"

"I think it's an Adler idea," Laurie continued, "sort of making life plots, mainly against parents."

"You can get them with guilt. It seems so clear. It seems so simple."

"It's easy enough to see the pattern and the script, but rewriting isn't as simple. It may go better now . . . Dr. Jason and I feel that part of what I was doing was getting near to being forty. My father didn't live much longer; I may have been trying to out-die him. That I had a deadline—literally—that I was trying to meet."

"And he wouldn't even know—your father, I mean."

"The scripts don't pay much attention to that. Anyway, people try to change their scripts unconsciously sometimes, and, also unconsciously, they've picked partners who won't let them. I think that happened with my first wife. I'm sure it probably happened with Berenger."

"How differently," I said, "we go about it—our rewrites. I need a thousand dress extras and dozens of special effects and you work it out with a sharp pencil and a theory, and we come to the same 'still point.' That's from a T. S. Eliot poem called 'Burnt Norton,'" I said proudly. "Where the dance is. Where the time before and time after doesn't matter, I think."

"You're reading."

"Oh. Yes. I ran into Nadia. She said it helps her when she is down. Reading." She had said "depressed."

I told Laurie about our fast talk: "It was just a moment, really. She was on her way to Leningrad, I think. She said I look younger. Not so many toxins. And she asked about you, of course. And about Emily. Nadia said she has a camera she doesn't need and she will give it to Emily when she comes back. If she remembers, she pointed out. So."

"So," he repeated. And kissed me on my all-right nose. "And you also have a new hat to get through the summer."

"You noticed the hat? With those sad eyes you had then!"

He nodded. "A serious summer hat. And sad eyes under it too."

"Laurie." I swallowed. It was like starting all over again. To speak of sex. Worse, without the speed hype. "Laurie," I repeated, "do you have fantasies about me now? Being away . . . or is that sort of tension kind of not— Damn. You know."

"Yes."

"It's not as easy to talk about this now."

"So, I've brought out your natural shyness, I think." He was really grinning.

"Well"—I shook my head—"I have these fantasies about you now and I can't tell you because it isn't a fair time."

"Your fantasies," he said, still almost laughing, "may be more preoccupying when there is something else to do. Especially something you aren't crazy about."

Has it occurred to him, I wondered, that this subject has come up right on the spangled heels of Nadia? She told me once I tend to libidinize everything.

She is right. And I like to. It's my way. Someday I will have to explain to her that it is more than that. I am understanding the principle of priorities. First things first is how it goes.

Laurie paid the restaurant check. He could now have money. I brought some to him from his salary check which they sent me every week. We walked out to the car through leaves beginning to fall.

"I think," he said, his arm around my shoulder, very lightly, "there are really only three ways to be about sex. You can be shy. Or far out, the other extreme—and you often find those extremes in the same person. Or . . ."

He kissed me on the cheek, helping me into the driver's seat. (When he was ready to do things, I noticed, he would just start handling them. When he was ready to drive, I felt, he would.)

"Or," he continued, "you can be something in the middle, where you can talk and behave openly, but only with someone you are really close to. Like me. With you."

"Except when we're being shy."

"Except then."

"Laurie," I said, deciding to leave the subject of sex because I didn't want him to sense any pressure from me, "Laurie, I was thinking of the Alanon people, and this kind of man/woman hostility at the meetings. They were more about that than drinking—the booze is the scapegoat. Or is that obvious?" I added that, but I had stopped worrying about being obvious.

After a moment he said, "You called affairs 'war stories,' remember, when we first met? I think that's your phrase, or it could be mine. It's like that in marriage. In divorcing. It's mainly the disillusionment; you expect to find reassurance and it isn't there. You get disappointed, then you get mad. I'm sure even

Berenger didn't mean it to work out the way it did—he was disillusioned."

"Yes, he thought I would wash a cleaner dish. Did you ever scream at a wife?"

"Well," he said, "I might have yelled something like 'Leave me alone.'"

"I could see that. I don't want to hear that." I thought of that hotel. That hostile, terrifying silence. His Not-Screaming had been worse than anyone else's shouting and hitting. I had felt it as a reproach. A failure in understanding.

I looked at the outline of his jaw, his face, the wave and perfect line of his hair against the glass window. The dark, gleaming blue. He is so beautiful. I can't resist him. "I want you soon . . ."

He reached out his hand and touched my knee. "Soon. Yes."

"I've been thinking about a lot of things, about trying to let go more. Something to think about, you know."

"Not to think about. Nothing needs to change—with you, with us. The thinking is pretty good. And the feelings."

He held me very tight in both arms. Now this is such a feeling . . . such a feeling.

I watched him walk across the lawn to his little house, with the light in the window. And because I could not have too much hope, I wondered, Will the reality be too much? The chaos. It seemed so neat, so perfect for him here.

Just enough of me to charm, not overwhelm . . .

It was a month later. I came to bring Laurie home. The turnpike was bordered in a celebration of color. California school discussions of autumn leaves had omitted any reference to magenta, or to trees of black light stuff.

So all I had expected was a little red, yellow and brown. This was very nice. I could almost hear a full studio orchestra warming up for the big number.

Laurie was standing waiting with his suitcase, which he

flipped into the back seat. Then he came around and took the driver's seat, holding me close to him, filling his hands with me. "To be continued . . ." he said. A grin. There was not a crack in the edges of his smile. I kissed it to be sure.

"What's new about the book?" he asked as he swung onto the turnpike to go home.

"Oh, not much," I said. "You know how it is with books— Easy Come/Easy Go."

EPILOGUE

It has been a few years.

We are in our apartment. There are the sounds of teen-agers and their music. Emily has been giving a party for Wright, who is visiting from California—a party that began with a "from five 'til . . ." a few days ago. What "from" goes "til" has not yet been established. The kids have been up most nights discussing politics, rock stars and films. The hottest arguments, of course, are between Wright and Emily—and now, at six-thirty on a Friday afternoon, they still go on while some of them help Emily make chili.

"You don't know what you're talking about."

"So prove it . . ."

Wright will go looking at some Eastern college campuses with Laurie tomorrow, which should put Emily's party back in her preferred calm focus.

Laurie now comes home, as always, between six-thirty and seven.

"There was a package in the package room, so I brought it up."

"Oh, the new sheets—the ones from the sale?"

"Sporting goods, I see," croaks Wright in one of his new voices. "Equipment for your playing field?"

"Oh, hilarious," Emily says. Arch. "So embarrassing . . ."

We go into our room and close the door. I want to see how the new sheets look, so Laurie and I make the bed. "They're fresh, nice; like a meadow," he says.

We grin at each other. It would be nice to get in this bed now and make love.

"I think they could hear us though," I say. "But the basic idea is good. Let's try the shower . . . It doesn't seem fair with how horny these adolescents feel; like rubbing salt, you know?"

"Fine, fine," he says, hanging his suit over the closet door. I throw my long skirt, with a sweep, onto my desk.

We turn on the shower and start gently soaping each other, drawing closer, kissing through the spill of the water, holding so closely. I try to get my leg around his waist.

"No . . . this way," I tell him, grabbing the shower curtain rod to pull myself up taller. The rod promptly collapses into a V. We start to giggle but the wanting is stronger.

"Here," he says, placing my hands around the ceramic towel bar at the other end, my back to him; now I place my leg on the ledge. The towel bar comes off, my leg slips—sliding off plastic bottles of shampoos and cream rinses that careen about our legs as we stand like laughing giants in a marina of pastel barges, the water thundering on our heads. We are up where the rain begins, laughing so hard I could cry with how happy we've learned to be.

"It's a conspiracy of architects—apartments built by legions of the decent." We sit in the shower, foot to foot, pushing each other's lightly back and forth. "Laurie?"

"Yes?"

"I'm not as free, somehow. I think I take the sex too seriously . . . that depresses me."

"Confuses you." He feels if we avoid saying we are depressed we learn to distinguish the degrees of difficulties.

"Actually, neither of the above. I just like to talk to you about it, and I'm in the habit of starting out with a complaint." I paused. "Laurie, can I ask you something and would you really tell me the truth even if it makes me mad, even if it's something I always ask but this time tell me the truth?"

"Sure."

"Laurie, you must have had just one drink—sometime—just one. Haven't you?"

There was a long pause, sound only of the shower, steam loping past his face like a pale horse—I don't want to hear. Of course he is probably drinking. Once a day, testing the latest moderation theory . . . he must be, or it wouldn't take him so long to tell.

"Okay. I've had a glass of wine twice. And I didn't like it. It just tasted very strong and funny . . . and that's all."

"True?"

"True."

"Laurie?" I sketched his eyebrows into circumflexes with my fingertips.

"Jill?" He pulled down my bangs, stroking the wet hair over my shoulders.

"Do you think I've taken speed? Do you think I'd take it again?"

"No. But you've thought about it."

"How do you know?"

"The part in this book where you talk about spacing out your speed to help you write the last part of the other book."

"And?"

"And I remember there were about two fivers left from that last batch you had. So I think you have them somewhere, which you should—to show yourself how you're not taking them."

"I thought about it, though; but it would be a last-ditch effort to louse this book up. And probably never finish it. Did you think I wouldn't? Finish this book?"

"No, you know that."

"I'm so frightened that I am. Finishing it.—Hey, just two glasses of wine?"

"Yes."

"That's incredible. It's funny."

"Why?"

"If it was one, I'd worry you'd try to test it by trying again, and if it was three, I'd worry that if it wasn't good the second time, why did you try again? Two seems right."

He nods. "You silly."

I wrap myself around Laurie. The steam covers our bodies. I raise my head from his shoulder to see his lovely face through the mist, smiling to himself the way he was when I saw him walking.

About the Author

This is the author's third book. Mrs. Robinson was born and raised in Los Angeles, where under her maiden name, Jill Schary, she had her own radio show, appeared on television talk programs and wrote for magazines. She is also the recipient of a fellowship from the National Endowment for the Arts.

Mrs. Robinson is the mother of a daughter and a son.

The Robinsons live in Greenwich Village.